TEAMWORK

Parents and Professionals
Speak for Themselves

T E A M W O R K

Parents and Professionals Speak for Themselves

Fred P. Orelove *&* Howard G. Garner, Editors

CWLA Press • Washington, DC

CWLA Press is an imprint of the Child Welfare League of America. The Child Welfare League of America (CWLA) is a privately supported, nonprofit, membership-based organization committed to preserving, protecting, and promoting the well-being of all children and their families. Believing that children are our most valuable resource, CWLA, through its membership, advocates for high standards, sound public policies, and quality services for children in need and their families.

CHILD WELFARE LEAGUE OF AMERICA, INC.
440 First Street, NW, Third Floor, Washington, DC 20001-2085
e-mail: books@cwla.org

CURRENT PRINTING (last digit)
10 9 8 7 6 5 4 3 2 1

Cover design by Jenny Geanakos
Photo credits for cover (clockwise from top): Tina Romero for the Arizona Department of Economic Security, Phoenix, AZ; Silver Spring Martin Luther School, Plymouth Meeting, Pennsylvania; Boys & Girls Aid Society of Oregon, Portland, Oregon; stock photo.

Printed in the United States of America

ISBN # 0–87868-602-9

Library of Congress Cataloging-in-Publication Data

Teamwork : parents & professionals speak for themselves / Fred P. Orelove and Howard G. Garner, editors.
   p.   cm.
   Includes bibliographical references.
   ISBN 0-87868-602-9
   1. Social service--Team work.   I. Orelove, Fred P., 1951-
II. Garner, Howard G.
   HV41.T345   1998   98-23708
   361'.0068'4--dc21

Contents

List of Figures

List of Tables

Part I:
The Context for Teamwork

Introduction to Teamwork

By Fred P. Orelove

Importance of Collaboration

There are few things more frustrating to a consumer than trying unsuccessfully to get something that he or she truly needs. Whether it is a product, such as a coffee maker, or a simple piece of information ("Where are your books on Zen Buddhism?"), the customer does not appreciate being stalled or given wrong information. It is even more aggravating to be told, "I don't know" and, with an expression that conveys "and I don't care," to be told, finally, "Why don't you ask someone else?"

When the customer is an individual with a disability or a family member, and the service is not a kitchen appliance or a book, but, rather, rehabilitation or education or respite care, the situation goes well beyond mere annoyance. Dissatisfied customers who seek help and support within the human service field—in hospitals and clinics, in schools and early intervention programs, in social service agencies, and so on—typically do not have a choice to "shop" somewhere else. Moreover, the stakes are much higher: the customer's physical, social, and emotional well-being. Finally, the territory is usually more complex and unfamiliar, and the rules are more cumbersome and harder to determine.

Customers with disabilities and family members often have multiple and complex needs for services and information. Because of the multiplicity of these needs, many find it necessary to seek support in a variety of settings (e.g., schools, clinics, welfare offices) from a variety of professionals (e.g., teachers, physical therapists, nurses, case workers). Unfortunately, many professionals in these settings often act as though each is the only person from whom support is being sought. There is little sense of understanding the situation from the perspective of the customer, who may get

---

Fred P. Orelove, Ph.D., is Executive Director of the Virginia Institute for Developmental Disabilities at Virginia Commonwealth University in Richmond.

either no information, wrong information, or conflicting information from professionals, each of whom views the customer from a different angle.

Operating solely from one's own disciplinary perspective, while occasionally useful and necessary, makes it difficult to meet customers' complex needs. To meet those needs requires professionals to collaborate with one another in a systematic way. Collaboration begins with the premise that professionals, and the agencies or programs in which they work, work **for** the customer. No matter the setting—a middle school or a social service agency—professionals from various disciplines must organize themselves around the **customers' needs**, not around their own administrative convenience.

Importance of Team Structure

Collaboration may begin because professionals in a particular program want to communicate more frequently or to work together more closely. Some individuals may recognize that they are not being as effective as possible working in isolation. In other situations, the supervisor may see the need for greater unity or efficiency.

The motivation for collaborating may differ across situations. In every case, however, the essential switch from an isolated to a collaborative method of operating comes when individuals organize themselves in a purposeful manner, i.e., in collaborative teams. The essence of collaborative teamwork is "work accomplished jointly by a group of people in a spirit of willingness and mutual reward." This definition implies that collaboration cannot be imposed, but rather must be entered into openly and freely, and that members of the team are working toward a common good. There may be several different "mutual rewards." For instance, team members may discover that working collaboratively reduces stress and competitiveness and increases productivity and creativity. The primary reward, of course, lies in enhanced support to, and reports of satisfaction by, the customer.

Why is team structure so essential to collaboration? First, because how we organize ourselves affects our daily behavior and interaction. As Howard Garner suggests in Chapter 2, service-oriented organizations that are built around departments (e.g., hospitals typically operate separate departments of occupational therapy and social work) often result in professional interactions that include territoriality, jealousy, distrust, and defensiveness.

Second, a collaborative team structure creates an important resource for problem solving and support. Johnson and Johnson (1989) have discovered that collaborative efforts to achieve mutual goals promote caring and committed relationships and skills critical for psychological well-being. This, in turn, leads to team members who seek out one another's perspectives when faced with a problem, which leads naturally to greater collective ownership of the problem and more creative solutions. Mutual support is also critical to preventing and resolving conflict situations that arise naturally in any team. Rather than ignoring or minimizing the conflict, collaborative teams tackle it directly and openly.

Third, collaborative teams work hard to identify and embrace common values and goals. At the same time, they seek to understand and to celebrate differences (in background, philosophy, approaches, and so forth). An understanding and acceptance of what is both common and different is powerful and comes from a deep sense of commitment and trust that grows from hard work over time.

Why Do Teams Struggle?

Given the many qualities that teams need to succeed, it should not be surprising that success often seems to elude professionals, resulting in feelings of frustration in both the professional and the customer. This section outlines several of the principal reasons why teams struggle.

Absence of Structure

Many teams do not operate successfully simply because they are teams in name only. These "pseudo-teams" may share a common name and space, and members may even attend the same meetings. Each member, however, comes with his or her own agenda and strategy. The overriding goal during meetings is for every person to present his or her ideas more forcefully and to "win."

A true team, on the other hand, is collaborative. Its members have a common purpose, and they conduct themselves in a manner that suggests that "winning" means reaching consensus for the good of the individual whom the team is designed to support. Collaborative teams are structured to make this happen. There are regularly scheduled meetings, for example, in which the members take responsibility for designing the agenda, conducting the meeting, and taking responsibility for following up on the decisions.

Failure to Understand One Another

It is not unusual for team members to fail to recognize each other's background, philosophy, or role on the team. Sometimes this leads to an overlap across disciplines for a particular function. For instance, various professionals (e.g., social workers, psychologists, rehabilitation specialists) see themselves, legitimately, as performing a counseling function. Each person, however, may view that function as his or her special province and may resent other members intruding on that domain. Moreover, different team members may approach the role from different philosophical or therapeutic directions, in turn confusing the consumer. On occasion, the opposite problem ensues: each professional assumes a particular service or support is being provided by someone else, thereby performing **no** service.

Failure to Take Advantage of Strengths

Groups of people who operate as individuals, and who do not take the time to get to know one another, also are unable to take advantage of each other's strengths. Those strengths may lie in a specific content area, in a particular clinical application, or they even may be in team process or leadership training. Understanding and building on one another's strengths lead to increased opportunities for collaboration and mutual support and allows members to represent each other honestly in dealing with families and consumers, thereby facilitating the best possible internal referral for a particular concern.

Professionals Trained in Isolation

Team members receive their training in universities, most of which organize programs in traditional, discipline-specific fashion. Thus, the model most professionals have is "uni-disciplinary," rather than collaborative. In coursework and field experiences, they see and hear individuals from the same profession speaking from their own disciplinary perspective. In fact, in the spirit of "professionalism" and "devotion to one's profession," the message routinely conveyed is, "Protect what you do, and do not let others practice what is yours." It is difficult to move from a model of training in isolation to working collaboratively in teams.

How Can Teams Overcome Challenges?

The difficulties that teams face are not insurmountable. Indeed, it is typical—and healthy—for teams to struggle, especially early in their development, and to continue to have conflict along the way. Like an infant becoming a toddler, a team falls down a lot as it learns to walk. This section describes several broad actions that teams can take to increase their chances at being successful.

Common Understanding of Purpose

All successful teams share a common purpose. That purpose needs to be more than, "We all work in the same place, and we all have the same supervisor." The purpose needs to be something that each person can buy into, that takes into consideration each person's personal vision, hopes, and desires. When a team member can see his or her own dream reflected in the team's overall purpose, that member will be immediately attracted to the purpose.

For instance, most professionals who work in rehabilitative services (as in other areas of human services) have a strong desire to make a difference in the life of an individual. A team working in a rehabilitation agency may develop a statement of common purpose, such as, "We do whatever it takes to enable each person we work with to find and maintain employment and to achieve personal success."

Reaching this point requires team members to talk with one another to discover their personal hopes and dreams. It is helpful, of course, for a leader to step forward or to emerge out of the group. Leaders typically communicate a shared vision and do so effectively, using clear visual images and metaphors that everyone can relate to [Kouzes & Posner 1995].

Respect for Specialized Training

As the preceding section suggested, team members rarely take time to learn about each other's desires. Even more fundamentally, though, members of the same team often fail to know each other's professional background, philosophy, values, or specialized knowledge and skills. Without this information, it is difficult to have mutual respect or to take advantage of individual strengths for the good of the whole.

The solution is rather straightforward. Team members must take time to share this information with one another and to engage in discussions around both commonalities and differences. Serious differences in values or philosophy will inevitably lead to differing approaches to treatment or intervention, catching the consumer in the middle. It is hoped that this book will help contribute a basic level of information about various disciplines; that knowledge, in turn, can act as a springboard for more intimate discussion among teams.

Team Structure

Teams struggling to be collaborative might first check to explore in what kind of model or structure they are working. Teams working in a **multidisciplinary** model, wherein each member works fairly independently, will find it almost impossible to be collaborative. A team organized within an **interdisciplinary** structure is better positioned to think and work collaboratively, and, finally, a team that functions in a **transdisciplinary** model will find collaboration most natural [Garner 1994; Orelove 1994]. (See Chapter 2 for a description of each model.) The hallmarks of the transdisciplinary model are that team members (i.e., across various disciplines) not only work together to assess, treat/educate, and evaluate, but that a person from one discipline shares and temporarily "gives up" parts of what he or she knows and does so that someone from another field can take on that function. (The model does **not** assume that all members can or should perform any given function at any time.)

Team Process

A collaborative team model, such as the transdisciplinary approach, works particularly well when the team has invested time and energy in good processes and procedures, both interpersonally and as a team. One thing team members can do is to support one another through sharing resources, skills, and technical expertise, and by providing moral support (i.e., listening and encouraging).

Teams that operate successfully also have clear rules about meeting. Not only do they meet regularly—an essential—but their meetings are well-organized. There is a clear agenda, developed in advance; the meeting time, location, and length are definite; and there are specific, jointly determined roles and guidelines for the meeting itself. For instance, members rotate turns being facilitator, notetaker, timekeeper, and so forth. For each item, there are clear and specific follow-up activities, with individuals assigned to be responsible.

Collaboration skills do not come naturally to most people. Fortunately, these skills can be learned [Rainforth et al. 1992]. The kinds of skills typically required of collaborative team members include exchanging information and skills, solving problems as a group, making decisions by consensus, and resolving conflicts. Numerous resources are available for teams to learn and maintain their skills in these areas.

Scope and Purpose of This Book

This chapter has implied to some degree that the information professionals have about the knowledge and skills of others typically is based on personal experience, stereotypes, or misinformation. What they know about parents as members of teams that are serving their children often is equally shallow or biased. Similarly, family members rarely have the opportunity to get to know the professionals or to understand their training and beliefs.

This book, therefore, has been written to provide both professionals and parents with a convenient source of information about the various points of view that are brought together in human service teams. It is offered in the spirit that trust—so critical to collaborative efforts—begins with understanding.

This chapter, as well as Chapters 2 and 3, provide a context for teamwork: what it is and is not, what works and does not work, what blocks collaboration, and what facilitates it. Chapter 3 focuses, in particular, on the role and involvement of parents on decision-making teams.

The second part of the book is devoted to descriptions of each of 10 traditional disciplines: medicine, nursing, physical therapy, occupational therapy, special education, social work, speech-language pathology, psychology, rehabilitation counseling, and gerontology. Each discipline-specific chapter provides a brief history of the profession, followed by philosophies in treatment and service, and a description of the services provided by practitioners in various settings. Each chapter also discusses the particular discipline's relationship to other fields, describes key issues about participating on teams, and explains professional preparation and credentialing for the profession. The chapter ends with a discussion of professional ethics.

It is critical to emphasize that the goal of describing individual disciplines is not to highlight differences between them, but rather the similarities. Even more important, when professionals come together to plan and deliver services (in collaboration with families), it is less important what an individual has to offer than what the **team** has to provide. Strong, collaborative teams are more than the mere sum of their parts—they are infinitely more powerful.

References

Garner, H. G. (1994). Multidisciplinary versus interdisciplinary teamwork. In H. G. Garner & F. P. Orelove (Eds.), *Teamwork in human services: Models and applications across the life span* (pp. 19-36). Newton, MA: Butterworth-Heinemann.

Johnson, D. W., & Johnson, R. T. (1989). *Cooperation and competition: Theory and research.* Edina, MN: Interaction Book Company.

Kouzes, J. M., & Posner, B. Z. (1995). *The leadership challenge.* San Francisco, CA: Jossey-Bass Publishers.

Orelove, F. P. (1994). Transdisciplinary teamwork. In H. G. Garner & F. P. Orelove (Eds.), *Teamwork in human services: Models and applications across the life span* (pp. 37-59). Newton, MA: Butterworth-Heinemann.

Rainforth, B., York, J, & Macdonald, C. (1992). *Collaborative teams for students with severe disabilities.* Baltimore, MD: Paul H. Brookes Publishing.

T E A M W O R K

Challenges & Opportunities of Teamwork

By Howard G. Garner

Introduction

"The children are our number one concern," says the educator. "Our patients are our first priority," say the physician and the nurse. "Our clients are the reason this program exists," say the social worker and the therapist. Individuals in the helping professions genuinely care about the people they serve. Being of service to other people and making a difference in those people's lives are the reasons helping professionals chose their fields in the first place. And when helping professionals evaluate the quality of their work, the criteria they value most highly relate to the positive effects of their programs, services, and interventions on their students, patients, and clients. The bottom line question in the helping professions is, "How successful are we in meeting the needs of those we serve?" The answer to that question almost always reflects how well professionals from different disciplines who serve the same individuals work together, how well they communicate essential information about the individual's strengths and needs, how well they make critical decisions as a group, how well they coordinate and integrate their services, and how consistently they pursue the same goals.

As we approach the year 2000, teamwork among professionals and parents has by necessity become a high priority in organizations that provide educational, health care, therapeutic, rehabilitative, and social services. The complexity of the problems people face today, and the many specializations within the helping professions, have made teamwork a necessity. Human service agencies are being held to new and higher standards of accountability. More attention is being paid to the need for transition planning and services as individuals develop, mature, and move across service systems. As a result of these influences, members of the various helping professions in-

---

Howard G. Garner, Ph.D., is Professor of Education at the Virginia Institute for Developmental Disabilities at Virginia Commonwealth University in Richmond.

creasingly are supporting the concept of teamwork among professionals from different disciplines, departments, and units, including families and the individuals being served. In many organizations, teamwork has become more than a concept or a philosophy. It has become the basis and guide for organizational change; the primary vehicle for communication, decision making, and service delivery; and the organization's means of monitoring and achieving consistency and quality.

A Brief History of Teams in Human Services

In recent years, teamwork has received renewed attention and priority, first in the business community and, more recently, in schools, hospitals, and social service agencies. Over the past 20 years, the widespread application of various team models in business and industry has been cited as a major ingredient in the phenomenal renewal and success of both Japanese and American industries [Deming 1982; Scherkenbach 1991]. In schools across the country, the team model has served recently as the basis for organizational restructuring and the empowerment of teachers and parents as active partners in school improvement efforts [Comer 1987; Maeroff 1993]. The changing field of health care is expanding the use of teams of physicians, nurses, therapists, and other specialists in almost every service area, including emergency rooms, chronic illness, geriatric care, and the treatment of patients with AIDS [Boyack & Bucknum 1991; Reilly 1990; Volberding 1989]. Social service agencies and schools are using treatment teams and interagency teams in planning and coordinating services to serve individuals and families who are facing such complex problems as child abuse, drug and alcohol abuse, and children with severe disabilities [Hawkins & Catalona 1991; McGonigel & Garland 1988; Watt 1985]. Human services organizations cannot afford the inefficiency of competition among professionals who need to work together to meet the needs of those they serve.

The speed with which teamwork is being adopted as "the new way of doing business" in human services has raised anxiety among some professionals, based in part on the assumption that teamwork is a new, and perhaps untested, phenomenon. But this is not the case. Teamwork has been advocated and used throughout much of this century. In the 1920s, during the development of child guidance centers, teams of psychiatrists, social workers, and psychologists became common practice [Ackerly 1947]. In the field of rehabilitation medicine, teamwork among the various medical and allied health disciplines also has a long history, with widespread application during and after World War II. The team concept had become so widely accepted that Garrett [1955] expressed concern that it had begun to lose its meaning. In other words, everyone agreed that teamwork was important and had begun to assume it would guide the interactions among professionals, clients, and families. Garrett regretted that this was not the case.

During the 1960s and 1970s, in residential programs for children and youth, the team model became the foundation for the organizational structure of Re-Education Schools serving students with emotional disturbances [Hobbs 1966] and of Positive Peer Culture programs serving adolescents [Vorrath & Brendtro 1985]. The use of these two treatment approaches continues to expand today, and advocates promote teamwork as an essential element of both.

Since the mid-1970s, teams have been used in special education programs by all public schools across the United States. Various federal laws (P.L. 94-142 in 1975, P.L. 99-457 in 1986, and P.L. 101-476 in 1990) have mandated the use of multidisciplinary teams of professionals, parents, and students (when appropriate) in the processes of assessment, determination of eligibility for special education services, and individualized planning. As a result, family members and professionals in many schools and communities have developed close partnerships in implementing best practices to meet the individual needs of children [Turnbull & Turnbull 1986].

Acknowledging the widespread use of teams during this century, Ducanis and Golin [1979] summarized the human services fields in which teams have been used. Their list included child abuse, corrections, exceptional children, chronic illness, long-term care, anesthesia, community mental health, dentistry, family health care, and rehabilitation services. In each of these areas of human services, several professionals from different disciplines work with the same student, patient, or client. When this occurs, the need for teamwork becomes obvious. Thus, it appears that teamwork is much more than the latest fad in the organization and delivery of human services. Teamwork has been around for a long time and will continue to be a necessity in response to a real need.

The Need for Teamwork Among Professionals and Parents

Ducanis and Golin [1979] described three major factors that have influenced and required the pursuit of teamwork in human services: These are the concept of serving "the whole client," the needs of the organization, and external mandates. A number of other advocates of teamwork have discussed, researched, and expounded on these three factors.

In regard to organizing to serve the "whole client," Whitehouse [1951] described the human organism as a dynamic, interacting, and integrated whole. All who are providing treatment to an individual must be prepared to respond in a dynamic and fluid manner to consider the interactive nature of the client's various needs. Recent emphasis and research on holistic medicine has confirmed Whitehouse's concerns and insights in this area [Kaslof 1978; Tubesing 1979].

With regard to the needs of the organization, Ducanis and Golin [1979] described the fragmentation that has occurred in health care and human services. Problems of miscommunication, the ineffective exchange of vital information, and confused lines of authority were discussed as necessitating a team approach. Garner [1977] described the chaos that occurs in departmentalized organizations as "a trip through bedlam." Under the departmental structure, employees are organized, not around the people being served, but according to the role, function, and title of the various professionals. Social workers, teachers, child care workers, physicians, nurses, psychologists, and therapists are assigned to separate departments where they develop loyalty to their respective discipline's philosophy, values, perspective, and self-interests. Garner [1982] detailed the distrust, absence of communication, inconsistencies, unresolved conflicts, territorial battles, and inefficiencies that are common in departmentalized organizations. He cited the negative impact these problems have on both the quality of services to clients and the morale and job satisfaction of professionals. Deming [1982] stated that the major problems of organizations are systemic and structural and advocated removing the departmental barriers that separate employees who need to work together.

The third major factor affecting the adoption of the team model by health care and human services organizations revolves around external mandates. Ducanis and Golin [1979] described the pressures and regulations from outside health care and human services organizations that have required the adoption of the team approach. They wrote, "In recent years the team approach has received considerable impetus from legislative mandates, state and federal government regulations, and the requirements of third-party payers. Team responsibility in assessment, diagnosis, and treatment was seen as one way to improve the quality of care and provide for professional accountability."

As mentioned earlier, in the field of special education, P.L. 94-142 in 1975 and its subsequent revisions mandated the use of teams in the processes of screening, assessment, determination of eligibility for services, and individualized program planning. Parents and students, when they are able to participate, are to be included as full team members in both discussion and decision making. Similarly, two professional education movements, the regular education initiative and the inclusive schooling initiative, have put pressure on schools to form teams of special and general education teachers and therapists to promote the full inclusion of students with disabilities in general education classrooms [Gamel-McCormick 1995]. As a result of such external pressures, health care, human services, and educational organizations have been encouraged, led, and required to develop teams to plan and deliver services.

In conclusion, it seems that whenever two or more disciplines are involved with students, patients, and clients, the necessity for efficient communication, coordination of services, shared decision making, and consistency inevitably arises. Teamwork is advocated as the answer to these necessities to meet the needs of the whole person, to meet the internal needs of the organization and its employees, and to fulfill external mandates on the organization for efficiency, fairness, and quality. Unfortunately, it takes more than advocacy and teamwork rhetoric to overcome the barriers that prevent professionals and organizations from experiencing the benefits of teamwork.

Barriers to Teamwork

In the helping professions where caring, concern, and service to others are highly valued, one might expect that the team concept would be relatively easy to implement. Supposedly, the helping professions are unlike the business world, where competing to get ahead and making a profit are seen as the dominant values. Most helping professionals pride themselves on their ability to communicate and cooperate to meet the needs of their clients. The problem seems to be "those other people." In spite of positive motives, high aspirations, and professional training, teamwork is often a cliché instead of a reality in many helping organizations. Why is teamwork so difficult to achieve? Why has the business community been able to use the team model in large complex organizations, while so many human services organizations remain stuck in dysfunctional, departmentalized structures?

Organizational Barriers to Teamwork

As noted earlier, many individuals have discussed how an organization's structure elicits either competitive or cooperative behaviors among its employees [Deming 1982; Garner 1982; Roy 1995; Scherkenbach 1991]. The departmental model has been criticized for producing behaviors that are barriers to teamwork. Many helping organizations assign their employees to departments organized around specific disciplines, such as social work, psychology, special education, therapy, nursing, and medicine. (The use of the departmental model follows the lead of universities that prepared the professionals in their respective disciplines.) These departments in hospitals, schools, and agencies are led by professionals trained and experienced in each specific discipline. The members of each department develop an allegiance to their departmental colleagues and department heads. They share a common perspective on the needs of the clients and how the organization is serving these clients. Each department has space and equipment (rarely viewed as sufficient) that has to be defended and protected against others who think their needs for space and equipment are more pressing. Each department has needs for additional positions to serve the long list of clients who need services, and each department has to constantly justify its need for the positions it currently has. Each department has certain privileges and treasured advantages that have to be defended—e.g., work schedule, salary, office space, and reputation—although the other departments always seem to have more.

Competition and jealousy among the departmental groups of employees is a common fact of life in many helping organizations. Pettiness and resentment drain energy and contribute to stress and low morale. Distrust among departments blocks communication, cooperation, and collaboration. In summary, Garner [1982] wrote, "The departmental models brings out the worst in us. In our departments, each profession builds its own little empire; each group protects its territory, power, and status. The interactions between staff from different departments frequently involve the feelings and behaviors of territoriality, attempts to control, jealousy, competitiveness, superiority v. inferiority, distrust, defensiveness, pettiness, disgust, frustration, anger, and resentment." Such behaviors certainly become major barriers and result in the recommendation for reorganization and restructuring to achieve the goals of real teamwork [Deming 1982].

Professional Barriers to Teamwork

Various professionals have analyzed and described the barriers that impede teamwork within human services organizations—even those not using the traditional departmental model.

Hunt [1979] discussed five common barriers that impeded health care teams in Great Britain, and these are relevant to many helping organizations everywhere. The professional barriers include educational preparation of team members, role ambiguity and incongruent expectations, status differentials, authority and power structures, and leadership styles. A brief discussion of each of these barriers follows.

Regarding **educational preparation** of team members, Garner [1988] analyzed the failure of universities to provide specific training in the skills required in interdisciplinary teams to students in all of the helping professions.

Although the training institutions recognize that their graduates will be required to work in interdisciplinary programs and pay lip service to the teamwork idea, most never provide systematic understanding of the role and contributions of other professional groups or the specific interpersonal skills required in a functioning team. In fact, the negative, critical, and cynical remarks of some professional educators about other helping professions serve to shape the perceptions and attitudes of the new graduates toward their future teammates and to lay the groundwork for interdisciplinary tension and conflict.

In most universities, professionals in the helping disciplines receive their training in isolation from one another and thus gain little understanding and appreciation of either the special knowledge and skills of other disciplines or the large overlap that exists among so many of the helping disciplines. This contributes to Hunt's second barrier, **role ambiguity and in-**

congruent expectations. Since professionals do not understand each other's roles and skills, this leads to confusion, perceptions of overlap of duties and responsibilities, and, eventually, conflict. Moreover, most helping professionals do not receive training in the skills of teamwork, such as facilitating a team meeting, engaging in consensus decision making, facilitating conflict resolution, and giving and receiving feedback. After graduation, they are expected to function as professionals on interdisciplinary teams without any preparation to do so.

The third barrier cited by Hunt is **status differentials among team members**, which include everything from the obvious (salary, work schedules, size and location of work areas) to the subtle (being listened to during meetings, public recognition, perceptions of who works the hardest). Inequities among team members can become major barriers to cooperation. Marwell and Schmitt [1975] reviewed 30 controlled experiments on two-person groups and discovered there were two basic factors that influenced the appearance and maintenance of cooperation: equity and interpersonal risk. The studies showed that when one partner is unequally rewarded (at a lower level), he or she tends to withdraw from cooperation and begins an individual style that is even less profitable. This occurred even when the inequity was not the responsibility of the other party. Commenting on this phenomenon, Garner [1982] stated, "The analogous situation in health services is the lack of cooperation by lowly paid paraprofessionals and certain professionals. Even though the highly paid medical doctors are not the ones who set the salary scales, they are frequently frustrated by the passive noncooperation of lower paid nurses, aides, and attendants who are essential to the implementation of the medical treatment." Further analysis of the research studies showed that cooperation did not flourish under conditions that involved high levels of risk when one partner could take advantage of the other. Cooperation occurred more frequently where face-to-face, personal relationships could build trust and overcome the risk factors.

In the discussion of the fourth professional barrier to teamwork, **authority and power structures**, Hunt [1979] distinguished between "authority," which is bestowed by the organization onto the position one holds, and "power," which is bestowed on an individual by others—colleagues, students, clients, and patients. Some team members have organizational authority but little interpersonal power. Some have power and credibility but little or no authority. Some have both, and some have neither. Conflict can arise in a team when one member attempts to use organizational authority to influence team decisions while others are using power they have received from other team members. Moreover, inequities of authority and power on a team can result in withdrawal and passive behaviors as discussed previously.

The final barrier to teamwork discussed by Hunt was **leadership styles**. Authoritarian leadership in a team results in passive or rebellious behaviors on the part of those team members who do not feel equally responsible for decision making and execution of team plans. Successful teams share both formal and informal leadership roles [Campbell 1992]. In addition to sharing responsibilities for facilitating the group meeting, time keeping, and recording team minutes, effective teams encourage their members to share such task leadership behaviors as initiating discussions, summarizing points of view, and testing for consensus. Maintenance leadership behaviors are also shared as members encourage and accept each other's contributions, bring harmony to difficult decisions, and seek compromise positions that everyone can support. Clearly, democratic leadership styles are more compatible with team processes than authoritarian styles.

In closing this analysis, it is interesting to note a common theme that runs through the discussion of barriers to teamwork. The absence of a shared understanding and appreciation of the skills that team members bring to the team from their respective disciplines contributes to a low level of trust among team members from different disciplines. Too often team members interact with one another based on old stereotypes and misperceptions rather than on up-to-date information and direct experience. If teams are to succeed, it is essential for team members to know one another well, both as professionals and as individuals. Team members obviously need to feel accepted, understood, valued, and even appreciated by their fellow team members.

One of the barriers to teamwork discussed earlier was incongruent expectations. Conflicts arise when some members expect the team to function in one way, to make significant decisions, while others expect the team only to serve as a forum for communication with team members' remaining free to take independent actions. Many of these differences of expectations are related to three models of teamwork in which there are significant differences in the team's tasks, goals, and authority.

Three Models of Teamwork

Teamwork among parents and professionals from various helping disciplines takes different forms. The three models of teamwork most often used in the fields of education, health care, and human services are multidisciplinary, interdisciplinary, and transdisciplinary [Garner 1994; Orelove 1994]. Teams based on all of these models may include professionals from a variety of disciplines, such as special education, social work, speech and language pathology, psychology, occupational and physical therapy, medicine, and nursing. However, the three models differ significantly in the authority of the team and the degree to which team members are expected to make decisions and implement them together.

The members of **multidisciplinary** teams maintain their primary loyalty to their own department or agency [Garner 1994; Pappas 1994]. For example, in interagency teams the members often represent a large organization or department, such as the school division or the departments of social services, mental health, and health. Each member functions independently when conducting assessments, making plans, and delivering services. Although team meetings serve as a place for communication and coordination, the team has little decision-making authority over the actions of its members. In the multidisciplinary team, each member's turf is protected and guarded. Team meetings tend to be leader-centered.

The members of **interdisciplinary** teams are primarily loyal, not to a department or agency, but to the individuals or group being served and to the team itself [Garner 1994]. Interdisciplinary teams recognize and value the overlap that exists among the various helping disciplines and therefore coordinate their services to achieve consistency and maximum effectiveness. Each member of the interdisciplinary team continues to work directly with the clients and to provide the services of his or her respective discipline. Members share responsibility for leadership of team meetings and the responsibility for facilitating the meeting is rotated among the members. Team decisions are made by consensus whenever possible. Mutual support and feedback are given to promote team functioning and professional development.

The **transdisciplinary** team shares many aspects of the interdisciplinary model but with one major difference—the use of role release in the provision of services [Orelove 1994]. The transdisciplinary model has members from various disciplines, where primary loyalty is to the students and the team. Like the interdisciplinary model, the transdisciplinary team values the overlap and interdependence of the various disciplines serving the same children. In this model, assessments and program planning are conducted collaboratively. Unique to the transdisciplinary team is the concept of role release. Team members release to one another some aspects of their knowledge, skill, and interventions. This can result in one or two members of the team working directly with the child and family while being monitored by the whole team that includes all the disciplines. Like the interdisciplinary model, the transdisciplinary team shares leadership, rotates the job of chairing the meetings, makes decisions by consensus (where a fair and open process allows input from all members), and provides support and feedback for team and professional development.

This brief overview of the three models of teamwork may spark a more in-depth study of the models of teamwork. If the members of a team have radically different assumptions about how the team should function, this will inevitably lead to conflict and dysfunction. A better understanding of the models of teamwork can lead teams to choose and implement the one that best meets their needs.

No matter which model of teamwork is used, teams inevitably go through several stages of team development. These stages are discussed in detail in the following section.

Stages of Team Development

Just as all children, adolescents, and adults go through stages of development, teams of professionals and parents progress through various stages of team development in order to achieve the highest levels of performance and quality services. As the members of a team first come together, add new members, or continue their work, they can benefit from carefully considering their team's stage of development and planning appropriate activities to assist them in progressing to the highest levels of team functioning.

The Forming Stage

Newly formed teams, as well as those that are adding new members, have to go through the first stage of team development—the "forming" stage [Tuckman 1965]. Changes of personnel due to staff turnover, transfers between teams, and newly hired employees will require a team to go back through this early stage. During the forming stage, a team needs to establish positive interpersonal relationships among all of its members. Issues of trust, team loyalty, and team identity need to be faced, acknowledged, and resolved. Each team member needs to feel accepted and valued as an equal team member in order to participate fully in the work of the team. During the forming stage, team members are usually careful about what they say and sensitive to the responses of others. When joining a new team or encountering a new team member, all team members ask themselves, "Is this a safe place where I can say what I think and feel?"

Team-building activities are appropriate during this early stage of team development. The goal of these activities is to break down the barriers that separate people so that open communication can occur about things that are familiar and nonthreatening. As members build trust, they will be able to communicate openly about issues that are more substantive and serious. Here are a couple of simple exercises that teams have found useful during the forming stage.

- Provide an opportunity for all team members to introduce themselves, to discuss their backgrounds and work experience, and to share the values that motivated them to want to work with students, patients, and clients.

- Organize ice-breaking activities that allow team members to disclose their personal interests, hobbies, likes, and dislikes.

- Participate in an activity to build team identity, in which the team members explore what they all have in common. This is an enjoyable exercise that takes no longer than 15 minutes but allows the team members to discover what they all share, as well as what makes each individual unique.

The Storming Stage

The second stage of team development is the "storming" stage, when differences of values and style begin to emerge. As the team's trust level increases, team members feel safer and are more willing to communicate what they really feel, think, and value. In addition, competition among team members begins to occur, especially around issues of control. Conflicts inevitably arise during this stage, and the team's future development requires the use of conflict resolution skills.

In order to avoid getting stuck in the storming stage, teams need to be proactive in choosing specific activities and strategies that will help promote their development to the next stage. The following are suggested activities for use during the storming stage.

- Acknowledge that differences of values and style are inevitable and even interesting. List on the board a few value statements and then create a scale (e.g., 1 to 10) that allows all members to describe how strongly they feel about each value. Then, allow discussion to explore the similarity and differences that exist in the team. Try to promote an atmosphere in which differences are valued and respected.

- Practice making a team decision about something that is playful and fun, such as a nickname or a theme song for the team. Spend some time brainstorming different possibilities, allowing for divergent and creative ideas. Then go through the process of trying to reach a consensus decision—one that everyone on the team can support. Encourage team members to express their different values about the nickname or theme song. Observe what happens when various team members' values come into conflict. Discuss the different roles that each team member plays in the effort to reach a solution that everyone can support.

Teams need to practice basic skills of communicating, problem solving, and decision making, just as an adult needs to practice basic skills that form the foundation for higher levels of performance. Too often professionals who work together in teams fail to recognize that teams can take responsibility for their own development. Once team members understand the stages of development they can choose specific activities to help the team progress to higher levels of team functioning.

The Norming Stage

Following the storming stage, teams enter the norming stage, in which the team is better organized, develops skills in problem solving and decision making, establishes procedures, learns to give feedback, and confronts issues. In this stage, the trust level is significantly higher, each member feels accepted and valued, and the team has a heightened sense of its own identity and purpose. In the norming stage the team recognizes its own values, traditions, and ways of working together. Team members can look back and reflect on how it used to be, "when we seemed to be in conflict all the time."

During the norming stage, teams can benefit from activities that allow them to explicitly identify their shared expectations regarding "how we do things." This can include expectations about meetings, their frequency, format, and style. This can include identification of the team's strengths, especially concerning the issue of shared leadership. During the norming stage, teams develop a sense of pride in their work and a willingness to take greater risks to achieve an even higher level of functioning.

The Performing Stage

The norming stage is followed by the performing stage that has also been described as a stage of mature closeness [Francis & Young 1979]. In this highest level of team functioning, the team is not only able to achieve its work goals efficiently but also to attend to the needs of the team members for professional development, support, and recognition. Teams in the performing stage are both flexible and creative. The team becomes efficient in identifying problems, gathering and analyzing relevant information, generating and combining creative solutions, and executing plans that require coordination and collaboration among team members.

Suggestions for assisting teams in making the transition to the higher stages of team development include the following:

- Use a structured team meeting format in which an agenda is developed at the beginning of the meeting with specific amounts of time assigned to each item.

- Encourage full participation by all team members. Ask team members what they think about issues and ideas if they do not volunteer them.

- At the end of every meeting, spend five to 10 minutes reflecting on the processes the team used during the meeting. Begin by saying what you liked about the meeting and then make suggestions for improvement.

Successful teams work their way through the forming, storming, and norming stages to perform at high levels of effectiveness and satisfaction. Once a team has achieved the performing stage, the whole team will work to maintain this level for two primary reasons. First, and most important, the members will see the benefits of teamwork to the students, patients, and clients. The collaborative and coordinated pursuit of common goals based on complete information produces a level of consistency that effects significant change that can be observed and measured. This is what helping professionals entered their fields to experience—to make a real difference in the lives of others. Once a team experiences this as a shared achievement, they will not want to let it go.

The second reason teams will work to stay at the performing level is the benefits experienced by the professionals themselves. In the performing stage, the members will be challenged and given the opportunity to grow professionally. They will learn from one another and expand their knowledge and repertoire of skills. As the trust level increases, team members become willing to ask for and then give helpful feedback to one another and to the team as a whole. For the first time in many careers, individual professionals can receive reliable feedback regarding the effects of their behaviors on both those being served and the other professionals with whom they serve. This provides a firm basis for growth and development within one's own profession. Thus, the observable benefits to those being served and the benefits to those who work together combine to produce teams that are cohesive and work to ensure their stability and continuity.

However, it must be noted once again that teams which have achieved higher stages of development may be required to go back through the previous stages under certain circumstances. First, when new people join the team, the team will need to develop a trusting relationship with the new member or members, who will need to learn the norms of the team. Of course, it will not take as long to progress through the various stages if there are only minimal changes in team membership. The strength gained through the team's experience will help the new members to quickly become fully contributing members.

A second factor that can require a team to return to previous stages of development is unresolved conflict. Even in the performing stage, teams will encounter conflicts of needs, values, roles and responsibilities, goals, philosophy, schedules, work styles, and more. The challenge is to resolve these conflicts as they emerge. Successful teams are able to do this, and they grow in confidence as they resolve more challenging conflicts. However, serious problems develop within teams that attempt to "sweep them under the rug" and then hope they will go away. As in life outside of work, unresolved conflicts affect subsequent communication, perceptions, interactions, and trust. Unresolved conflicts may even escalate, create high levels of stress, and eventually force changes in the team—either having to return to the storming stage or having certain team members leave the team. When the latter occurs and new members are added, the team is forced to return to the forming, storming, and norming stages. Thus, one can see that the life of a team is a dynamic and ongoing process that requires attention, energy, and understanding.

Conclusion

Successful teams provide quality services to the students, patients, and clients they serve. Successful teams create a work environment that is stimulating, supportive, and challenging for the adults who work together. However, no one said teamwork is easy to achieve. It requires more than commitment, dedication, new knowledge and skills, hard work, and concentrated effort. It requires schools, health care institutions, and human services agencies that are carefully organized to create and support teams in pursuit of their primary mission. It requires administrators who share the values of teamwork and who can provide leadership in the formation and development of teams within the organization. It requires team members who are trained in the skills of team communication, consensus decision making, and conflict resolution. It requires a new level of understanding and appreciation of each other's professional skills, knowledge, and experience.

We can no longer afford to do our jobs in isolation from one another. That way of working is not cost effective, nor does it produce the highest levels of positive change and growth in those we serve. And in some cases it may even be dangerous, such as when professionals make critical decisions without complete information. The days are long past when the teacher worked alone in his classroom, the doctor worked alone in her office, therapists interacted only with their patients, and only the social worker communicated with the family. We live in a complex world with complex problems that require the knowledge and skill of a wide range of helping professionals. We know more than ever about the human body, mind, and even spirit. But that increased knowledge and skill are not contained within any one discipline. What we know and the skills we have learned can benefit our students, patients, and clients only when we integrate them into a whole—when we function as a team. We are willing to do that because the people we serve are our highest priority.

References

Ackerly, S. (1947). The clinic team. *American Journal of Orthopsychiatry, 17,* 191-195.

Boyack, V., & Bucknum, A. E. (1991). The quick response team: A pilot project. *Social Work in Health Care, 16,* 55-68.

Campbell, L. J. (1992). Team leadership. In *Guide to interdisciplinary practice in rehabilitation settings* (pp. 93-112). Skokie, IL: American Congress of Rehabilitation Medicine.

Comer, J. (1987). New Haven's school-community connection. *Educational Leadership, 44,* 13-16.

Deming, E. (1982). *Out of crisis.* Cambridge, MA: Massachusetts Institute of Technology, Center for Advanced Engineering Study.

Ducanis, A. J., & Golin, A. K. (1979). *The interdisciplinary health care team.* Germantown, MD: Aspen.

Francis, D., & Young, D. (1979). *Improving work groups: A practical manual for team building.* San Diego, CA: University Associates.

Gamel-McCormick, M. (1995). Inclusive teams serving included students: Regular and special education teams working in integrated settings. In H. G. Garner (Ed.), *Teamwork models and experience in education* (pp. 157-174). Boston: Allyn & Bacon.

Garner, H. G. (1977). A trip through bedlam and beyond. *Child Care Quarterly, 6,* 167-179.

Garner, H. G. (1982). *Teamwork in programs for children and youth: A handbook for administrators.* Springfield, IL: Charles Thomas.

Garner, H. G. (1988). *Helping others through teamwork.* Washington, DC: Child Welfare League of America.

Garner, H. G. (1994). Multidisciplinary versus interdisciplinary teamwork. In H. Garner & F. Orelove (Eds.), *Teamwork in human services: Models and applications across the life span* (pp. 37-56). Boston: Butterworth-Heinemann.

Garner, H. G. (1995). *Teamwork models and experience in education.* Boston: Allyn & Bacon.

Garner, H. G., & Orelove, F. P. (Eds.) (1994). *Teamwork in human services: Models and applications across the life span.* Boston: Butterworth-Heinemann.

Garrett, J. G. (1955). Social psychology of teamwork. In M. R. Harrower (Ed.), *Medical and psychological teamwork in the care of the chronically ill* (pp. 67-70). Springfield, IL: Charles Thomas.

Halstead, L. (1976). Team care in chronic illness. *Archives of Physical Medicine and Rehabilitation, 57,* 507-511.

Hawkins, J. D., & Catalona, R. R. (1991). *Communities that care.* Seattle, WA: Developmental Research and Programs, Inc..

Hobbs, N. (1966). Helping disturbed children: Psychological and ecological strategies. *American Psychologist, 21,* 1105-1115.

Hunt, M. (1979). Possibilities and problems of interdisciplinary teamwork. In M. Marshall, M. Preston-Shoot, & E. Wincott (Eds.), *Teamwork for and against: An appraisal of multi-disciplinary practice.* Birmingham, England: British Association of Social Workers.

Kaslof, L. J. (Ed.). (1978). *Holistic dimensions in healing: A resource guide.* Garden City, NY: Doubleday.

Maeroff, G. (1993). Building teams to rebuild schools. *Phi Delta Kappan, 74,* 512-519.

Marwell, G., & Schmitt, D. (1975). *Cooperation: An experimental analysis.* New York: Academic Press.

McGonigel, M. J., & Garland, C. W. (1988). The IFSP and the early intervention team: Team and family issues and recommended practices. *Infants and Young Children, 1,* 10-21.

Orelove, F. (1994). Transdisciplinary teamwork. In H. G. Garner & F. P. Orelove (Eds.), *Teamwork in human services: Models and applications across the life span* (pp. 37-56). Boston: Butterworth-Heinemann.

Pappas, V. (1994). Interagency collaboration: An interdisciplinary application. In H. G. Garner & F. P. Orelove (Eds.), *Teamwork in human services: Models and applications across the life span* (pp. 37-56). Boston: Butterworth-Heinemann.

Reilly, C. H. (1990). The geriatric consult team: Service and advocacy for elders. *Nursing Administration Quarterly, 14,* 21-24.

Roy, S. (1995). The process of reorganization. In H. G. Garner (Ed.), *Teamwork models and experience in education* (pp. 85-101). Boston: Allyn & Bacon.

Scherkenbach, W. (1991). *The Deming route to quality and productivity: Road maps and roadblocks.* Washington, DC: Ceepress Books.

Tubesing, D. (1979). *Holistic health: A whole-person approach to primary health care.* New York: Human Sciences Press.

Tuckman, B. W. (1965). Developmental sequences in small groups. *Psychological Bulletin, 63,* 384-399.

Turnbull, A. P., & Turnbull, H. R. (1986). *Families, professionals, and exceptionality: A special partnership.* Columbus, OH: Merrill.

Volberding, P. A. (1989). Supporting the health care team in caring for patients with AIDS. *Journal of the American Medical Association, 261,* 747-748.

Vorrath, H. H., & Brendtro, L. K. (1985). *Positive peer culture* (2nd ed.). New York: Aldine.

Watt, J. W. (1985). Protective service teams: The social worker as liaison. *Health and Social Work, 10,* 191-197.

Whitehouse, F. (1951). Teamwork: An approach to a higher professional level. *Exceptional Children, 18,* 75-82.

LeRoy G. Schultz
Emeritus Professor
West Virginia University
Morgantown, WV 26506

T E A M W O R K

Beyond Good Intentions: Full Inclusion of Parents on Decision-Making Teams

By Irene H. Carney & Bonnie Atwood

The concept of interdisciplinary teamwork enjoys support among most practitioners of human service professions. The ability to organize and maintain a truly interdisciplinary approach, however, has eluded many agencies and individual service providers. Several authors have described the challenges inherent in requiring professionals to temper their own discipline-specific values and priorities for the sake of planning by consensus [Garner 1988; Orelove & Sobsey 1991]. What may be even more challenging, however, is having professional team members recognize and value the contribution that parents can make to team process and decisions.

The notion of parent-professional partnership and parent involvement in services has been the subject of numerous articles, chapters, and books [Carney 1991; National Center for Clinical Infant Programs 1985; Lynch & Stein 1982; Peters 1982; Shelton et al. 1987; Turnbull & Turnbull 1990; Yoshida et al. 1978]. Early writings on this topic established a rationale for involving parents [Peters 1982; National Center for Clinical Infant Programs 1985]; explored the extent to which parents participated in the development of Individualized Educational Plans (IEPs) [Cone et al. 1985; Lynch & Stein 1982; Yoshida et al. 1978]; and means by which parents might realize more active planning roles [Goldstein & Turnbull 1982; Brinkerhoff & Vincent 1986].

Other publications have detailed approaches to teaching parents how to teach their children [Filler & Kasari 1981; Shearer & Loftin 1984] or how to modify their child's behaviors [Baker et al. 1980; Koegel et al. 1978]. As Carney [1987] noted, much of the literature of the 1970s and early 1980s described ways in which parents could become more like profession-

---

Irene H. Carney, Ph.D., is Director of the Sabot School in Richmond, Virginia. Bonnie Atwood is a lobbyist with David Bailey Associates in Richmond, Virginia.

als in understanding and interacting with their child with special needs. More recently, however, several authors (many of them parents) have questioned whether this professionalization of parents is necessary or even desirable. Featherstone [1980], for example, noted that parents have many obligations to their children that limit the extent to which parents can and wish to become responsible for teaching their child at home. Turnbull et al. [1984] also detailed the many functions that families fulfill for their members and note that other family needs (e.g., economic or health related) may preempt parents' active participation in a child's early intervention, school, or vocational program. Other authors [Diamond 1981; Greenspan 1988; Kogan et al. 1974] have pointed out that emphasis on the parents' role as teacher or therapist may interfere with the parent-child relationship as a source of acceptance, nurturance, and fun. Yet another body of literature details the way in which services affect the family system [Carney 1987; Harris 1983; Turnbull & Turnbull 1990].

Those authors and others have contributed to a greater understanding of the complexity of parent-child relationships and of family life. They have also underscored the ways in which families differ from one another [Berger & McLean 1981; Turnbull et al. 1984] and the ways in which families change over time [Carney 1991; Turnbull et al. 1986; Wikler et al. 1981]. These realizations have led, in turn, to a shift from emphasis on parent involvement in professional services to a growing belief that professional services should be more individualized, flexible, and responsive to families.

The terms "family-focused" and "family-centered" began to appear in the professional literature on disabilities in the late 1970s [Bristol & Gallagher 1977]. These authors and their contemporaries argued that professionals who are concerned about an individual with disabilities (particularly those concerned with children) need to understand that person in the context of her or his family. Proponents of family-centered services also assert that program decisions should have the following goals:

- Be based on assessment that include consideration of family needs and preferences [Bailey & Simeonsson 1984],

- Aim to reduce family stress [Bristol & Gallagher 1977],

- Foster close relationships between the individual with a disability and other members of the family [Bristol & Gallagher 1977], and

- Be individualized to suit unique family characteristics [Bailey 1987].

Concern regarding the impact of services on families has also inspired the notion of "family empowerment." Dunst et al. [1988] define empowerment as a process that enables families to meet their own needs by

- giving families access to and control over the resources they need,

- promoting families' problem-solving and decision-making abilities, and

- facilitating families' mastery of behaviors they need to interact effectively with others.

While family-*centered* services aim to make programs more responsive to family needs, the empowerment approach asserts that service providers should support families in such a way that families can meet their own needs.

The 1986 amendments (P. L. 99-457) to the Education of the Handicapped Act (P. L. 94-142) bear the imprint of the literature on family empowerment, family focus, and family-centered services. This law (now referred to as IDEA—Individuals with Disabilities Education Act) expands parents' roles substantially beyond the role mandated by P. L. 94-142. Part H, the section of the bill pertaining to infants and toddlers, dictates that services be delivered according to an Individualized Family Service Plan (IFSP). In this radical departure from many professionals' established practices, multidisciplinary decision-making teams must consider not only the concerns and preferences, but also the service and support needs, of parents and other family members as well as those of the infant or toddler receiving services. In some states, implementation of the law is exceeding the letter of the law by means of policies that give parents the option to exercise substantial control over the answers to such questions as the following: Who will constitute family's team? Who will provide the service coordination required by the law? and "Will the child and family, in fact, participate in early intervention?"

While P. L. 99-457 may be the most clear-cut example of a family focus, Bradley and Knoll [1990] argue that the entire field of developmental disabilities is shifting from an emphasis on "mass-produced" services to an emphasis on individuals, families, and life in the community. Bradley and Knoll assert that families are at the center of a new paradigm for services in developmental disabilities. If we accept their assertion to be true, we must also renew our concern with parents' access to participation in decision-making teams.

Facilitating Parent Involvement in the Team Process

Parent involvement in the team process has numerous benefits to both the parents and the professional members of the team. It is generally accepted that parents have information to which no other team member has access, and that parents' views are essential for making informed and effective decisions. It is also true that parents are more likely to accept and support a plan in which their opinions and ideas are reflected. How, then, can other team members facilitate parents' participation?

The teams that are best prepared to include parents in decision making are those that adhere to basic components of effective team functioning. These components, which have been detailed elsewhere [Garner 1982; Garner 1988; Orelove & Sobsey 1991], will not be discussed at length here. Several characteristics, however, are meaningful for this discussion:

- A desire to understand the child or adult in question as an individual, rather than as a label or diagnosis;

- Interest in and respect for the contributions of each member of the team;

- Openness to a variety of possible outcomes from the team's efforts; and

- Commitment to and skill with facilitative communication practices, including a shared framework for resolving differences.

Most of these characteristics reflect the attitudinal climate of the team. Effective teams, it appears, are those on which members approach the child or adult with questions and one another with interests, openness, and respect. Such teams also approach their task with flexibility and creativity, avoiding or rejecting foregone conclusions regarding the outcomes of their work.

The following sections will explore these attitudinal aspects of team functioning as they related to parent participation in the team process. This chapter will also discussion problem-solving and conflict-resolution practices that support parent-professional communication.

Attitudinal Influences on Parent Involvement

Attitudes Regarding the Child or Adult in Question

How do attitudes regarding a student, patient, or client affect parents' involvement with team decision making? Several parents have offered an answer to that question in accounts of their personal diagnostic and program-planning experiences. Turnbull and Turnbull [1990], for example, quote Halperin's [1989] reaction to the ways in which professional participants in a team meeting regarded her son and his behavior:

> I was told that my child was a behavior problem, dyslexic, hyperactive, and a general "pain in the neck." He was always clowning around and disrupting classes. This child was the light of my life, yet no one had anything positive to say about him. No one suggested that his clowning was a need to cover for his feelings of inadequacy. No one realized that it is easier to let others think he was funny than reveal that he couldn't do the work.

The members of this team clearly neglected to solicit the parent's perspective on her son's behavior and to consider that perspective in attempting to understand their student. Moreover, the team's negative and clinical ways of discussing this adolescent led his mother to conclude that the "experts" with whom she was meeting neither liked nor understood her child. A parent's reaction to such a discovery might include a range of such emotions as anger and disappointment. Parents are not, however, likely to respect or trust professionals who appear to bring so little interest, insight, or empathy to their roles as human service providers.

Lipton [1982] reports similar experiences and reactions following her daughter's enrollment in an early intervention program:

She was around other babies. I was around other parents. That was the good news. The bad news was the recurrent trauma of meeting with the experts. There were doctors who, after observing her for a few minutes, made pronouncements about Chloe's intelligence or possible lack of it, they used her in their lectures to students, making prognoses on a child they didn't know, talking about Chloe as if she and I were not in the room. One said she would walk by the time she was four. Another said she would never walk. Some of the experts were kind and tickled Chloe. Some were cold and "professional." Often their words seemed to have no relation to my strong-willed baby ... I began to dread the "multidisciplinary" team meetings. They were a cross between a postmortem and a Peter Seller's satire on the awkward professional ... After a few months of these experiences, I developed a mistrust of these experts; their judgments often seemed ludicrous and based on so little. And when they finally talked about the future for handicapped kids, the choices seemed so limited ... After obsessively evaluating the opinions of these experts, I decided I had to follow my own instincts about Chloe, take their ideas with a grain of salt, and have confidence in my own feelings. I knew her best after all. It was Chloe's joy, vitality, and determination that motivated me to fight the assumptions and the labelling which made an object of her.

This passage illustrates several attitudes and practices that erode parents' confidence in professional team members:

- Drawing conclusions about a child's current and future ability on the basis of a brief observation;

- Talking about students or clients in their presence as if they could not hear, understand, or care about what is being said;

- Failing to interact with the child or adult during evaluations or meetings;

- Making final pronouncements on what the child will or will not be able to accomplish or experience; and

- Failing to see or talk in terms of a child's qualities, such as the "joy" or "determination" that a parent might emphasize.

These parent authors have a clear message for professionals: Get to know our children for who they are and what they can do, as well as in terms of their deficits and needs. Find something to like about them and show it. Consider *why* they do the things that you may find confusing or irritating. Believe in them—in terms of what they might be able to accomplish now and experience in the future. And treat them as you would want for yourself or your child to be treated—with friendliness and respect. Wiegle [1990] put it in these words:

> What I ask from professionals is that you stand next to me, that you believe that those kids that you work with are O.K. Too often I feel that the professionals who are working with me pity me, pity my child. I do not want to have to fight against the people who are here to help my children. I want you to know that they were born with the same rights and responsibilities as every child within our country. I want you to help me help them lead the best lives they possibly can. I want you to value them. I want you to value me.

Wiegle speaks to professionals' attitudes toward people with disabilities and to team members' views of and impact on parents. Attitudes toward parent participants in teamwork is the next area of consideration.

Attitudes Regarding Parents

One of the characteristics of effective teams is members' openness to and interest in the perspectives and recommendations of other participants. Are parents viewed as valuable members of interdisciplinary teams? A family-centered approach to services implies that parents and other family members have history, information, and perspective that are critical to the development of responsive and effective plans. The history of parent involvement in planning, however, is one, by and large, of parents as passive recipients of information and plans.

In an excellent review and discussion of parent participation in development of educational plans, Turnbull and Turnbull [1990] noted that, while some parents are active participants, the majority are not. They based this conclusion on their review of research on parent involvement in IEP development. They cited, for example, Lynch and Stein's [1982] finding that, of 400 parents of students with disabilities, only 71—or 18%—reported participating in the development of their child's IEP. Turnbull and Turnbull listed several barriers to parent participation, including professionals' attitudes toward parents. Fuqua et al. [1985] reported teachers' conclusions that parent apathy was at fault for parental noninvolvement in school activities. Vincent et al. [1980] listed several negative assumptions that professionals hold:

- Parents are not willing to work with their child,

- Parents have unrealistic expectations,

- Parents do not know what is best for their child,

- Parents do not know how to teach their child effectively,

- Parents need professionals to help them solve their problems, and

- Parents contribute to the child's problems.

Sonnenschein [1981] suggested that professionals see parents as maladjusted, less observant and intelligent than professionals, and adversarial. Halvorsen [1982] further noted that apathy and parents' problems with judgment and understanding are among the reasons professionals have given for parent noninvolvement.

All of these analyses of professionals' attitudes toward parents arose in the early years of the implementation of P. L. 94-142. By 1986, Lipton asserted that parents, as a group, were in transition from "passive and uncertain participation" in planning to a more confident and assertive role. She also observed that professionals were "getting used to" parent involvement in team planning. "Getting used to" does not, however, constitute real openness to or interest in collaborating with parents. In fact, there are a number of ways in which professionals continue to communicate to parents that they have second-class status in team planning.

Meeting logistics. Parents are placed at a psychological disadvantage in a variety of subtle and not-so-subtle ways. Scheduling meetings, for example, is usually done by the professionals and at the convenience of the professionals. Location, date, time, and child care (sometimes including extraordinary child care arrangements) are just some of the factors a parent will have to consider before attending the team meeting.

Time to plan and prepare is a courtesy naturally extended to anyone who is expected to be an active member of the team. The implicit assumption that parents have no need to prepare is illustrated by the experience of one parent who was dropping her child off at school when the principal saw her and ("as long as you're here") pressured her to attend a meeting about her child's alleged behavior problems. (This is one of the most unsettling topics that a parent can face at a meeting; it is not tackled without emotion, however hidden.) Dressed in a sweatsuit and sneakers, this mother looked around the room at the professionals in their tailored suits. This was a parent who was clearly intimidated by the other team members, and to this particular parent, and many others, appearance is of great concern.

An alternative approach might have facilitated this parent's involvement in the team process. Consider, for example, how the parent might have felt had school staff let her know that they had some concerns and asked her to observe for specified behaviors at home and in the community and asked the mother if she could meet with staff for a discussion and checked with her about her availability. Clearly, if parents are to be truly included in the team process, mothers and fathers need to have the same information and preparation time as have other members.

Meeting linguistics. The language used by professional team members often suggests discrepancies between professionals' perceptions of their own importance and the value of parent participants. Parents frequently note that professionals' use of unfamiliar jargon has the effect of keeping parents on the periphery of discussions about evaluation results, program options, and possible goals. Professionals often, for example, use acronyms as shortcuts. The names of disciplines (O.T., P.T.); evaluation instruments (WISC-III); and educational categories (ED, LD, EMR, ADD, SPH) are often shortened to these "codes" that only other professionals are likely to understand. Professionals can also tend to substitute technical terms for more readily understandable words (e.g., "upper and lower extremities" for arms and legs).

The ways in which team members address one another can also convey distinctions between parents and all other participants. Do all team members, for example, address one another using first names, while the parent is expected to address them using courtesy titles? Is the parent called by her or his first name without having invited others to do so? Do professionals assert the superiority of their role by prefacing their remarks with the phrase "... in my humble opinion"?

What Can Professionals Do?

If teams truly want parents to feel like valuable players, then they have to think about how all aspects of the team process will affect parent members.

A number of authors have provided specific guidance for professionals who wish to reexamine their attitudes toward parents and their practice of interacting with mothers and fathers. Their collective suggestions include professionals' taking another look at their attitude toward parents, taking responsibility for involving parents, and taking the time to make interactions with parents truly collaboration.

Take a Look at Attitudes

Shelton et al. [1987] address health care providers in their manual on family-centered health care. These authors assert that health care professionals must recognize that families provide constancy in children's lives while services and personnel often change. Kaiser and Hayden [1984] also exhorted their special education colleagues to understand and value parents' contributions:

> Special educators must appreciate that parenting can be every bit as important and helpful a thing to do as teaching or therapy. The parent role must not be inadvertently disparaged on the basis of its departure from standard professional trappings. A parent's effectiveness must not only be judged through criteria measuring his or her successive approximations to the professional therapists and teachers providing treatment.

Parents ask professionals to heed the message conveyed by Atwood [1991] who recalled her conversation with a mother who stated, "All the doctors and therapists think their area is most important. They all have their little, single point of focus ... What they ask you to do is important, but so is a day in the park, so is a trip to Grandma's."

Not only do parents provide their children with experiences that professionals typically do not, but parents also have information that can help professionals to more fully understand their students and clients. There are, for example, a number of factors that influence children's' behavior, including fatigue or changes in relationships or routines—dimensions of the child's life most familiar to parents. Parents can also help professionals to evaluate behavior in terms of the child's behavioral history. Behaviors that professionals have identified as a problem (e.g., inappropriate verbalization) may actually represent an improvement over earlier means of acting out such as physical aggression. Parents and professionals may also have different definitions of what is considered "acceptable" behavior—a difference that could interfere with behavior change efforts, unless parents are actively involved in setting goals and planning strategies.

When parents' information and perspectives are considered trivial or inaccurate, parents' full inclusion on the team is compromised. Parent participation is also sometimes limited by the attitudes that parents are rivals or "outsiders." Professionals are sometimes less open to input from colleagues in other agencies or fields. In a similar vein, professional team members may be closed to parents' contributions, asserting that parents don't understand the nature or practical realities of the treatment setting. People with disabilities do not, however, *live* in the school or clinic or hospital. Nor do they stay forever in most residential settings. Even though parents' perspectives may reflect a reality other than the one in which professional team members work, mothers' and fathers' concerns and views *must* be taken into account if programs are to reflect and make a difference in students' or clients' larger world and lives.

Interest in and openness to parents' input may be particularly difficult to summon when the family is economically or culturally different from most other members of the team. In that case, it would seem even more important to actively solicit information and recommendations from parents. Listening to parents can help professionals to better understand the values, patterns, and barriers that influence the family's priorities as well as the child's learning and behavior.

Take Responsibility for Involving Parents

Fran Smith, a professional in the field of disabilities and mother of two children with special needs, sums up teamwork this way:

> In a successful team, everyone is committed, knows their role, and has the skills to do the job. Newcomers, however, may feel intimi-

dated and may not play their role very well. Parents are newcomers to the service delivery team. Professionals should support and encourage parents to participate effectively as knowledgeable, skilled team members. The team will function best when there is an atmosphere of trust in which parents feel respected, heard, and supported as equal members of the team [personal communication].

Several strategies for professionally mediated parent involvement have been demonstrated and verified through model demonstration and research. Among the earliest of these was a study by Goldstein and Turnbull [1982], in which higher levels of parent participation resulted from simple modifications of the meeting routine for a special education team. The changes involved having one team member take responsibility for introducing the parent and other team members to one another, pausing frequently during the meeting to see if parents needed clarification or further information, and making sure parents had an opportunity to assert their priority concerns and recommendations.

Brinkerhoff and Vincent [1986] also demonstrated a means for increasing parent-professional collaboration. These authors reported on a project where parents and educators learn to link children's educational goals to their daily routine at home. Brinkerhoff and Vincent encourage professionals to incorporate parents' observations of their child into assessment and parents' priority goals into program plans.

Walker [1989] also provided training to both parents and professionals in hopes of improving collaboration. Walker's training aimed to improve skills in taking another's perspective, providing positive reinforcement, and maintaining frequent contact. This author did not find change in specific communication behaviors, but she did document an increase in participants' interest in parent-teacher communication and cooperation.

Take Time to Make Interactions Truly Collaborative

Perhaps the most comprehensive list of guidelines for professionals in this regard is furnished by Turnbull and Turnbull [1990]. These authors are specifically concerned with parent involvement in the development of the IEP and the IFSP. Their advise, however, is pertinent for teams in many settings. Turnbull and Turnbull offer detailed lists regarding preconference preparation, initial conference proceedings, review of evaluation results, development of goals, determination of placement, and conference conclusion. Their suggestions imply a careful, patient process. As attested to by many parents cited in previous pages, many agencies opt for a more efficient process that, unfortunately, minimizes the involvement of parents.

Even when planning is conducted carefully and patiently, differences among members' perspectives and concerns may result in stalemates or in conflict. An educator and a physical therapist, for example, may disagree about whether it is important for a student with physical disabilities to eat in a cafeteria with the rest of his class and school in order to have a "normalized" mealtime, or whether that child should eat in a quiet, secluded place to promote relaxation and improved oral-motor patterns. An educator and a psychologist might differ about the most appropriate approach to behavior change. A parent and a speech therapist might conflict over whether to aim for verbalizations or an alternative means of communication. All of these represent fundamental and difficult differences. In this event, teams may need a concrete approach to examining and resolving their differences. One such approach—principled negotiation—has been applied to many types of conflict from interpersonal disputes to international negotiations. Principled negotiation may hold promise for teams who need a means of moving beyond differences toward consensus decisions.

Apply Components of Principled Negotiation

Principled negotiation is the term that Fisher and Ury [1983] have used to describe one approach to conflict resolution. Through their work with the Harvard Negotiation Project, these authors have applied this approach to such diverse disagreements as tenant-landlord disputes, conflicts between local governments and their citizenry, and such international tensions as the Middle East Crisis of the 1970s. Fisher and Ury's approach addresses actions or decisions that are stalemated by conflict. Their approach could also be adopted in a proactive way, however, as a general approach to decision making in teams.

The basic elements of principled negotiation include the following:

- Separating the people from the problem;

- Focusing on interests, not on positions;

- Creating options for mutual gain; and

- Using objective criteria to evaluate outcomes.

Separating the People from the Problem

Bailey and Simeonsson [1984] suggested that in an ideal team, conflict is not necessarily absent but stems from substantive issues. Examples of productive conflict might include those cited earlier, such as differences regarding values (e.g., integration) or strategies (such as the use of aversive consequences for behavior). Conflict that is rooted in personality differences, however, threatens the team's effectiveness. Fisher and Ury substantiated this observation and asserted that decision makers will be unable to generate effective decisions if they blame problems on individual participation in decision making.

For example, one of the explanations educators have given for lack of parental involvement on IEP teams is parent apathy [Turnbull & Turnbull 1990]. If a teacher were to apply the "separate the people from the problem" approach in this case, the problem might be stated not as the parents' lack of concern, but as the teacher's frustration with the difficulty of obtaining information from parents that might aid in planning. With the problem restated in this way, the potential for solving the problem is greatly improved. The teacher is unlikely to change a parent or the parents' investment in the team. The teacher, however, could well find a means of obtaining needed information from parents, such as removing logistical barriers to parents' attending meetings or securing information by means other than the team meeting.

Fisher and Ury suggested several ways out of the trap of blaming another person for difficulties in the decision-making process. They highlighted the need for clear and consistent communication. They also advocated the practice of recognizing and acknowledging the emotional by-products of conflicts, such as anger, distress, frustration, and confusion. Finally, they emphasized the importance of checking perceptions rather than making assumptions about why people behave as they do or believe what they profess. Fisher and Ury proposed that by transcending personality differences, parties involved in conflict can begin to view one another as allies in the effort to solve a difficult problem.

Focusing on Interests, Not on Positions

One of the most logical yet novel features of principled negotiation is the emphasis on *interests* rather than on positions. Fisher and Ury provided a succinct description of the difference between the two when they noted, "Your position is something you have decided upon. Your interests are what caused you to decide." A parent team member, for example, may advocate for direct occupational therapy for his son, arguing that the indirect or integrated therapy model that the rest of the team supports does not provide sufficient structure or intensity. Upon exploration, it may become apparent that the father has taken this position because his child, at age 9, does not yet demonstrate the strength and dexterity necessary to manage snaps and zippers and is, therefore, still dependent on others for dressing. The father took a position on a model for service delivery. His real interest, however, had to do with his concern that his son needed to become more independent. With this additional information on the table, the team has the opportunity to construct a plan in which the teams' service delivery preference is adopted, but the father's priorities for instructional goals are respected and addressed.

Fisher and Ury observed that this approach is effective in resolving disagreements for two reasons. First, focusing on interests helps parties in conflict to find a common ground. In the example above, the parent and professional team members upheld opposing positions regarding the appropriate and desirable model for occupational therapy services. All team members, however, could agree that independent dressing was an appropriate goal. They all shared an interest in seeing this student develop the skills he needed to dress himself.

Second, focusing on interests helps team members to identify different paths to the desired end. In the example, the team could elect to find or create more frequent opportunities for the student to practice snapping and zipping throughout the school day. They could also choose to modify the child's clothing, for example, with sticky closures, so that the elusive snapping and zipping skills would no longer be necessary.

On the subject of how to identify interests, Fisher and Ury suggested taking the others' perspectives and trying to imagine or understand why they take the positions they do. The authors recommended making a list of interests that might be influencing all parties. They also emphasized that the most powerful and influential interests reflect basic human needs such as security, recognition, and control over one's life. Once team members are aware of the interests at work in their decision making, they are able to generate options among which they ultimately will choose.

Creating Options for Mutual Gain

"The key to wise decision making," Fisher and Ury [1983] asserted, "lies in selecting from a great number and variety of options." A team can best generate a large menu of options through the process of brainstorming. Brainstorming is an approach with which most team members are like to have experience and includes the following steps:

- Defining your purpose;

- Choosing participants and a facilitator;

- Creating an informal and relaxed atmosphere;

- Seating participants side by side, facing a flipchart or chalk-board;

- Clarifying ground rules, including the rule that no idea is to be criticized;

- Brainstorming; and

- Selecting the most promising ideas and then inventing improvements on them.

In the context of interdisciplinary team work, these activities would most likely take place in preparation for a program planning meeting, such as an IEP meeting. A more formal meeting, however, could be the setting in which the final decision is discussed and agreed upon. Fisher and Ury listed several considerations that can enhance the effectiveness of brainstorming. Three of their suggestions may be particularly useful for transdisciplinary teams.

First is the idea of making sure that parties who hold different positions, particularly parties who disagree with one another, participate in brainstorming together. In the case of parent and professional team members, this implies that both groups should create the list of options that the team will finally consider. Program planning, as it is most frequently practiced, is characterized by professionals determining what recommendations they will make to parents. Parents are, in fact, often unaware of any options other than those that are preselected and presented to them. The process of reviewing all options together gives all participants equal access to information in addition to ownership of the problem.

A second and related consideration is that brainstorming groups look through the eyes of different experts. An interdisciplinary team has the resources, in the form of its members, to consider possibilities from the perspectives of several professional fields, as well as through the parents' expertise.

Third, Fisher and Ury caution that there may not be one best answer. Teams may find their best and most creative plans by selecting combinations or parts of several different options. Once the team has reached consensus on how they will proceed, they can complete the process of principled negotiation by identifying what objective criteria they will use to evaluated their decision.

Using Objective Criteria to Evaluate Outcomes

Interdisciplinary teams traditionally have been concerned with criteria that indicate whether or not a student is achieving or progressing toward specific goals and objectives. These criteria can also be the means by which team members choose to evaluate their plans.

When plans have been constructed through principled negotiation, however, teams might also wish to evaluate their plans in terms of whether the interests of team members have been met.

Summary

In summary, principled negotiation provides a framework that confronts and makes constructive use of differences among team members. In groups that adopt this approach, individual members can accomplish the following:

- View one another as allies in the challenge of fashioning a mutually agreeable and effective plan,

- Explore one another's perspectives in order to better understand differences and to find shared interests,

- Map several different paths to a solution, and

- Use objective criteria to ensure the effectiveness of the plan.

Conclusions

The field of developmental disabilities is moving toward a family-centered approach to services. Recent developments in the field underscore the need to engage parents as active participants on decision-making teams. Including parents may, however, require attitudinal and behavioral adjustments on the part of professional team members.

As teams and individual professionals strive to work collaboratively with parents, they may need to reexamine their attitudes toward the individuals with disabilities with whom they work—moving toward a more positive and holistic view of students, patients, and clients. Service providers may also need to reframe their perspectives on parents and parent involvement.

In addition to the attitudinal and emotional aspects of parent-professional collaboration, several behavioral practices may require review and revision. Parents' inclusion is influenced by such practices as where and when meetings are held, how participants address one another, whether professional jargon replaces more readily understandable terms, whether professionals actively assume responsibility for eliciting parents' views, and whether the team has and uses a shared approach to resolving differences.

Commitment to full inclusion of parents as team members promises to move the field from a long-held ideal to a practical reality. Responsiveness to parents' roles and contributions, furthermore, is essential to the development of truly effective plans.

References

Atwood, B. (1991). Personal communication.

Bailey, D. B. (1987). Collaborative goal-setting with families: Resolving differences in values and priorities for services. *Topics in Early Childhood Education, 5*, 59-71.

Bailey, D. B., & Simeonsson, R. J. (1984). Critical issues underlying research and intervention with families of young, handicapped children. *Journal of the Division of Early Childhood, 9*, 39-48.

Baker, B. L., Heifetz, L. J., & Murphy, D. (1980). Behavioral training for parents of retarded children: One year follow-up. *American Journal of Mental Deficiency, 85*, 31-38.

Brinkerhoff, J. L., & Vincent, L. J. (1986). Increasing parental decision-making at their child's individualized educational program meeting. *Journal of the Division for Early Childhood, 11*, 436-458.

Carney, I. H. (1987). Working with families. In F. P. Orelove and D. Sobsey, *Educating children with multiple disabilities: A transdisciplinary approach* (pp. 407-429). Baltimore, MD: Paul H. Brookes Publishing Co.

Carney, I. H. (1991). Working with families. In F. P. Orelove and D. Sobsey, *Educating children with multiple disabilities: A transdisciplinary approach.* 2nd edition (pp. 407-429). Baltimore, MD: Paul H. Brookes Publishing Co.

Cone, J. D., Delawyer, D. D., & Wolfe, V. V. (1985). Assessing parent participation: The parent/family involvement index. *Exceptional Children, 51*, 417-424.

Diamond, S. (1981). Growing up with parents of a handicapped child: A handicapped person's perspective. In J. L. Paul (Ed.), *Understanding and working with parents of children with special needs* (pp. 23-50). New York: Holt, Rinehart, & Winston.

Dunst, C. J., Trivette, C., & Deal, A. (1988). *Enabling and empowering families: Principles and guidelines for practice.* Cambridge, MA: Brookline Books.

Featherstone, H. (1980). *A difference in the family.* New York: Basic Books.

Filler, J. & Kasari, C. (1981). Acquisition, maintenance, and generalization of parent-taught skills with two severely handicapped infants. *Journal of the Association for the Severely Handicapped, 6*, 30-38.

Fisher, R., & Ury, W. (1983). *Getting to yes.* New York: Basic Books.

Foster, M., Berger, M., & McLean, M. (1981). Rethinking a good idea: A reassessment of parent involvement. *Topics in Early Childhood Education, 1* (3), 55-65.

Fuqua, R. W., Hegland, S. M., & Karas, S. C. (1985). Processes influencing linkages between preschool handicap classrooms and homes. *Exceptional Children, 51*, 307-314.

Garner, H. G. (1988). *Helping others through teamwork: A handbook for professionals.* Washington, DC: Child Welfare League of America.

Garner, H. G. (1982). *Teamwork in programs for children and youth: A handbook for administrators.* Springfield, IL: Charles C. Thomas.

Goldstein, S., & Turnbull, A. P. (1982). Strategies to increase participation in the IEP conference. *Exceptional Children, 48,* 360-361.

Greenspan, S. I. (1988). Fostering emotional development in infants with disabilities. *Zero to Three, 9,* 8-18.

Halperin, L. (1989). Encounters of the closest kind: A view from within. *NASP Communique, 17,* 6.

Halvorsen, A. T. (1982). *Models of parent involvement in the educational process of their severely handicapped children.* Paper presented at the meeting of the Association for the Severely Handicapped, Denver, Colorado.

Harris, S. L. (1983). *Families of the developmentally disabled.* New York: Pergamon Press.

Kaiser, C. E., & Hayden, A. H. (1984). Clinical research and policy issues in parenting severely handicapped infants. In J. Blacker (Ed.), *Severely handicapped young children and their families* (pp. 275-318). New York: Academic Press.

Koegel, R. L., Glahn, T. J., & Hieminen, G. S. (1978). Generalization of parent-training results. *Journal of Applied Behavior Analysis, 11,* 95-109.

Kogan, K. L., Tyler, N., & Turner, P. (1974). The process of interpersonal adaptation between mothers and their cerebral palsied children. *Developmental Medicine and Child Neurology, 16,* 518-527.

Lipton, D. J. (1982). Parents and professionals. In M. Peters (Ed.), *Building an alliance for children: Parents and professionals* (pp. 25-48). Seattle, WA: University of Washington Program Development Assistance System.

Lynch, E. W., & Stein, P. (1982). Perspectives on parent participation in special education. *Exceptional Education Quarterly, 3,* 56-63.

National Center for Clinical Infant Programs. (1985). *Equals in this partnership: Parents of disabled and at-risk infants and toddlers speak to professionals.* Washington, DC: Author.

Orelove, F. P., & Sobsey, D. (1991). *Educating children with multiple disabilities: A transdisciplinary approach* (2nd ed.). Baltimore, MD: Paul H. Brookes Publishing Co.

Peters, M. (Ed.). (1982). *Building an alliance for children: Parents and professionals.* Seattle: WA: University of Washington Program Development Assistance System.

Shearer, D. E., & Loftin, C. R. (1984). The Portage Project: Teaching parents to teach their preschool children in the home. In R. F. Dangel & R. A. Polster (Eds.), *Parent training* (pp. 93-126). New York: The Guilford Press.

Shelton, T. L., Jeppson, E. S. & Johnson, B. H. (1987). *Family-centered care for children with special health care needs* (2nd ed.). Washington, DC: Association for the Care of Children's Health.

Sonnenschein, P. (1981). Parents and professionals: An uneasy relationship. *Teaching Exceptional Children, 14,* 62-65.

Turnbull, A. P., Summers, J. A., & Brotherson, M. J. (1984). *Working with families with disabled members: A family systems approach.* Lawrence, KS: University of Kansas, Kansas University Affiliated Facility.

Turnbull, A. P., Summers, J. A., & Brotherson, M. J. (1986). Family life cycle: Theoretical and empirical implications and future directions for families with mentally retarded members. In J. J. Gallagher & P. M. Vietze (Eds.), *Families and handicapped persons: Research, programs, and policy issues* (pp. 45-65). Baltimore, MD: Paul H. Brookes Publishing Co.

Turnbull, A. P., & Turnbull, H. R. (1990). *Families, professionals, and exceptionality: A special partnership* (2nd edition). Columbus, OH: Merrill Publishing Company.

Vincent, L. J., Lalen, S., Salisbury, C., Brown, P., & Baumgart, D. (1980). Family involvement in the educational process of severely handicapped students: State of the art and direction for the future. In B. Wilcox & R. Yort (Eds.), *Quality education for the severely handicapped: The federal investment* (pp. 164-179). Washington, DC: U.S. Department of Education, Office of Special Education.

Walker, B. (1989). Strategies for improving parent-professional cooperation. In G. H. S. Singer & L. K. Irvin (Eds.), *Support for caregiving families* (pp. 103-120). Baltimore, MD: Paul H. Brookes Publishing Co.

Wiegle, L. (1990). *What parents have to teach professionals.* Paper presented at the conference, "Where the Heart Is: Home, Family, and People with Disabilities," Richmond, Virginia.

Wikler, L., Wasow, M., & Harfield, E. (1981). Chronic sorrow revisited: Parents' vs. professionals' depiction of the adjustment of parents of mentally retarded children. *American Journal of Orthopsychiatry, 51,* 63-70.

Yosida, R. K., Fenton, K. S., Kaufman, M. J., & Maxwell, J. P. (1978). Parental involvement in the special education pupil planning process: The school's perspective. *Exceptional Children, 44*, 531-534.

Part II:
Professional Disciplines

Medicine

By Allen C. Crocker

A Brief History of Medicine

Medical teaching and practice in the modern setting, pertinent to coordinated action and public planning, has a surprisingly recent history. Only in the last century, for example, did the health and diseases of childhood emerge as a specialized branch [Cone 1979]. Jacobi opened the first children's clinic in New York City in 1860, and accepted the first professorship of pediatrics (then also called pediatry or pedology). The Children's Hospital in Boston began in 1869; by the end of the century there were several dozen such hospitals in the United States. The American Pediatric Society was started in 1888, the American Academy of Pediatrics in 1930, and the American Board of Pediatrics in 1933. In 1961 the research base was reinforced by founding of the National Institute of Child Health and Human Development.

Current Philosophies of Treatment and Service

"Modern medicine," Starr wrote, "is an elaborate system of specialized knowledge, technical procedures, and rules of behavior. By no means are these all purely rational" [1982]. This system has a preeminently humanistic goal, namely the relief of disease or disorder through biologically derived understanding. The traditional preoccupation with rectification of pathology is

Allen C. Crocker, M.D., is Program Director for the Institute for Community Inclusion at Children's Hospital, Boston, Massachusetts. Appreciation is expressed to Priscilla Osborne, M.S., R.P.T, for her contribution regarding the relationship between the pediatrician and the developmental physical therapist and to Gerald A. Tuttle, Ph.D., for his comments on the composition and relations among members of specialized medical teams.

underlined by the "Chief Complaint" terminology that opens a medical history. Another major activity is intercession for prevention of disorder where the knowledge base allows—either for the individual (health promotion) or for populations (public health). And a forward look now widely respected suggests that medicine can join in building an expanded concept of health that is stronger than simply the absence of disease.

Because of the direct contact involved with persons served, the universality of individual fears and hopes (mortality), and the aura of scientific foundations, a respect and trust for the medical practitioner prevails. In turn, the profession often assumes the demeanor of authority that exercises extended judgments (regarding such concerns as competence, fitness, disability, illness, and sanity).

The last three decades have seen a challenge to medical authority, as consumerism has brought a more rounded relationship to the exchange. Shared decision making, second opinions, rigorously informed consent, access to records, confidentiality, privacy, and respect of individual (or cultural) taste are essential in the new partnership and are included sometimes in a patient's "Bill of Rights." The profession has also undergone change in current times as it becomes perceived as a "vast industry," or as Starr puts it, "the social transformation of American medicine" [1982]. The cost of medical care has risen in the past 20 years, assuming more than 13% of the gross national product, while disturbing numbers of the population (a sixth in many areas) remain uninsured or underinsured for dependable coverage. Technological advancements (diagnostic and therapeutic) hold both promise and alarm, for personal and economic reasons. Individuals often find medical corporations and defensive medical behaviors discomforting. In this setting of revision and modified prestige, the medical worker is clearly trying to find a valid role that involves a refreshed partnership with clients and that invokes the best of new knowledge and remains aware of societal obligations.

Successful medical treatment draws on a sequence of special features. Some are found as well in other human service encounters, some are fully expressed only in the medical setting. The treatment milieu is basically a two-party interaction, involving a *petitioner* (active or passive) and a service *provider* (directly and personally committed or sometimes operating within an institutional design). The typical interaction can be diagrammed in the following fashion:

Patient:	Physician:
• Request for assistance	• Indication of capacity to assist
• Description of concerns	• Identification of specifics of these concerns and their content
• Sharing in discovery process	• Search and analysis, guided by domains of expressed concern, interpretation
• Understanding, agreement	• Consideration of elements of intervention
• Compliance	• Prescription
• Reciprocation	• Ongoing evaluation
• Continuing components, potential closure	• Therapeutic conclusions, adjustment
• Payment	• Record keeping, billing

Undergirding a favorable prospect for this developing process is a dynamic that needs trust each way and desires to improve health and assist in the improvement process. The financial consequences of the contract can be intrusive. We hope this can be controlled and tensions lightened; a discussion of this is beyond the scope of the present chapter. Some moderation in the zeal for costly comprehensiveness may be appropriate, regarding the consumption of societal resources.

Services Provided in Various Settings

Statistics are available for the distribution of medical professionals holding the M.D. degree, and these indicate the characteristics of the service patterns:

- In 1993, there were 670,000 physicians in the United States, an increase from 334,000 in 1970.

- Of these, 82% were involved in regular patient care (60% in office-based practice) and 152,000 physicians were hospital based (58% as residents and most of the rest as full-time staff).

- Some 7,800 physicians (1.2%) were employed as medical faculty; 14,500 in administration; and 14,700 in research.

- By declared area of specialization, the largest number of physicians were in internal medicine (111,000); family practice

(52,000); pediatrics (46,000); general surgery (38,000); psychiatry (37,000); and obstetrics/gynecology (36,000).

- In contrast, there were only 4,800 child psychiatrists and 4,800 workers in physical medicine/rehabilitation.

- Men comprised 81% of the country's physicians in 1993.

- Of the females, 86% were in patient care, 1.5% in administration, and 1.9% in research [Roback et al. 1994].

We have established a variety of settings for the provision of medical services. To some extent, the environment is a marker of the following expectations:

- A traditionally gentle form of free enterprise exists in usual office practice, solo or group, which has flexible components and may even include home visitation.

- A contract for a specified range of service, with near or total prepayment, characterizes subscriptions of health maintenance organizations (HMOs). The physician has no choice; the patient has some.

- Limited physician selection occurs in the setting of hospital treatment areas and school clinics. Emergency medicine now generally has its own expert teams, prescribed by the system.

- Basically, no freedom of selection occurs at all in residential facilities for persons with mental retardation, mental illness, or certain severe chronic disorders (or in prisons).

- Good will, but only moderate flexibility, is found in the formation of the physician/patient dyad in special project settings, such as community health centers and certain categorical outreach programs.

Clearly, services are what people make them. Young physicians in training are given moderate (but probably inadequate) exposure to atypical treatment habitats that could allow their mental preparation for resilience in later service provision. The current cultural scene has an intense preoccupation with the cost involved in entering the medical treatment process. This preoccupation presses for crisply defined service encounters, codification of the interaction, and utilization review.

Statistics from the American Medical Association report that physicians currently work an average of 59 hours a week, 47 weeks a year [Gonzalez 1994]. For practitioners, the income is substantial—highest for radiologists, surgeons, and anesthesiologists, lowest for those in pediatrics or general practice. In 1992, professional liability claims were filed at an annual rate of 8.9 per 100 physicians (14.8 for obstetricians, 6.9 for pediatricians, 2.4 for psychiatrists) [Gonzalez 1994].

Relationship to Other Disciplines

Modern practice incorporates a large knowledge base and also a consumer demand for coordinating diverse resources. These forces require the physician to look more broadly for allies and to resist traditional assumptiveness and isolation, often a substantial cultural adjustment. For illustration here, pediatrics and, more specifically, the paradigm of developmental and developmental/behavioral pediatrics, show this evolution well [Levine et al. 1992].

Physicians seeing children, both in crises and in well-child care, have a number of tactical advantages. Their offices are predictable sites for encounters with young children, often the only systematic community-based contacts for this in early life. The pediatrician has ready access to diagnostic instrumentation, has approval for formal and informal interventions, and possesses the predominant means for uncontroversial reimbursement of services. These opportunities can be an important force for prevention and advocacy or can be diffused by avoidance of appropriate referral and partnership activities.

For the developmental pediatrician, there are countless territories where potential collisions may occur with other experts in child study and treatment, and where skills and outreach are needed to assure maximum effectiveness, as indicated by the following examples:

- Child abuse (with child welfare);

- Family conflict (social work, counseling);

- School function problems (special education, school psychology);

- Developmental stress (clinical child psychology);

- Difficulties in special skills (habilitative therapies);

- Incomplete support for child health (nursing); and

- Behavioral syndromes (behavioral psychology).

Further, the developmental pediatrician may collide with other specific medical fields, including those for mental health (child psychiatry) and specific disorders of the central nervous system (neurology). Interdisciplinary familiarity and respect are an obvious requirement [Friedman 1985].

In the last several years, the Society for Developmental and Behavioral Pediatrics (incorporating many developmental pediatricians) has invested much effort in considering the proper domain of its specialty for the clarification of families, reimbursement plans, training programs, and its own scholarly activities. The pressure to respond to the call for medically related input in the formation of individualized educational programs within the regulations of P. L. 94-142 and P. L. 99-457 has heightened this assignment.

In a helpful review, Perrin [1992] has described the expected activity of the two leading medical disciplines/specialties in the developmental field.

- The *primary care pediatrician* provides the following:

  - The newborn exam (extended if needed) and parental counseling;

  - Continuing developmental follow-up in early life, with referral for early intervention in situations of risk or disability, anticipatory guidance, parent conferences on common developmental/behavioral problems, counseling on chronic illness; and, later,

  - School readiness assessment, school conferences, planning and guidance in disability or chronic illness, counseling for teen issues, and health education.

- The *developmental pediatrician* or developmental/behavioral specialist in the current system offers the following services:

  - Furnishes neurodevelopmental assessment in situations of risk, suspected delay, or specific disorders;

  - Makes referral for more specific testing and assessment;

  - Facilitates access to parent support services;

  - Provides consultation and assistance in situations of chronic illness, disability, and/or specific behavioral problems; and

  - Advises schools and community programs.

Personal experience in pediatric practice provides a useful example of the dynamics between physicians and other health care professionals. The pediatrician and the *physical therapist* share common concerns regarding the quality of motor function in children, yet each brings his or her own areas of expertise to the evaluation and treatment of a child with a motor disability. To understand the children with motor dysfunction, it is important to integrate the findings of both, as well as that of other team professionals. The pediatrician offers important diagnostic and/or descriptive information concerning health and neurological function. The physical therapist describes the neuromotor system in terms of functions in a developmental framework, to supplement the diagnostic information of the physician. Treatment by the physical therapist is based on the findings of the physician, other team members, and the physical therapy assessment, all of which are necessary to plan a therapeutic approach. Effectiveness is monitored by the physical therapist and feedback provided to the physician regarding goals and the progress toward these.

Many times the relationship between the pediatrician and the physical therapist begins with a referral to the therapist from the physician. Although numerous states have Independent Practice Acts that allow physical therapists (and occupational therapists) to practice without specific referral from a physician, the referral process continues to be the primary initiation of the communication between the two professionals.

The most important part of the referral process is to establish and continue the exchange between the M.D. and the R.P.T. concerning the treatment of the child. Currently, most insurance companies and other reimbursement programs, including Medicare and Medicaid, require a physician's referral for physical therapy before allowing payment of this service. Also, in some institutional settings (hospitals, for example), a physician's referral for physical therapy services is required by the Joint Commission for the Accreditation of Health Organizations. Therefore, physical therapy is closely tied to physician referral for a number of reasons. It should be remembered, however, that this is a referral process and not a process requiring the physician to provide specific "orders" for the physical therapist. The referral system allows the physical therapist to use his or her own professional expertise to evaluate and provide treatment for the child. In acute medical situations, more direct input is necessary from the physician and he or she is clearly the team leader. In developmental situations, an open team approach is more reasonable, with equal input from each discipline.

Key Issues Regarding Participation in Teams

The physician has come late to the role of an egalitarian contributor to the actions of teams with diverse disciplines. Medical training still tends to foster the concept of the physician as a sturdy and resourceful personal problem solver. Further, societal approbation has generally endorsed the assumption by physicians of political, social, and cultural authoritarianism, a situation not well-suited to a shared dynamic. The need to command or control can be a subtle extension of the starched white coat, reinforced by higher salary, longer educational investment, and concurrent diverting organizational responsibilities. Physicians have learned of the special insights offered by other discipline colleagues (in the developmental services scene, for example) while chairing multidisciplinary teams; their capacity for turn-taking in the interdisciplinary model may be more constrained (see Figure 1).

It is encouraging to note that physicians currently in training, perhaps especially pediatricians, have come to appreciate the professionally expanding and fulfilling aspects of practice shared with other therapists, behaviorists, and social scientists. Similarly, educators and child care workers have

Figure 1. The Dynamics of Interactions in Some of the Assessment or Treatment Teams on Which Physicians Find Themselves*

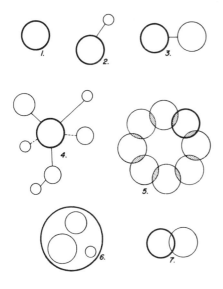

1. Solo practice
2. Consultation
3. Partnership
4. The multidisciplinary team
5. The interdisciplinary team
6. The transdisciplinary team
7. Collaborative practice

The bold circle in each diagram represents the coordinator or communicator; in some settings, this will be the medical member.

* **Source:** Crocker, A. C., & Cullinane, M. M. (1983). The function of teams. In M. D. Levine, W. B. Carey, A. C. Crocker, & R. T. Gross (Eds.), *Developmental-behavioral pediatrics* (pp. 990-993). Philadelphia: W. B. Saunders, Co.

found physicians to be sympathetic team members when a good exchange of professional insights can be assured [Crocker & Cullinane 1983]. Ultimately, of course, it is the realization that good outcomes in human services require coordinated contributions that assure appropriate teamwork from physicians. City, state, and federal projects often insist upon complementary efforts by medical and other workers, and the consumer movement will not tolerate an incomplete conceptualization of the total health support potential.

Some teams with medical membership are firmly structured on an expedient basis, sanctioned by a necessary accountability for technological achievement. These include, for example, the group that is addressing the solution of a complex neurosurgical intervention or an organ transplant. In the traditional formula of public clinics for children with special health care needs (state-directed Title V programs), such as those for young persons with cerebral palsy, spina bifida, or muscular dystrophy, a medical director (orthopedist, neurologist) serves as chair. This individual often is employed as a salaried consultant with intermittent responsibility, while the sustaining and coordinating functions are provided by agency staff persons on the team, such as the nurse clinician, social worker, and physical or occupational therapist. Teams for the treatment of children with cleft palates have members with well-identified functional contributions. The chair is commonly the plastic surgeon and intimately involved are the otolaryngologist, the speech pathologist, the audiologist, and the orthodontist. Supporting members include the nurse, psychologist, social worker, and prosthodontist.

The presence of medical members of teams may also be ordained by law, agency regulation, or accreditation requirement. Examples include competency assessment for court actions (such as for guardianship decisions) and in institutional reviews boards (IRBs) or human rights panels. In the latter situation, the specific views of a physician are required in analysis of programmatic health risk, chemical restraint, questions of infectious disease transmission, etc. Obviously a need exists to assure responsible and accurate contributions to the deliberations, while at the same time accommodating other concerns based in the team about particular and general human factors.

The term "medical model," now not infrequently used in a pejorative or scolding fashion, refers to organizational design where attention to health (and/or disease) concerns are preeminent, perhaps unfairly. The principal abuse of this model was historic in the state residential facilities for persons with mental retardation, where the institutions were run as monolithic hospitals, residents were called patients and lived in wards, and the superintendent was a physician.

In the larger scene of long-term care for persons with special needs, medical directive dominance has waned rapidly during the past two decades, but some residual fear regarding medical models still exists in community-based services. There is a concern that medical pronouncements, with insinuations of illness, will subvert the thrust toward normalization in behavioral and educational planning [Crocker 1989]. Improved social awareness by physicians, better exchange at levels of scholarship and public planning by all professionals, and actualization of consumer movement expectations, can serve to avoid the unilateral promulgation of the "medical model" and the distress that its concepts produced. The physician member on the modern team should provide a balanced view regarding necessary health-related services.

Levels of Training, Licensure, and Certification

There are currently 126 active medical schools in the United States (45 states, plus the District of Columbia and Puerto Rico) [Roback et al. 1994]. The total pool of applicants to these U.S. medical schools was 26,915; that same year there were 13,135 graduates (33.2% women) [Moore & Priebe 1991]. The schools with the largest number of graduates now practicing in the United States are (in order) the University of Illinois, Indiana University, University of Minnesota, University of Michigan, Jefferson Medical College, State University of New York/Brooklyn, Harvard Medical School, Northwestern University, Ohio State University, and the University of Tennessee.

Modern medical education has become much more comprehensive than was characteristic of the formula traditional for many decades. The latter held that the first two years must be strictly scientific and preclinical, and the last two would then encompass a stylized experience with each of the clinical specialties. Medical students had long expressed pervasive discontent with such substantial postponement of encounters with patients and with a schedule that underplayed the broader personal and societal implications of human maladies. Consumers have also insisted that the preparation of physicians be more invested with social and ethical training.

Present curricula now include guided contact with patients beginning in the first year, such as in small group tutorials. Overall, the social and behavioral sciences are strongly represented throughout, as is work on the doctor/patient relationship and on preventive medicine and health care policy. There is still the initial obligation to complete anatomy, biochemistry, physiology, pharmacology, developmental and molecular biology, pathology, microbiology, and the neurosciences, but the previously mentioned elements are interlaced.

Further, there are often new structures introduced for the student body that set the scene for ongoing coordination, advisory relations, more faculty contact, and student stimulation and reflection. At Harvard, for example, this includes continuing membership for all students in one of five academic societies, staffed with Masters, Educators, Senior Fellows, Tutors, Preceptors, and Advisors [Harvard University 1994].

Also of relevance is the greater capacity now for independent study and research during the major four years, plus the opportunity for joint degree programs. The latter at Harvard include the M.D. plus a Master of Public Health (five years), Master of Public Policy (five years), or Ph.D. (average of seven years).

Medical education is notably expensive, with annual tuitions for private schools having risen 400% (after adjustment for inflation) since 1960, now averaging $17,794. More than four out of five students must take on educational loans, and the average debt at the time of graduation for these trainees is $46,224. It has been observed that the nearly unavoidable obligation to borrow large amounts of money may have significant long-lasting effects on choices about careers [Hughes et al. 1991].

Licensure for medical practice in the United States is regulated by state boards. Applications are accepted after one year of graduate (residency) training by the majority of the states; eight require two such years. In 1992, 19,760 initial license were issued by diverse routes [Bidese 1994]. The majority of the new U.S. graduates have obtained certification via the National Board of Medical Examiners, a three-part qualification ordinarily begun during the school years (completed by 12,200 in 1992). There has also been a uniform Federal Licensing Examination (FLEX), introduced in 1968 and periodically updated, accepted by all state boards and used by a variety of candidates. Some 13,000 FLEX exams were given in 1992, with a 72% pass rate. Both the National Board and the FLEX examinations are now gradually being replaced by the new United States Medical Licensing Examination (USMLE). Graduates of schools outside the United States, Canada, and Puerto Rico must complete the examination of the Education Commission for Foreign Medical Graduates (ECFMG); this also includes a listening comprehension English test. In 1992, 11, 800 ECFMG certificates were issued.

Re-registration is required by state boards of medicine annually or biannually. This is without examination, but 30 states demand concurrent completion of Continuing Medical Education credits [Bidese 1994].

Advanced professional qualification is documented by completion of "specialty boards," now available in 23 formal examinations. There has been a strong growth in pursuit of such certification, with virtually all residency programs now oriented to assisting the trainee in this preparation. By 1986, 79% of all U.S. practitioners had become board-certified. The largest numbers completing current examinations are (in order) for internal medicine, family practice, pediatrics, psychiatry and neurology, obstetrics/gynecology, radiology, and surgery [Moore & Priebe 1991]. Basic board examinations can be taken following three to five years of graduate training, varying with the field; subspecialty certification is not uncommon after additional, usually Fellowship-level, study. In 1990, among the candidates for pediatric specialty boards, 21% indicated that they planned further work and career orientation in one of the seven established subspecialty areas (cardiology, neonatology, hematology/oncology, etc.) and another 12% in the noncertified subspecialties (developmental/behavioral, etc.). Of considerable interest is the growing number of women medical graduates currently entering American hospital residency training programs. In 1989, 54% of first-year pediatric residents were women, as well as 50% of those in obstetrics/gynecology, 48% in psychiatry, 39% in family practice, 16% in general surgery, and 5% in orthopedics [Moore & Priebe 1991].

Professional Organizations and Leading Journals

The giant among professional medical organizations is, of course, the American Medical Association, currently with 290,000 members. It is generally accorded with having an essential role in defining the vocational mission and standards in medicine, albeit while executing complex political behavior. It publishes the medical journal with the world's largest circulation, the *Journal of the American Medical Association* (JAMA), 336,000 weekly copies average during 1994. A representative active state medical association, the Massachusetts Medical Society, has 15,700 members. It, in turn, publishes a weekly with extraordinary prestige, the *New England Journal of Medicine,* now at 231,000 circulation (63,000 foreign). The most influential pediatric organization, the American Academy of Pediatrics, has 46,600 members (compared to a recent figure of 27,200 board-certified pediatricians in the

United States), and reaches actively into the areas of health planning and advocacy for children. Its journal, *Pediatrics*, also has strong professional prominence, and a circulation of 57,000. *The Archives of Pediatrics & Adolescent Medicine* has a circulation of 33,000 in 85 countries.

Standards of Ethics

As would be expected, strong ethical tracks exist that acknowledge the special opportunities of medical workers and the ameliorating elements that should enrich those human service circumstances. The aggregate of medical ethical concern and tradition is well presented in the review of Reiser et al. [1977]. For team functions, there would seem to be four predominant areas of special interest:

- **Personal behavior.** Accountability and grace are expected in physician actions, whether in the Hippocratic affirmation ("I will use treatment to help the sick according to my ability and judgment"), or the American Medical Association Principles ("Physicians should merit the confidence of patients entrusted to their care, rendering to each a full measure of devotion"). Fellow team members should be able to expect an earnest identification with human need, in an atmosphere of respect for the client.

- **Mobilization of resources.** There is the requirement that the physician on the team will reach by all reasonable means for diagnostic accuracy about health-related conditions, especially as these bear on family counseling, insights about expected natural history of the related conditions, and potential interventions regarding primary or secondary disability. While it is true that quality health care is not a full entitlement in our culture [Crocker 1989], persons with disadvantage or reduced choices deserve particular diligence in the application of health maintenance efforts. This also involves the intelligent and humanistic utilization of habilitation and rehabilitation measures for human improvement, by best current understanding.

- **Human issues in modern technology.** The now somewhat awesome potential for invoking advanced biomedical approaches for human problems requires simultaneous creativity and vigilance. The medical team member will gain by sharing with colleagues the broader implications of the effects of new genetic counseling techniques, fetal manipulation, supports to extremely low birthweight newborn infants, complex surgical repair, organ transplantation, research investigations, and experimental medications. Gains and losses may have new definitions.

- **Maintenance of values.** Throughout team operations, the autonomy and special values of the person served must remain ascendant. It would be tragic if the physician representative did not preserve this central concept and provide leadership in language, personal gesture, relation to family, and public stance. Love is the touchstone.

Practice standards and guidelines exist in many spheres that offer direction for performance in human service activities, often with ethical insinuations. For the child with special needs, for example, it is now acknowledged that services must be more user-directed: family-centered, community-based, and coordinated. Adult programs have parallel guides. Medical services can grow in this format [Crocker 1992]. And teams with physicians can actively engage these considerations.

Summary

There are now 670,000 physicians in the United States, 60% of them in office-based practice, and the remainder on hospital staffs, in research, in administrative positions, or as medical faculty. Self-revision by the profession, and greater exercise of strength by consumers, has led to more nearly a partnership in the formulation of clinical service plans. At present, 79% of American physicians are specialty-board certified. Women now constitute 19% of doctors and 33% of new graduates.

Much interaction occurs in medical settings between doctors and nurses, agency personnel, behavioral scientists, teachers, therapists, and managers. Membership on larger teams, however, is a relatively modern experience for physicians; it is increasingly successful as trust develops and control is balanced. Some teams have a prescribed medical presence (e.g., competency team, institutional review boards), while in others the physician simply shares common clinical hopes.

It is expected that physicians will bring to team action a substantial devotion to the client, the capacity to make good use of clinical resources, appropriate interpretation of new technology, and an orientation to values and standards in service.

References

Bidese, C. M. (1994). *U.S. medical licensure statistics and current licensure requirements*. Chicago, IL: American Medical Association.

Cone, T. E., Jr. (1979). *History of American pediatrics*. Boston: Little, Brown & Company.

Crocker, A. C. (1989). Partnerships in the delivery of medical care. in I. L. Rubin & A. C. Crocker (Eds.), *Developmental disabilities: Delivery of medical care for children and adults* (pp. 3-9). Philadelphia, PA: Lea & Febiger.

Crocker, A. C. (1992). Expansion of the health-care delivery system. In L. Rowitz (Ed.), *Mental retardation in the year 2000* (pp. 163-183). New York: Springer-Verlag Publishers.

Crocker, A. C., & Cullinane, M. M. (1983). The functions of teams. In M. D. Levine, W. B. Carey, A. C. Crocker, & R. T. Gross (Eds.), *Developmental-behavioral pediatrics* (pp. 990-993). Philadelphia, PA: W. B. Saunders Co.

Friedman, S. B. (1985). Behavioral pediatrics: Interacting with other disciplines. *Journal of Developmental and Behavioral Pediatrics, 6*, 202-207.

Gonzalez, M. L. (1994). *Socioeconomic characteristics of medical practice 1994*. Chicago, IL: American Medical Association.

Harvard University. (1994). Harvard Medical School Course Catalog 1994-95. *Official Register of Harvard University*. Cambridge, MA: Author.

Hughes, R. G., Barker, D. C., & Reynolds, R. C. (1991). Are we mortgaging the medical profession? *New England Journal of Medicine, 325*, 404-407.

Levine, M. D., Carey, W. B., & Crocker, A. C. (Eds.). (1992). *Developmental-behavioral pediatrics* (2nd ed.). Philadelphia, PA: W. B. Saunders Co.

Moore, F. D., & Priebe, C. (1991). Board-certified physicians in the United States, 1971-1986. *New England Journal of Medicine, 324,* 536-543.

Perrin, J. M. (1992). The breadth of developmental and behavioral services. *Journal of Developmental and Behavioral Pediatrics, 13,* 7-10.

Reiser, S. J., Dyck, A. J., & Curran, W. J. (Eds.). (1977). *Ethics in medicine: Historical perspectives and contemporary conclusions.* Cambridge, MA: MIT Press.

Roback, G., Randolph, L., Seidman, B., & Pasko, T. (1994). *Physician characteristics and distribution in the U.S.* Chicago, IL: American Medical Association.

Starr, P. (1982). *The social transformation of American medicine.* New York: Basic Books, Inc.

T E A M W O R K

Nursing

By Eunice Shishmanian & Mary Challela

A Brief History of Nursing

Nursing has had a long and heroic history. From earliest times people who were ill or infirm were cared for by family members or concerned neighbors. The emphasis was on curing illness, tending with childbirth, or helping those who were dying. There was little beyond that, and there was no such person as a "trained nurse."

Modern day nursing came into being as a consequence of Florence Nightingale's experiences with the wounded soldiers during the Crimean War [Torres 1980]. The first schools of nursing in the United States were founded in 1873 at Bellevue Hospital in New York City, the Connecticut Training School in New Haven, and the Boston Training School [Leddy & Pepper 1989]. The first formally trained American nurses graduated from Bellevue in 1873. These early nurses were given a formal knowledge base and supervised practice. Otherwise, their duties were the same as less formally prepared nurses: tending to the hygienic, nutritional, and environmental needs of patients and following doctors' orders. In addition, they were responsible for preparing meals, cleaning patient areas and kitchens, and performing other necessary duties. Hours were long, with few hours off each week [Friedman 1990].

By the end of the 1890s, nursing leaders began to seek education standards for the schools of nursing, including licensure and registration for graduate nurses as a means of stabilizing and upgrading the quality of nursing. By 1923, 48 states, the territory of Hawaii ,and the District of Columbia had licensure laws in place [Friedman 1990].

The number of nurses continued to increase in the 1930s, along with the number of hospitals and patient care requirements, all of which brought

Eunice Shishmanian, M.S.R.N., is retired from the Institute for Community Inclusion at Children's Hospital in Boston. Mary Challela, R.N., D.N.Sc., F.A.A.M., is retired from the Shriver Center, Waltham, Massachusetts.

pressure on the hospitals' governing bodies to hire graduate nurses instead of placing the burden of care on nursing students. Although the University of Minnesota established a three-year diploma program with the College of Medicine, the first university school with its own dean was set up at Yale University in 1923. However, hospital-based schools of nursing remained the predominant model until the mid-1970s [Leddy & Pepper 1989]. The hospital-based educational programs were medically oriented and illness focused, with faculty that consisted of physicians and nurses whose preparation was primarily in hospitals. While recommendations regarding nursing education focused on the need to broaden the scope and experience of students to include prevention of illness, health promotion and follow-up, the psychosocial needs of patients, and community practice, it was not until 1950 that these critical elements received much attention [Friedman 1990].

During the 1950s, another track for educating nurses developed that combined general and technical instruction within a higher education setting. The purpose of this model was to produce the "technical" nurse who would be educated in two-year community colleges for direct care of patients. Thus, three different types of nursing education programs evolved:

- The hospital/diploma,

- The university/baccalaureate degree, and

- The community college/associate degree.

These programs all prepare students for different levels of nursing but for the same licensure, which became the criterion for practice in the role of registered nurse [Leddy & Pepper 1989]. These factors, along with the increasing demands on nursing, gave impetus to specialization in nursing and the rapid development of master's degree programs in accredited schools [Lambert & Lambert 1989].

The 1970s saw a growing awareness of the need to describe in theoretical terms what nursing is and what nurses do. The academic community emphasized the development of nursing theories through research. Simultaneous with the move toward the baccalaureate program came the need and push for advanced education at the master's and doctoral levels [Lambert & Lambert 1989]. The master's-prepared nurse has become the specialist, and the doctoral nurse the research and leader [ANA 1980].

As a result of the expansion of knowledge and explosion of technologies in the 1980s, there were vast changes in the types of treatment and the scope of medical and nursing practices in hospitals. These changes were soon reflected in the community, along with the recognition of the importance of prevention of illness and disabilities and of rehabilitation. Cost containment became an issue, particularly with health insurance companies. At that time, it became clear that the same level of nursing practiced in the hospital was needed in other settings: schools, homes, community programs, and in the workplace.

As the 21st century approaches, nursing has a new definition: "The diagnosis and treatment of human response to actual or potential health programs." This definition means that nursing has four defining characteristics:

- Observable human responses to potential or health-related problems, such as self-care limitations, pain, and emotional problems related to health, which result in a nursing diagnosis;

- Theory applications;

- Nursing action or intervention; and

- Evaluation of the effects of actions on what was observed.

Nursing addresses the health needs of individuals, which includes preventive aspects, care during illness, and rehabilitation activities throughout the life span. Nursing reaches people in all walks of life, and within various educational and social settings. Unlike most other health care professionals, nurses as caregivers are responsible for providing care and coordinating health care services 24 hours a day in a variety of health care settings. These include hospitals, neighborhood health centers and clinics, health maintenance organizations, long-term care facilities, schools, and private and group practices.

Current Philosophies of Treatment and Services

The philosophy of nursing is based on the worth and dignity of the individual. Each person is a unique being with important needs, who has the right to sufficient information to participate actively in health care discussions, thus retaining an appropriate degree of autonomy. By virtue of its definition, nursing has an orientation of care that promotes wellness, as well as care during illness. Over the past years, there has been a gradual transition from a disease-oriented focus to that of attaining, maintaining, and regaining good health. Even terminology reflects this change. Health care, a broader term, is replacing the more limited term of medical care at health centers. (Care of the sick continues to be the major responsibility of the hospital.) In addition, there has been an increasing realization that each individual must take considerable responsibility for his or her health and should be supported to develop and achieve this goal. Toward this end, nursing care is planned with consideration of the physical, intellectual, psychosocial, spiritual, and cultural needs of the person.

Standards are the mechanism by which the nursing profession describes the responsibilities and accountability of its practitioners, and therefore standards reflect the values and priorities of the profession. Standards also provide direction for and evaluation of nursing practice, and describe a competent level of care and professional performance regardless of setting and practitioner. Moreover, standards are defined as qualitative statements that stipulate explicit and valid expectations of nursing practice. They outline specific patient outcome criteria that are essential for evaluating the effectiveness of nursing interventions. These criteria provide a creative framework that encourages and supports the nurse in assuming responsibility and accountability for professional practice. The parameters for safe, consistent, and quality interventions are delineated in standards of nursing practice. Guidelines, which are derived from standards, describe recommended courses of action in specific areas of clinical practice and particular client needs. Figure 2 on the next page summarizes the relationships among nursing practice, nursing process, and standards of nursing practice [ANA 1980].

Nursing recognizes and supports the nation's efforts to create quality accessible services at affordable costs. The field has responded in several ways to assist the reorganization of health care, congruent with the philosophy of the discipline. Nursing has promoted the development of improved comprehensive nursing roles in different settings and has taken an active approach by demonstrating a unified stance as a profession. Nursing has presented an agenda for immediate health care reform in the document, "Nursing's Agenda for Health Care Reform" [ANA 1991]. The agenda is

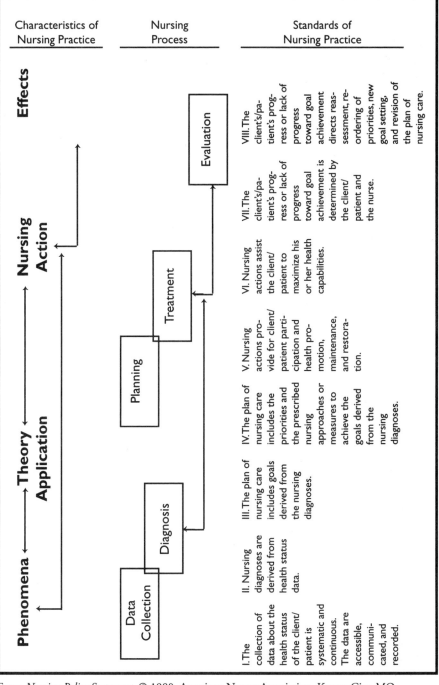

Figure 2. Defining Characteristics of Nursing Practice

directed at the current crisis in health care. The plan, a product of consensus building within organized nursing, addresses restructuring, reorienting, and decentralizing health care service in order to promote access to services cost containment, and the assurance of quality care.

Furthermore, the agenda emphasizes primary health care services, health promotion, and restorative services in a cost-efficient manner that includes consumer responsibility and participation in health care decision making. It assures that services are appropriate, cost effective, and accessible with the focus on consumer needs and participation.

Relationship to Other Disciplines

Historically, as nursing developed as a profession, other disciplines began to emerge and define themselves in areas once considered the province of nursing, such as social work, psychology, nutrition, and rehabilitative therapies. These disciplines overlap with nursing, often creating blurred boundaries and a confusion in expectations by professionals and consumers [Friedman 1990].

As part of the health care system, nurses share responsibility for the health and well-being of citizens along with professionals from other disciplines. Each discipline has its own areas of expertise, specific characteristics, and responsibilities. As members of the interdisciplinary team, each professional brings a discrete core of knowledge and particular perspective to the health care goal; however, many of the disciplines share a common knowledge base.

Since nursing is a dynamic and generalist discipline that responds to the needs of individuals and society, the field's boundaries are flexible. The Nursing Social Policy Statement [ANA 1980] speaks to its intersections with other professions and its extensions into other domains. Nursing frequently intersects with some disciplines, such as medicine. Few problems ensue when there is shared collegiality and respect. Similarly, there is much sharing of domains with rehabilitative therapies and social work. There is a difference, however, between a general knowledge and skill that is derived from a common knowledge base and a specific core of knowledge and skill that comes only from a prescribed course of study and practice.

To avoid conflicts, it is important for each discipline to identify clearly its area of expertise and to respect those of others. These conflicts should be expected and confronted, because they force all parties to take another look at what is happening, to identify and discuss the source of the conflict, and to come to a common course of action in the best interest of the client. This is negotiation, one part of the interdisciplinary process that leads to professional growth and improved client outcome [Brill 1976]. An example might be how to deal with a "feeding problem" of a 2-year-old child who refuses table food and has been fed only strained food. Questions one might ask include: Are the child's teeth in good condition? Does he have normal oral motor coordination? Do the parents consider this a major objective at this time?

The representative of each discipline involved focuses on the area of most concern to that discipline, but, once all team members discuss the overall goal (i.e., to ensure good nutrition and normal progression of feeding skills), a constructive plan is developed to address everyone's concerns. The first steps are to discuss the issue with the parents to find out their interest and concerns, to assess the child's nutritional status and oral motor capabilities, and to review the pediatrician's medical work-up. The nurse assumes the responsibility to interview the parents in more detail to assess their general concerns, their living habits, particularly with respect to mealtime, and the child's developmental history and general health profile. During this assessment, the nurse also gathers information on dietary habits and a general nutritional history; this is shared with the nutritionist who makes an in-depth assessment of the child's nutritional status.

Key Issues Regarding Participation in Teams

Nursing has a unique role on the interdisciplinary team, whether in the hospital, where the emphasis is to achieve wellness, or in the community or school setting, where the emphasis is to maintain health. Nursing, by virtue of its broad base of knowledge and skills may dovetail, overlap, or be distinctly separate in its role. To be an effective team member, the nurse must identify the role clearly and specifically, recognize the need for and deal with overlap, know the boundaries and territories of expertise of other disciplines, and develop influence in sharing the power distribution of the team [Challela 1979].

Families play a significant role in the patient's care, and they must be invited to participate on the team to the degree to which they are interested and are capable. Comprehensive and effective care is planned with regard for a full range of needs and should be addressed in ways to assist clients to reach, adapt to, and sustain their health potential. The environment should encourage self-care to the level possible, fostering independence and interdependence as needed. Compassionate care should be given within a climate of trust. If transitions are planned, there must be continuity in the therapeutic plan.

Challela [1979] outlined the nursing role on the team as follows:

- **Promotion and maintenance of health** of the client and family by identifying those issues that might interfere with functioning or potentially cause problems. Possible needs to be addressed may be a chronic illness, nutritional deficiency, environmental hazards, or public health measures, such as immunizations and accident prevention. The nurse also assesses and addresses nutrition, elimination, sleep/rest patterns, activity/exercise routines, the person's perceptions of his or her health, and sexuality/reproductive issues as they relate to and affect the client's needs and the proposed program.

- **Facilitator of growth and development** relative to the person's age, diagnosis, and potential. In the case of children, this includes anticipatory guidance for parents, helping them to be aware of the next stage of development in order to promote its accomplishment.

- **Provider of supportive counseling** for parents/caregivers and family to enhance their interactions with the family member involved and their development as a functional unit. The nurse is cognizant of the values and beliefs of the family/client and suggests measures to support their coping skills.

- **Teacher** for the client and family members in the areas of self-care skills and decision making to enhance potential development based on the principles of growth and development and mental health. The nurse teaches strategies to develop sensitivity to the cues the client presents to alleviate stress. In addition to the client and family, the nurse also teaches other team members principles of good health and how to use the services of the nurse effectively to identify potential health problems. An example of this is promoting safety in the environment.

Levels of Training, Licensure, and Certification

Nursing has three levels of basic academic preparation: diploma, associate degree, and baccalaureate degree, all leading to eligibility to take the registered nurse licensure examination and the designation of registered nurse, yet varying widely in scope, amount of education, and practice. Although the American Nurses Association in 1965 stated that the baccalaureate degree is the entry point for the "professional nurse" and the diploma and associate degree is the "technical nurse," in reality there has been little or no difference in levels of responsibility assigned in the work settings in hospitals.

Many studies have been done to clarify and differentiate between the technical and professional levels of practice. In 1984 and 1985 ANA reaffirmed the 1965 position statement and formally established two categories of nurses. The National League for Nursing and the American Association of Colleges of Nursing supported these standings in 1986 [Leddy & Pepper 1989]. Currently, there are 21 nursing organizations that support the baccalaureate as the educational preparation for professional practice [Lambert & Lambert 1989].

One study [Young et al. 1991] of 14,000 full-time nurse graduates of all three types of programs looked at the types of activities the nurse in the hospital engaged in, such as health histories or evaluations of patient outcomes, and the number of times these activities were performed. Results demonstrated that the baccalaureate-prepared nurse performed more complex tasks and spent less time in routine low-skilled work in comparison with the diploma-educated nurse.

These complex tasks included evaluating patient outcomes, performing psychosocial examinations, and conducting physical examinations, and determining nursing diagnoses categorized as "higher nursing skills," including assessment, data analysis, priority setting, and evaluating outcomes.

Another conclusion of the study was that baccalaureate-prepared nurses allocated their time differently from the nurses within the other two levels of preparation in functions performed. Nurses at all levels participated in prevention activities and health promotion.

Within the profession, the ANA has defined two levels of professional practice: the generalist and specialist. Specialization in nursing practice permits new applications of knowledge and refined nursing practices to flow from the specialist to the generalist.

The generalist provides care to individuals whether healthy or ill. The generalist uses a comprehensive approach to health care and can meet the variety of needs of people in hospitals, home, and community. The generalist may be prepared in a diploma, associate degree, or baccalaureate educational program; however, the type of education program determines the amount of independence and expertise of the practitioner and, therefore, his or her responsibilities. Generalists in nursing form the majority of the nursing profession and therefore provide a comprehensive approach to health care.

The specialist in nursing is an expert in a defined area of practice. Specialization is a narrowed focus in one part of the nursing field involving the application of a broad range of theories to the needs of individuals and groups. This includes specific age groups, specific types of practice, specialized fields, and the education of practitioners. Specialization involves empirical and controlled research to clarify discrete fields and areas to generate new theories and approaches to the solution of health problems. The nurse specialist is educated at the master's and doctoral levels.

Nurse specialists may hold a variety of titles: clinical nurse specialist, nurse practitioner, educator, etc., all of whom are educated at the master's and doctoral levels. The clinical nurse specialist has advanced knowledge and skills in a specialized area of practice, such as maternal, child, community health, or geriatrics, and can address the needs of the particular population in any setting. The nurse practitioner has advanced skills in physical assessment, preventive aspects of illness, and the diagnosis of minor illnesses, and often functions in such primary care settings as clinics, schools, physicians' offices, and other community settings.

The nurse specialist at the doctoral level is prepared to initiate and carry out research for the purposes of generating hypotheses, testing existing theories and developing new ones that affect the health and well-being of society on the health continuum. The doctoral nurse possesses the skills

Table 1. Scope of Nursing*		
Practice	**Education**	**Role**
Generalist	Diploma	Generalist
	Associate Degree	
	Baccalaureate Degree	
Specialist	Master's Degree	Clinical Nurse Specialist
		Nurse Practitioner
	Doctorate	Educator
		Researcher

* From *Nursing Policy Statement,* © 1980. American Nurses Association, Kansas City, MO. Reprinted with permission.

necessary for developing curricula to meet the emerging trends in the health care system to ensure adequate preparation of competent professional nurses (Table 1).

Licensure is the legal basis for practice established by law in the individual states and is accomplished by means of a written test complied by a pool of experts throughout the country under the auspices of the National Council of State Boards of Nursing. Nurses may receive reciprocity to practice in different states by means of applying to the desired state, meeting required test scores, and paying a fee. Fees and frequency of renewal varies between states. Most states require evidence of continuing education units of credits as a condition of license renewal.

Certification refers to a formal recognition of expertise in a specialty area via a written examination and evidence of practice under the auspices of the ANA. It is reserved for those nurses who have pursued education beyond basic preparation, received the endorsement of their peers, and demonstrated special knowledge and skills that surpass those required for licensure. Evidence of continuing education and practice are requirements for periodic review.

Services Provided in Various Settings

Nursing is the art of applying scientific principles of health care to the individual and family throughout the life cycle to promote the optimum well-being of the total person in society. Toward this end, nursing includes the following:

- Health promotion;

- Prevention of illness and disability;

- Assessment; and

- Care during illness and follow-up, as needed.

These measures are accomplished by counseling, education, and/or direct physical/psychological care as determined by the person's age, health condition, and environmental circumstances in schools, the workplace, home, residential settings, clinics, hospitals, prisons, and shelters.

Health promotion and **prevention of illness and disability** include teaching the essentials of good health, safety and prevention, the importance of immunizations, how to establish and maintain a healthy life style by being aware of the dangers of alcohol, smoking and drugs, and the importance of good nutrition and dental care. Health promotion and prevention of illness and disability also include identifying the need for and referring the person to appropriate services as indicated. Examples of these are genetic or family counseling, housing assistance, and a comprehensive medical work-up by a physician or a psychiatric evaluation.

Assessment and maintaining well-being include taking data on the individual's general health status, developmental history, family and home environment, ethnic/cultural background, community resources, and other relative factors that influence health and well-being. In school and community settings, assessment might include periodic visual, auditory, and developmental screenings or the response to treatment of an acute or chronic illness. In the hospital, assessment includes gathering information that might affect treatment, as well as the patient's response to specific treatments or medications.

Care during illness occurs either in the hospital, at home, or in community settings established for persons who are ill or recovering from illness. In these instances, care includes a variety of activities related to getting well and preventing further complications or disabilities:

- Coordinating the care plan with other disciplines and being responsible for the direct or indirect care of patients throughout 24 hours, 7 days a week.

- Monitoring vital signs (temperature, pulse, respiration, blood pressure);

- Carrying out treatments and medications ordered by the physician; assuring that nutrition, fluid, and elimination needs are met;

- Providing an environment to promote healing;

- Supporting the patient and family in their response to illness;

- Initiating or participating in follow-up planning; and

- Mobilizing aftercare resources.

Throughout all contacts with people, regardless of age, health, or developmental status, the nurse initiates or participates in teaching and counseling activities to promote health, prevent illness and disability, and help people to achieve an optimum level of wellness. Implicit in health education and counseling are the importance of maintaining the integrity of the individual, encouraging autonomy, and recognizing that everyone is influenced by the culture and attitudes of the greater society. The goal of nursing is to demonstrate the value of each person's contribution to society and society's obligation to provide assistance as the person strives to achieve good health, recover from illness, cope with disability, and enjoy the opportunities that lie ahead.

Professional Organizations and Leading Journals

The American Nurses Association represents the profession at the national level and incorporates the state nurses associations within its governing body. It was formed in 1911 by the "amalgamation of alumnae associations" of schools of nursing. The National League for Nursing (NLN) was established in 1893 from the former American Society of Superintendents of Training Schools for Nurses. It consists of nurses and other individuals interested in the nursing profession. One of its major functions today is the national accreditation of nursing education programs [Friedman 1990].

Indicative of the heterogeneity, yet specialization in nursing, is the plethora of nursing organizations. Some of these related to the practice setting, such as the community or hospital, while others relate to a practice role such as educator, administrator, or researcher. In addition, several organizations acknowledge achievement by means of peer recognition, where admission is by invitation only. (See Table 2.)

Nursing is prolific in its publications. *The American Journal of Nursing* is the organ of the ANA, written primarily for the clinician. Each specialty area publishes and disseminates new information, emerging trends, and issues through specialized journals. Other publications address specific areas of concern to the clinician, researcher, educator, and administrator (see Table 3 on page 88).

Standards of Ethics

The professional nurse's education and practice promote an understanding of the nature of human values. Ethical thinking embodies concepts of human values and personal philosophy. This background enables the development of a philosophy that guides the making of ethical judgments. Each nurse enters the profession with goals, values, and self-concept and, in addition, makes a commitment to uphold the values and moral obligations of the profession's code of ethical practice. This code is the framework for conduct in carrying out nursing responsibilities. The nurse makes ethical decisions within these guidelines and obligations established by the profession.

The ANA has provided leadership in documenting the primary goals and values of nursing in *The Code for Nurses with Interpretive Statements*. This informs both the nurse and society of the profession's expectations and requirements in ethical matters. The values applicable to clinical practice guide the nurse to the following standards:

- To provide services with respect for human dignity and the uniqueness of the individual;

Table 2. Professional Nursing Organizations

American Academy of Nursing
American Association of Colleges of Nursing
American Association of Nurse Anesthetists
American Nurses Association
American Psychiatric Nurses Association
Association of Black Nursing Faculty in Higher Education
Association of Community Health Nursing Educators
Association of Critical Care Nurses
Association of Rehabilitation Nurses
Emergency Nurses Association
International Society of Nurses in Genetics
NAACOG, Organization for Obstetric, Gynecologic, and
Neonatal Nurses
National Association of School Nurses
Nurse Consultants Association
Orthopedic Nurses

- To safeguard the client's right to privacy of information;

- To ensure safety for the client by protecting the client from inconsistent, unethical, or illegal practice by others;

- To be responsible and accountable for individual nursing judgments and action;

- To maintain competence in nursing;

- To exercise informed judgment using individual competence and judgment in seeking consultation, accepting responsibilities, and delegating nursing activities to others;

- To participate in the development of the profession's body of knowledge;

Table 3. Leading Nursing Journals

Advances in Nursing Science
American Journal of Maternal Child Nursing
American Journal of Nursing
Image, Journal of Nursing Scholarship
Journal of Advanced Nursing
Journal of Gerontological Nursing
Journal of Nurse Midwifery
Journal of Nursing Administration
Journal of Nursing Education
Journal of Obstetric, Gynecologic and Neonatal Nursing
Journal of Pediatric Nursing
Journal of Psychosocial Nursing
Journal of School Nursing
Nurse Educator
Nursing Clinics of North America
Nursing Outlook
Nursing Research
Oncology Nursing Forum
Pediatric Nursing
Public Health Nursing
Rehabilitation Nursing

- To participate in efforts to improve standards of nursing;

- To participate in maintaining conditions of employment conducive to high-quality nursing care;

- To participate in maintaining the integrity of nursing to the public; and

- To collaborate with health professionals and citizens in promoting community and national efforts to meet the health needs of the people.

In determining how to act when confronted with a dilemma, the code provides a framework that guides a process of thinking. Based on the context in which the situation is occurring, a fitting response can be determined by posing three questions:

- What is the right thing to do in this situation?

- What is the good thing to do and for whom is it good?

- What is the most fitting response based on the context in which the problem presents itself?

Nurses are advocates for patients and clients and are committed to good health care. They have no vested interest, such as financial gain, except in what is the best care for the client, which places them in a strong advocacy position. They seek to provide options so clients may have a voice in determinations that influence their care. Ethical issues often differ for the nurse in contrast to other professionals. "Ethical rounds" is a format that can be used for reflection and clarification of the elements of decision making around actual or hypothetical situations. An interdisciplinary team requires sufficient opportunity for its members to discuss and articulate the professional values and viewpoints each discipline brings to the situation. There is a need for planned opportunities in a calm setting to allow team members to go beyond the question of what to do. Consideration of the ethical dilemma in a variety of learning settings allows time for this reflective thinking to occur.

Summary

In conclusion, the nursing role on the interdisciplinary team has been shaped by its history and philosophy. It has evolved from caring for and helping the "infirmed" with a minimum of preparation, to being expert clinicians, educators, and researchers. Nursing embodies the holistic perspective of the individual with a broad knowledge base and skill level. The nurse synthesizes information from other disciplines which is then integrated into a cohesive plan of care for the client and family. Finally, the nurse, as caregiver and healer, provides and coordinates health care in a family-centered approach throughout the life cycle.

References

American Nurses' Association. (1980). *Nursing: A social policy statement.* Kansas City, MO: Author.

American Nurses' Association. (1985). *The code for nurses with interpretive statements.* Kansas City, MO: Author.

American Nurses' Association. (1991). *Nursing agenda for health care reform.* Kansas City, MO: Author.

Brill, N. (1976). *Teamwork: Working together in the human services.* New York: Lippincott.

Challela, M. (1979). The interdisciplinary team: A role definition for nursing. *Image, 11,* 9-15.

Friedman, E. (1990). Troubled past of invisible profession. *Journal of the American Medical Association, 264,* 2851-2859; *23,* 2977-2981; *24,* 3117-3122.

Lambert, C. E. Jr., & Lambert, V. (1989). *Perspectives in nursing.* East Norwalk, CT: Appleton-Lange.

Leddy, S., & Pepper, J. M. (1989). *Conceptual basis of professional nursing* (2nd ed.). Philadelphia, PA: Lippincott.

Torres, G. (1980). Florence Nightengale. In *Nursing theories* (pp. 27-28). Englewood Cliffs, NJ: Prentice Hall.

Young, W., Lehrer, E., & White, W. (1991). The effect of education on the practice of nursing. *Image, 23,* 105-108.

T E A M W O R K

Physical Therapy

By Beverly Rainforth & Pamela Roberts

A Brief History of Physical Therapy

The Early Years

With no formal "reconstruction" or rehabilitation program in place at the beginning of World War I, the Surgeon General of the U.S. Army called on a group of prominent physicians to study established European programs. That same year, 1917, the Surgeon General established The Division of Special Hospitals and Physical Reconstruction to implement physical, educational, and vocational Reconstruction Aid Programs that provided rehabilitation for those injured in the war. Both physical and occupational therapy grew out of these Reconstruction Aid Programs.

Originally called Physiotherapy, the field incorporated existing but separate therapeutic interventions documented as far back as 3000 B.C. Muscle training, massage, water, and electrical applications formed the basis of the physical therapists' skills used to restore function and prevent disability following disease, injury, or the loss of a body part. Spurred on in the 1920s and 1930s by civilian needs associated with industrial accidents and polio epidemics, the profession was well established by World War II. A professional journal was founded and educational programs accredited.

Today, physical therapists use the therapeutic effects of such physical agents as heat, light, electricity, water, and sound waves, as well as massage, exercise, and manual and developmental techniques to assist persons of all

Beverly Rainforth, Ph.D., P.T., is Associate Professor of Special Education, State University of New York at Binghamton. Pamela Roberts, M.A., P.T., is Associate Professor and Program Director, University of Connecticut, Storrs. Preparation of this chapter was supported, in part, by Grant #H086V40007 from the U.S. Department of Education to Allegheny-Singer Research Institute and State University of New York at Binghamton. The positions presented herein do not necessarily represent policies of the U.S. Department of Education, and no official endorsement should be inferred.

ages to reach optimal function. Physical therapists contribute to wellness and to reduction of the incidence and severity of physical disability, bodily malfunction, and pain.

Several federal and state mandates affected the growth of the profession. For example, physical therapy was identified as a reimbursable service under Medicare and Medicaid legislation in 1965. As a result, hospital-based and outpatient physical therapy grew in scope for both the elderly and the poor. Physical therapy services were also covered by private insurance.

With passage of the Rehabilitation Act of 1973, the public and those paying for services recognized physical therapy's role in evaluating and eliminating architectural barriers and maximizing access to public buildings, employment, and education for all persons regardless of handicap. In 1975, the Education for All Handicapped Children Act (EHA) explicitly named physical therapy as a related service and part of the educational team mandated to plan and implement free, appropriate public education programs in least restrictive environments for all children. In 1986, the EHA was amended to establish services for infants, toddlers, and preschool children. As a result of these mandates, physical therapists have expanded their services into a variety of settings, such as child care centers, preschool programs, public schools, and community-based supported work environments. In 1990, the Individuals with Disabilities Education Act (IDEA) reauthorized the EHA and its amendments, reasserting the importance of physical therapy as a service in early intervention and educational programs.

Even more recently, managed health care has grown in popularity as employers looked for ways to decrease their group health insurance costs. Industrial physical therapists now work both to prevent injury and to maintain and restore health after injury or disease. The health fitness wave of the 1980s expanded opportunities for physical therapists to provide services to amateur and professional athletes of all ages. In the 1990s, the growing elderly population challenges physical therapists to provide innovative and cost-effective residential and community services.

Physical therapy, which serves infants and their families, children and adults with developmental disabilities, employees and elderly citizens who are well and at risk, victims of disease or trauma, and persons recuperating from surgery, has grown in both breadth and depth through more than 75 years of existence.

Current Philosophies in Treatment and Services

Early in the history of the profession, physical therapy focused primarily on helping stabilize or improve a patient's medical status under the direction of a physician. Current philosophies in treatment and service require physical therapists to deal with issues that are more complex in terms of professional competencies and, at the same time, more practical in terms of the consumer's quality of life.

Diagnostic Problem Solving

The physical therapist is a diagnostician of movement function and dysfunction who identifies the probable structural, physiological, and behavioral responses that lead to the consumer's abilities, limitations, potentials, and concerns. A comprehensive physical therapy assessment includes appropriate referrals from, referrals to, and ongoing communication with other members of health and education teams.

A recent conference established the following principles regarding the practice of physical therapy and fulfillment of the physical therapist's role as diagnostician [APTA 1991]. Anatomy, physiology, applied physiology, pathology, neuroscience, behavioral science, human growth and development, biomechanics, and kinesiology are the foundations for physical therapy decisions. The scope of the physical therapist's clinical decisions for evaluation, treatment, and treatment modifications extend across the musculoskeletal, cardiovascular/pulmonary, and neuromuscular clinical sciences. Decisions require consideration of relevant moderating factors, including but not limited to age, gender, ethnicity, culture, family support, community context, and individual as well as group motivations.

Functional Outcomes

Watts [1985] discussed important considerations when determining outcomes of physical therapy services. "Outcomes are described in terms of attributes of value to the patient, such as survival, changes in level of function, [and] amount of discomfort..." [Watts 1985]. Therefore, physical therapists work toward the following:

- Achieve the outcomes that matter most to the individual being treated,

- Minimize the risk of particularly dangerous or unpleasant consequences, and

- Limit excessive use of scarce resources.

By focusing primarily on functional movement, the physical therapist works closely with the consumer and family to identify congruent goals and to work systematically to meet those goals. It is essential that the goals are meaningful to the consumer.

Often the setting of practice influences the level and type of functional emphasis. For example, working in a home care setting as a member of a hospice team with a person who is terminally ill, the therapist will focus on the person's overall comfort and the ease of care provided by the family. In a school setting, the therapist will focus on the ability of the student to take full advantage of the learning opportunities offered there.

Health Promotion and Disease Prevention

As more has been understood about disease and dysfunction over the past half century, physical therapy has naturally moved into the area of health promotion and disease prevention. The physical therapist integrates health teaching and consultation with consumers and their families, empowering consumers and families to take control of their own health. By accepting a health promotion and disease prevention perspective, physical therapy has begun contributing to meeting the U.S. Goals for the Year 2000 and the Education Goals for Health Professions for the Year 2005 [Shugars et al. 1991]. The addition of screening and health, fitness, and mobility education have expanded physical therapist service models beyond the typical rehabilitation procedures to a broader base model in physical therapy departments of major hospital, public, and private education settings as well as private physical therapy clinics.

Trend Toward Accountability for Treatment Effectiveness

In the 1970s, insurance companies and public policy began to emphasize cost containment in health care settings. Hospitals and other institutions, such as nursing homes and visiting nursing services, were mandated to evaluate the need for and cost of particular services. Physical therapy research to compare the results of alternative treatment approaches and to identify standards for quality and cost-effective services became an important national professional effort. The profession has adopted the idea that "quality care" is a multidimensional concept that includes access to care, efficiency and outcome of that care, as well as coordination of the care received across disciplines and levels of intervention. There is increasing recognition that the interactions between and among those providing care impact on quality, so more information is being shared about referral relationships, case management issues, and roles and responsibilities of therapists in various settings and on various types of teams.

Because mobility, functional movement, and access impact heavily on the multidimensional "quality of life" factors and outweigh medical stability as a more traditional unidimensional measure, credit for the importance of physical therapy has grown. Researchers are starting to show that what physical therapists do indeed makes a difference. Although clinical research on efficacy has been an emphasis, many more specific studies are necessary. Databases of physical therapy patient outcomes help inform those who oversee health care costs and help mold the decisions therapists make toward "best practice."

Services Provided in Various Settings

Although physical therapists share a common set of skills, responsibilities, and roles, there are numerous variations to meet the goals of different service settings.

Medical Settings

Congruent with the traditional model of curative health care, physical therapists in conventional general hospital settings often focus primarily on restoring function through the direct service model of care. Consumers may receive specific physical therapy interventions daily or even twice daily in order to decrease pain, increase range of motion, increase strength and endurance, and begin returning to such basic activities of daily living as getting into and out of bed, walking short distances, and transferring to or from a chair. Specific activities and interventions are determined through assessing problems and setting goals that will facilitate the person's return home or to a rehabilitation or skilled nursing care residential facility.

Team interactions in the medical environment require sharing information and discussing expectations so that professionals, family, and consumer can agree on a general vision for the consumer. Often that shared vision affects the quality of life for the consumer and family, both for the immediate future and for longer range, especially when the consumer is coping with an irreversible disease or disability.

Inpatient Rehabilitation Settings

In these settings, physical therapists often work on teams intended to provide specialized services to consumers with particular types of needs. The idea of coordinated multidisciplinary services has been valued since the emergence of rehabilitation hospitals and skilled nursing facilities and has resulted in assembling stroke teams, developmental teams, traumatic brain injury teams, and hospice teams. Even with these teams, however, services may be a series of isolated single interventions rather than coordinated and collective solutions and strategies to help consumers reach their maximum potential.

Effective teams commit themselves to a shared vision and to consistent strategies for interventions. A good example of a rehabilitation team is one in which team members set consistent cognitive demands and communication interaction methods for persons with traumatic brain injuries. While team members typically have priorities corresponding to their discipline, the team as a whole agrees on a general approach. For example, with a 19-year-old young man recovering from an automobile accident, the speech therapist works on functional conversation, the occupational therapist focuses on dressing and self-feeding, and the physical therapist works on walking and functional wheelchair tasks. The general approach with this young man, his family, and nursing staff is planned to challenge and empower him to participate fully in all services. Consistent verbal directions or cues, a structured schedule, and general limitation of extraneous and distracting sensory stimuli are integrated into all services the team provides. The young man's ability to take full advantage of his services improves when the team coordinates their overall approach and strategy for his care.

Along with others involved in the consumer's rehabilitation, the physical therapist is an important member of this type of well-developed interdisciplinary team. The physical therapist role in the rehabilitation setting expands past direct service to include education, consultation, and planning with the consumer, family members, and other professionals.

Early Intervention Programs

At least 20 years ago, physical therapists who worked in early intervention realized that they could not effectively meet the needs of infants and toddlers with disabilities by merely providing direct treatment services to babies. Physical therapists understood that young children with disabilities had numerous needs, that services from multiple service providers were hard for young children to integrate, that multiple services increased stress on families, and that parents were important members of the decision-making and service provision team. In response, physical therapists assumed roles as transdisciplinary team members in early intervention programs, with parents recognized as the primary interventionists for their child [Patterson et al. 1976].

Federal early intervention law now requires many of the best practices advocated two decades ago. A physical therapist may be selected as case coordinator for a young child with many gross motor needs, reducing the number of professionals with whom parents must communicate and coordinate while ensuring high-quality services. As parents identify typical family daily routines, physical therapists help identify needs and methods for better positioning (e.g., an adapted infant seat); postural control (e.g., sitting with good alignment); and mobility (e.g., rolling or crawling to get a toy). Addressing these needs both allows the child to participate more successfully in the daily routines, and reduces the need for parents to add "treatment sessions" to already busy schedules. Finally, physical therapists integrate their methods with those from other disciplines into a comprehensive intervention that parents and other caregivers help implement. Although physical therapists may provide direct treatment to infants and toddlers, first priority is placed on working with family members to help them address their child's needs.

Special Education Programs

In special education, physical therapy is provided as a related educational service and intended to assist a child to derive greater benefit from the educational program than if physical therapy were not provided. The

Pediatric Section of the American Physical Therapy Association identifies two levels of service that might be written into a student's Individualized Education Program to meet his or her unique needs [Martin 1990]. Indirect services involve the physical therapist and other members of the educational team exchanging information to improve the amount or quality of the student's participation. Indirect services may involve general consultation or specific child/procedure consultation. General consultation is aimed at information sharing and problem solving, such as determining a furniture arrangement that enables a student to move her wheelchair around her classroom more independently. Specific child/procedure consultation is aimed at providing more consistent intervention, so a teacher and teaching assistant might learn to apply a student's splints, teach him to stoop to get toys from a shelf, and teach him to ascend and descend stairs as he goes to lunch. The physical therapist would work directly with the student to assess his abilities and needs and to determine effective intervention strategies, but would use treatment time to help classroom staff improve their skills.

Special education teams place high priority on indirect services, because students can work on motor skills several times each day, not just when the physical therapist is present. Direct services are the hands-on treatment provided by the physical therapist. These are not necessarily provided in a separate room, however, and may be provided while a student is walking to the bus, playing at recess, participating in homemaking class, or working at a community-based vocational site. Whether physical therapy is provided through indirect or direct services, the relevance of physical therapy to the educational program is improved when assessment and treatment occur in the student's routine educational activities. Rainforth et al. [1992] provide a thorough description of physical therapist roles and strategies for fulfilling those roles in special education settings.

Home and Residential Programs for Children and Adults

Home and residential programs may be provided in a person's natural home or in a licensed residence. In residential programs, as in educational programs, physical therapists are part of a team charged with developing and implementing an integrated, individualized plan to assist the child or adult to achieve purposeful outcomes [Accreditation Council 1989]. Purposeful outcomes of physical therapy are gross motor abilities needed to assume and maintain upright postures (e.g., sitting, kneeling, standing); to travel from one location to another (e.g., rolling, crawling, walking, driving a wheelchair, transferring in/out of a car); and to participate in daily living activities (e.g., to use a broom, to play T-ball). A physical therapist is also concerned with whether a child or adult has strength, coordination, range of motion, and endurance to achieve these purposeful outcomes.

Residential programs offer physical therapists unique opportunities to work closely with families and paid caregivers to address these needs in the context of daily living activities. For example, assessment may show that a child has delayed gross motor development with poor range of motion and coordination in the arms, legs, and trunk. In cooperation with caregivers and other team members, the physical therapist designs procedures to work on these needs each day during the morning dressing routine. Such procedures might include gently moving specified body parts until the child relaxes; helping the child make choices by reaching toward preferred clothing; stretching shoulders, elbows, wrists, hips, knees, and ankles while putting on shirts, pants, socks, and shoes; prompting the child to push arms into sleeves and legs into pants and to roll from side to side as pants and shirt are pulled toward the waist; prompting the child to lift her head and push with her arms while assuming a sitting position; and positioning the child in an adapted wheelchair. The physical therapist designs similar procedures for other activities where the team determines needs and opportunities exist.

With a geriatric population, the emphasis may be less on habilitation or rehabilitation, per se, and more on maintaining wellness and existing abilities. Comfort, ease of personal care, and participation in meaningful activities are more likely to be high priority for aging consumers. Physical therapists have an important role in maintaining this population's physical activity, which is critical to maintain both physical and mental health. When physical therapists provide services in a person's home, they have particular responsibility to determine and abide by each individual's personal preferences. This responsibility applies whether a person resides in his or her natural home or in a congregate living facility, and whether or not the person is able to articulate preferences through conventional means.

Community Services for Persons with Disabilities

Physical therapists in community programs assume similar roles and address similar needs as in residential programs. A particular need in the community is for mobility, which involves the person's access to and endurance when travelling within or among work, leisure, public transportation, and other community living environments [York 1989]. For example, while working in a small office, a person may have sufficient endurance and coordination to walk holding furniture and may have no need for physical therapy services. This person may be unable to walk from the bus stop to the office, however, requiring assessment of alternate means of mobility (e.g., carpool to office, manual or power wheelchair); accessibility of public transportation and the office building; and utility of alternate mobility in relation to other community activities (e.g., grocery shopping, attending art class). Assessment may reveal that several alternatives are feasible, but that the person will need physical therapy services to learn new travel skills and to improve stamina during community travel.

Because many adults with physical disabilities use adapted equipment for travel, positioning, and participation in various activities, physical therapists in community services often make recommendations for adaptations. In a job where workers usually stand, for example, a physical therapist might help adapt the work station for a person in a wheelchair or recommend a parapodium or supine stander. If a stander is used, the physical therapist would teach a job coach or coworkers how to use the equipment safely. When a person with physical disabilities uses any position (e.g., sitting) for long periods of time, the physical therapist guides planning for position changes at regular intervals throughout the day. Using an effective positioning plan helps protect the person from deformities while it improves circulation, respiration, and other bodily functions.

Industrial Settings

The physical therapist consults and provides environmental adaptations in work environments. In these settings, therapists emphasize education about body mechanics and posture to decrease work-related injury and dysfunction, such as low back pain, carpel tunnel, and cervical stress syndromes. In addition, when injury occurs, on-site physical therapy with supervised exercise and environmental adaption programs often allow workers to progress slowly toward full participation in the job, decrease sick days, and minimize recurrent injury or dysfunction. Other team members in industrial settings may include physicians, nurses, human resource personnel, as well as community agency personnel who provided health and social services to injured workers.

Physical therapists may also provide screening services in industrial settings. General health and fitness screening have become one way that employers try to decrease their health insurance costs. Screening programs can identify workers with significant dysfunction early in the course of disease or dysfunction and thereby prevent or limit disability. This early intervention can increase productivity and decrease the more expensive crisis intervention health care costs associated with full blown injury or disease.

Relationship to Other Disciplines

Physical therapists have skills and responsibilities that complement and overlap with many other disciplines. The growing shortage of physical therapists in almost all service settings and geographic areas makes it essential that available physical therapy services be maximized. Table 4 shows several areas of need and some disciplines that may contribute to addressing those needs. When referring to this table, it is important to realize that disciplines often contribute different perspectives on one area of need. For example, an important daily living activity for a child with severe disabilities is mealtime. While a physical therapist may focus on sitting posture and head control, an occupational therapist may focus on use of utensils, a speech therapist may focus on oral motor skills for eating and communication skills to indicate preferences, and a special education teacher may focus on learning style and steps in the various tasks composing mealtime. Family members and friends are important members of the team also, since they provide important information about eating habits and feedback about the utility of various methods during typical mealtimes.

To use team members most effectively, it is important to determine the consumer's specific needs and then determine who can best address those needs, recognizing that skills vary among professionals within the same discipline. Physical therapists' skills vary tremendously, depending upon initial preparation, work experiences, and continuing education. One physical therapist may not have the skills to address the previously mentioned child's needs at mealtime; another may have skills in positioning, oral motor aspects of eating, and using utensils. Because occupational therapists and physical therapists have many overlapping skills, programs for children and

Table 4. Needs Addressed by Physical Therapy and Other Disciplines

Area of Need	Other Disciplines
Gross motor development	
Birth to 18 months	Occupational therapy
	Nursing
	Education
18 months to 6 years	Occupational therapy
	Education
6 years to adulthood	Physical education
	Adapted physical education
	Recreation/leisure
	Education
Daily living activities	Occupational therapy
	Education
	Speech therapy [eating]
	Rehabilitation counselling
Adaptations	Occupational therapy
	Rehabilitation engineering
	Orthotics and prosthetics

adults with developmental disabilities often adopt a "developmental thera-pist" model in which one therapist serves as "primary therapist" for a team and the other therapist serves as consultant. This approach maximizes use of available staff and reduces the number of team members who must coor-dinate on a daily basis.

Key Issues Regarding Participation in Teams

While there are many issues shared by all disciplines, there are also unique issues that affect how physical therapists participate in teams.

Shortage of Physical Therapists

There is a national shortage of physical therapists, which will not be remedied soon. Because improved recruitment and retention by employers will not increase the number of therapists available, programs must focus on using available expertise more efficiently. One approach is for physical therapists to coordinate and integrate their methods with those from other disciplines and with other team members accepting responsibility for daily implementation of intervention plans. Another approach is to identify areas of overlap between physical therapy and other disciplines, so other team members might fulfill roles traditionally assigned to physical therapists. Teams cannot afford to have rigid territorial boundaries drawn around the practice of physical therapy or other disciplines; rather, flexibility needs to characterize decisions about who provides services and how. Finally, when physical therapy is a low priority relative to other needs, consumers and their teams may benefit from focusing on the higher priorities rather than dilute the impact of all services.

Professional Preparation for Teamwork

The majority of today's physical therapists were prepared to work in multidisciplinary teams in medical settings (e.g., Rainforth 1985]. The medical terminology routinely used by physical therapists has further served to categorize physical therapists as medical professionals and sometimes to alienate them from consumers and other team members. Current regulations, accreditation standards, and best practices call for interdisciplinary and transdisciplinary teamwork in a variety of nonmedical settings, however. Some physical therapists have actively sought information about new roles and responsibilities; others have clung to traditional roles and resisted change.

While therapists often report that they are well prepared to function in a team, those beliefs are not always supported by behavior in actual work settings. Therapists who use accountable decision making with functional outcome assessments as measures of their success have been found to also practice with high levels of team interaction. Their team interactions often include establishing shared visions, setting goals that are consumer and family centered and congruent with those of other professionals, sharing roles with team mates, and overlapping roles and responsibilities with team mates.

The definition of a "master clinician" is broadening to include not just those therapists who generate and choose alternative and successful strategies specific to individuals and their situations, but also those therapists who seek out and use interdisciplinary and transdisciplinary strategies to provide coordinated, congruent, effective, and efficient service.

Consumer-Oriented Services

The traditional medical model in which many physical therapists were prepared was a paternalistic model. Professionals were viewed as "experts" who advised patients and their families regarding the correct course of action and compliance was expected. Patients often were defined in terms of their diagnosis or disability, and referred to as "the CP child" or "the quad." These attitudes are changing, and physical therapists now recognize that a "patient" is a consumer of physical therapy services and the most important member of the team. The consumer is viewed as a person, not a diagnosis; when a diagnosis or disability is relevant to a discussion, the person is referred to as "a child with cerebral palsy" or "a man with quadriplegia." Physical therapists also recognize that consumers have the right to be active members of the decision-making team, and physical therapists have the responsibility both to encourage that participation and respect the outcomes [Bradley & Knoll, no date]. Operationalizing this philosophy requires physical therapists to adopt new strategies, however.

First, the team needs a shared vision of a desirable future for the consumer. A consumer may indicate that a desirable future would be to attend college, or to live in a supported apartment, work in a local small business, and enjoy a variety of leisure activities with family and friends in the local community. Then the physical therapist can help the consumer identify abilities and supports necessary to make the vision a reality. Physical therapy services are provided to address the needs, goals, and priorities the consumer identified. Adequacy of services is evaluated in terms of consumer satisfaction with processes and outcomes. Although many physical therapists find this change in roles challenging at first, helping to empower consumers enables them to experience new levels of satisfaction.

Traditional Referral and Reimbursement Models

In most states, physical therapists are still required, by law, to have a physician referral prior to providing services. In some service settings, physical therapists are the only members of the team with this professional constraint. For some settings and agencies, reimbursement for physical therapy services is contingent upon the physical therapist providing direct hands-on treatment, which limits the scope of available services and supports. These constraints have created frustration among consumers, physical therapists, other professionals on their teams, and employers. Fortunately, changes are underway in these systems.

The number of states seeking and gaining direct access for physical therapy services by consumers increases each year. In "direct access states" the physical therapist's increased autonomy has not decreased interactions with other health professionals. Instead, interdisciplinary collaboration has increased to include relevant referral both to physical therapists from physicians and others and from physical therapists to other health, education, and social service providers.

Patient education, home evaluations, and adaptive equipment consultations are now listed as reimbursable interventions, despite an insurance system that is still oriented primarily toward fees for medical services. While the number of consumers and the number of therapists working in managed care, health maintenance organizations, and prospective payment systems is increasing, a full transition away from the medical model, crisis intervention, fee-for-service system has yet to occur. Change is slow. The American Physical Therapy Association is working to increase the scope of reimbursable services. Concurrently, studies are helping to identify the patterns of physical therapy service with outcomes correlated with decreased health care costs. Minimizing the frequency and duration of services while still reaching the consumer's, family's, and society's goals for independence and maximum functional abilities is a goal of the profession.

With the advent of educational payment for physical therapy as a related service under P.L. 94-142, physical therapists' reliance on medically oriented insurance reimbursement diminished. Unfortunately, a new trend of school systems to bill public and private medical insurance providers confuses the educational versus medical benefits of physical therapy and hinders broader interdisciplinary and transdisciplinary approaches in these nontraditional settings. Professional organizations and consumer advocacy groups at the federal and state levels have begun to identify strategies to address this problem.

Levels of Training, Certification, and Licensure

Today, physical therapist and physical therapist assistant educational programs are accredited by the Commission on Accreditation in Physical Therapy Education of the American Physical Therapy Association (APTA). Standards for the preparation of physical therapists were first set in 1928. Until 1936, the American Physiotherapy Association held sole responsibility for enforcing standards in education. The American Medical Association (AMA) assumed responsibility for setting and enforcing standards from 1936 to 1977. In 1977, The American Physical Therapy Association was recognized as an independent accrediting agency by the U.S. Commissioner on Accreditation in the U.S. Office of Education and by the Council on Postsecondary Accreditation. In 1983, the APTA became the sole accrediting agency for physical therapist and physical therapist assistant educational programs.

Physical Therapist Preparation and Credentialing

Completion of an accredited entry-level educational program prepares the physical therapist to sit for a nationally run licensure examination required for state level licensure. All accredited programs must meet the *Evaluative Criteria for Accreditation of Education Programs for the Preparation of Physical Therapists*, adopted in 1990 with an effective date of January 1, 1992. As of June, 1992, 55 programs met these standards through master's entry-level programs, while 75 educational programs met these standards through baccalaureate degree. The American Physical Therapy Association supports a transition to postbaccalaureate preparation for entry into the profession [APTA 1985]. Four baccalaureate degree programs have plans for transition to master's entry-level programs during 1992. Because entry-level programs prepare therapists for broad areas of physical therapy across many settings, entry-level preparation cannot make the new therapist an expert in all areas of physical therapy evaluation, decision making, and interventions.

In addition to basic entry-level preparation leading to licensure, therapists often acquire advanced master's degrees or doctoral degrees in areas of specialization or in related education, management, and basic science fields.

The changing knowledge base in physical therapy requires other lifelong learning strategies for the therapist to keep up with the field. Numerous continuing education programs are offered, often with continuing education credit or certificates of completion. Some states require continuing education for licensure renewal.

Physical Therapist Assistant Preparation and Credentialing

The APTA first authorized the training of physical therapist assistants (PTAs) in 1967 and approved the first programs in 1971. The specific legal recognition of the physical therapist assistant differs from state to state, with some states requiring licensure of the PTA and other states simply defining the role through statutory language in physical therapist licensure. In states that require PTA licensure, a nationally available examination is offered to graduates of accredited physical therapist assistant programs. Currently there are 124 PTA entry-level programs in the United States.

PTAs are trained primarily at the associate degree-level and work under the supervision of a physical therapist in the delivery of physical therapy services. Their duties include assisting the physical therapist in implementing treatment programs according to the plan of care, training patients in exercises and activities of daily living, conducting treatments, using special equipment, administering modalities and other treatment procedures, and reporting to the physical therapist on the patient's responses [CAPTE 1992]. The PTA's role varies with the setting but includes team interactions as delegated and coordinated through the physical therapist. PTAs do not carry out initial evaluation and assessments but often are delegated responsibility for interventions in the plan of care, which is designed and modified by the physical therapist.

Certified Advanced Clinical Specialists

In 1978, the American Physical Therapy Association established the specialist certification program to provide formal recognition for physical therapists with advanced clinical knowledge, experience, and skills in a special area of practice. The program evolved from the membership of special interest sections of the APTA as a means to encourage and facilitate professional growth. Coordination of the standardized application and examination process is provided by the American Board of Physical Therapy Specialties, which governs the process. Councils representing each of the specialty areas are appointed to delineate the advanced knowledge, skills, and abilities for each area, to determine the academic and clinical requirements for certification, and to develop the certification examination.

To be eligible for certification, therapists must have achieved a required number of hours of clinical practice in the specialty area within the last 10 years, demonstrate evidence of knowledge in the competency areas, meet any additional requirements specified by the individual specialty council, and pass an examination. Currently seven areas for specialty certification exist: cardiopulmonary, clinical electrophysiologic, geriatric, neurologic, orthopaedic, pediatric, and sports. The first specialists were certified in 1985, with average yearly increases of more than 25% since that time [ABPTS 1992].

Professional Organizations and Leading Journals

The American Physical Therapy Association (APTA)

The American Physical Therapy Association represents more than 53,000 physical therapists, physical therapist assistants, and students, comprising about 60% of the therapists practicing in the United States. The object of the APTA, as stated in its Bylaws, is "to meet the physical therapy needs of society, to meet the needs and interest of its members, and to develop and improve the art and science of physical therapy including practice, education, and research" [APTA 1989]. Physical therapists (Active members), physical therapist assistants (Affiliate members), and students of any physical therapy curriculum make up the constituency. The APTA monitors the ethical practice of physical therapy by addressing questions regarding the competency of those practicing in the profession and taking actions as necessary.

The APTA is governed by a Board of Directors that implements policies set by the House of Delegates, which is made up of delegate representatives from each state chapter. In addition, the APTA has Sections that consist of members who have common interests in special areas of physical therapy.

Sections of the American Physical Therapy Association

Sections include the seven specialty certification areas listed previously and numerous other special interest areas. Listed below are the areas of common interest represented by APTA Sections.* Sections promote the interests of their members and often collaborate with the Association to provide information or respond to issues specific to the area of common interest. Many sections offer either a journal or a newsletter for communication with members. Sections have representation in the House of Delegates, the APTA's policy-making body.

Acute Care	Neurology
Administration	Ob-Gyn
Aquatic Physical Therapy	Oncology
Cardiopulmonary	Orthopedics
Clinical Electrophysiology	Pediatrics
Community Health	Private Practice
Education	Research
Geriatrics	Sports Therapy
Hand Rehabilitation	Veterans Affairs
Health Policy and Legislation	

Physical therapist assistants are members of the Affiliate Assembly. Students of physical therapy programs are members of the Student Assembly. Each of these assemblies have representation in the APTA House of Delegates. The assemblies often sponsor continuing education programming and issue forums, allowing the APTA to better meet the needs of its physical therapist assistant members and student members from all types of programs.

The Foundation for Physical Therapy Research

The Foundation supports research in physical therapy through solicitation of funding from a broad base of sources. Ongoing grant programs support individual research projects and doctoral level students. In addi-

---

* Names and addresses of section leaders are available from Component Services, APTA, 1111 N. Fairfax St., Alexandria, VA 22314. Assemblies of The American Physical Therapy Association.

tion, the Foundation has recently supported the creation of a Center of Excellence for Physical Therapy Research. The Foundation sets short-term and long-term priorities for research that will move the profession forward in accounting for its knowledge base and the efficacy of practice.

Leading Journals

The official journal of the APTA is *Physical Therapy*, a monthly publication with subscription for members included in Association dues. It is available to nonmembers through an annual subscription rate. This refereed journal includes research reports of interdisciplinary interest in research, education, and practice. Official documents of the organization and special lectures are routinely published. Abstracts of articles in *Physical Therapy* are included in several health and social science indexes. The first journal of the APTA, *P.T. Review* appeared in 1921. The name was changed to *Physiotherapy Review* in 1949 and to the *Journal of the American Physical Therapy Association* in 1962. The present name, *Physical Therapy*, began in 1970. Those doing literature reviews should be aware of these name changes.

The APTA also publishes a less formal, monthly magazine, *PT Today*, which includes short articles about professional issues and Association business, resources of interest to physical therapists, governmental affairs updates, and member features. The APTA also publishes the weekly *PT Bulletin*, a mixture of short articles and classified job and product advertisements. Several APTA sections sponsor or publish refereed journals, including *Pediatric Physical Therapy*, *Journal of Orthopaedic and Sports Physical Therapy*, and *Physical Therapy Education*.

Two other journals, not affiliated with the APTA but of particular interest to physical therapists, are *Physical and Occupational Therapy in Pediatrics* and *Physical and Occupational Therapy in Geriatrics*. Depending upon their interests and areas of practice, physical therapists may be interested in numerous other journals from the fields of medicine, allied health, education, child development, psychology, and the many branches of science.

Standards of Ethics

Since 1935, the APTA and the predecessor organizations have set a *Code of Ethics* for physical therapists. Although binding only on APTA members, the standards set through the Association have more broadly influenced standards of practice and legal regulations. Beginning in 1982, the APTA also approved *Standards of Ethical Conduct for the Physical Therapist Assistant*. Revised on many occasions, the most recent versions of the *Code of Ethics* and the *Guide for Professional Conduct* for physical therapists, and the *Standards of Ethical Conduct* and the *Guide for Conduct of the Affiliate Member* for the physical therapist assistant are available on request from the APTA. The Code and Standards are shown Appendix A. The *Guides for Conduct* are longer documents that briefly expand on each of the principles in the Code and Standards.

Several areas of the guides address behaviors appropriate in team situations. The principles require therapists to "be responsive and mutually supportive of colleagues and associates." Under Principle 5, guidelines for fees, the therapist should "attempt to ensure that providers, agencies, or other employers adopt physical therapy fee schedules that are reasonable and that encourage access to necessary services." By making recommendations for physical therapy consultation and management of services, when appropriate, rather than always direct, individual services, physical therapists can influence important decisions that affect both access to and the cost of services.

Under Principle 7, the guidelines allow for and encourage a consumer advocacy and protection role. This role is especially important when the team considers the person with a disability as a contributing and valued member of the team. Physical therapists have responsibility to inform and educate people with disabilities and their families about the scope and limitations of the physical therapist's role.

Summary

Physical therapy is a relatively young profession, which is evolving and expanding along many dimensions. There are ongoing changes in professional preparation, treatment approaches, settings for practice, team member roles, and relationships with consumers. These changes are all related to increased professional visibility and accountability and ultimately influence how physical therapists contribute to the health of our society.

References

Accreditation Council on Services for People with Developmental Disabilities. (1989). *Standards for services for people with developmental disabilities.* Landover, MD: Author.

American Board of Physical Therapy Specialties. (1992). *Specialist certification in physical therapy* (brochure). Alexandria, VA: Author.

American Board of Physical Therapy Specialties. (1985). *A decision for change: Raising entry level education of physical therapists.* Alexandria, VA: Author.

American Board of Physical Therapy Specialties. (1989). *Bylaws: American Physical Therapy Association.* Alexandria, VA: Author.

American Board of Physical Therapy Specialties. (1991). *Proceedings: Impact I conference.* Alexandria, VA: Author.

Bradley, V. J., & Knoll, J. (no date). *Shifting paradigms in services to people with developmental disabilities.* Cambridge, MA: Human Services Research Institute.

Commission on Accreditation in Physical Therapy Education. (1992). *Revision of the evaluative criteria for accreditation of education programs for the preparation of physical therapist assistants* (second draft). Alexandria, VA: Author.

Martin, K. (Ed.) (1990). *Physical therapy practice in educational environments: Policies and guidelines.* Alexandria, VA: Pediatric Section, APTA.

Patterson, E. G., D'Wolf, N., Hutchison, D. J., Lowry, M., Schilling, M., & Siepp, J. (1976). *Staff development handbook: A resource for the transdisciplinary process.* New York: United Cerebral Palsy Association of America, Inc.

Rainforth, B. (1985). *Collaborative efforts in the preparation of physical therapists and teachers of students with severe handicaps.* Unpublished doctoral dissertation, University of Illinois at Urbana-Champaign.

Rainforth, B., York, J., & Macdonald, C. (1992). *Collaborative teams for students with severe disabilities: Integrating therapy and educational services.* Baltimore: Paul H. Brookes Publishing Co.

Shugars D. A., O'Neil E. H., & Gader, J. D. (1991). *Healthy America: Practitioners for 2005, an agenda for action for U.S. health professional schools.* Durham, NC: The Pew Health Professions Commission.

Watts, N. T. (1985). Decision analysis: A tool for improving physical therapy practice and education. In S. L. Wolf (Ed.), *Clinical decision making in physical therapy* (pp. 7-23). Philadelphia, PA: F.A. Davis Company.

York, J. (1989). Mobility methods selected for use in home and community environments. *Physical Therapy, 69,* 736-747.

Occupational Therapy

By Winnie Dunn

A Brief History of Occupational Therapy

The first workers in the occupational therapy profession were called reconstructive aides. Reconstructive aides worked during World War I to rehabilitate disabled soldiers and civilian patients [Willard & Spackman 1978]. These workers addressed the fact that war veterans needed something beyond wound repair; they needed to have something useful to do. The reconstructive aides enabled individuals to recapture purpose in their lives. This simple concept is the basis of occupational therapy: individuals need to engage in purposeful activities that give meaning to their existence and provide a means for organizing life.

After World War I, occupational therapy expanded beyond serving those with physical impairments to include those with mental illness; these two primary arenas continued to expand through World War II. After World War II, services for individuals with developmental disabilities and pediatric disorders emerged and this emphasis continues today.

There are many federal legislative rules and regulations that address the need for occupational therapy as part of comprehensive services. Laws expand and clarify the scope of occupational therapy. For example, with the passage of P. L. 94-142, occupational therapy services expanded to serve children within schools. This legislative action led to many reforms in the service provision approaches and strategies classically used by occupational therapists, because educational environments are different from medical ones. The Americans with Disabilities Act will move professions like occupational therapy into a clear community focus and emphasize the importance of integration into all life environments.

Winnie Dunn, Ph.D., O.T.R., F.A.O.T.A., is Professor and Chair of the Department of Occupational Therapy Education at the University of Kansas Medical Center, Kansas City, Kansas.

Current Philosophies of Treatment and Services

Occupational therapy emphasizes that individuals need and want to participate in meaningful activities in their lives. Occupational therapists consider activities of daily living (ADL), work, and play/leisure as the three key performance areas. Table 5 presents a list of the performance areas addressed by the occupational therapist. Three core principles guide the occupational therapy service provision process. First, the individual's needs are considered in relation to desired outcomes. Second, desired outcomes occur in relevant contexts. Third, collaboration produces pertinent methods for functional outcomes.

Needs Are Related to Desired Outcomes

When individuals cannot perform ADL, work, or leisure tasks (see Table 5), the occupational therapist analyzes task performance to determine why the problem exists. The occupational therapist considers the sensorimotor, cognitive, and psychosocial aspects of performance. Table 6 presents the list of performance components in these categories. The occupational therapist uses skilled observation, interview, records review, and history taking and formal and informal assessment to obtain pertinent information. The occupational therapist always keeps a focus on the desired performance outcome (Table 5) throughout comprehensive assessment, because performance in life tasks is the focus of occupational therapy services. Individual referral sources, other team members, or family members may identify performance problems. For example, it is irrelevant to create an intervention based on a low visual perception test score if there are no indications that selected ADL, work, or play/leisure activities are affected. Specific performance component deficits (Table 6) are considered only if they interfere with the individual's ability to perform necessary or desired life tasks.

Desired Outcomes Occur in Relevant Contexts

The contexts in which individuals perform tasks can facilitate or create barriers to performance [Dunn et al. 1994]. For example, if the day care center is too noisy, the baby may not be able to get to sleep; if the desk is too crowded, the individual may not be able to find the work for the meeting.

Table 5. Performance Areas Addressed in Occupational Therapy

Activities of Daily Living	Work & Productive Activities	Play or Leisure Activities
1. Grooming	1. Home management	1. Play or leisure exploration
2. Oral hygiene	- Clothing care	2. Play or leisure performance
3. Bathing/showering	- Cleaning	
4. Toilet hygiene	- Meal preparation/cleanup	
5. Personal device care	- Shopping	
6. Dressing	- Money management	
7. Feeding and eating	- Household maintenance	
8. Medication routine	- Safety procedures	
9. Health maintenance	2. Care of others	
10. Socialization	3. Educational activities	
11. Functional communication	4. Vocational activities	
12. Functional mobility	- Vocational exploration	
13. Community mobility	- Job acquisition	
14. Emergency response	- Work or job performance	
15. Sexual expression	- Retirement planning	
	- Volunteer participation	

If the desk is equipped with compartments and bins, however, and objects are sorted in them, the individual may be more successful.

Objects, persons, and places are all part of the context. The occupational therapist considers the features of the context and how they might be contributing to or interfering with the individual's performance. The occupational therapist uses this information to determine whether the context needs to be adapted (i.e., to become more "user friendly") for the individual, or whether the individual can improve sensorimotor, cognitive, or psychosocial skills to manage the context more successfully [Dunn 1990]. Many times, both strategies are useful.

Occupational therapists encourage the use of natural contexts for interventions, because they contain inherent properties that support functional behavior. For instance, the bathroom contains sinks, which may remind us to wash our hands; the preschool has peers who respond spontaneously to a child's actions. When interventions can support an individual

Table 6. Performance Components Addressed in Occupational Therapy

Sensorimotor Component

1. Sensory
   a. Sensory awareness
   b. Sensory processing
      - Tactile
      - Proprioceptive
      - Vestibular
      - Visual
      - Auditory
      - Gustatory
      -Olfactory
   c. Perceptual skills
      - Stereognosis
      - Kinesthesia
      - Pain response
      - Body scheme
      - Right/left discrimination
      - Form constancy
      - Position in space
      - Visual closure
      - Figure/ground
      - Depth perception
      - Spatial relations
      - Topographical orientation
2. Neuromuscular
   a. Reflex
   b. Range of motion
   c. Muscle tone
   d. Strength
   e. Endurance
   f. Postural control
   g. Postural alignment
   h. Soft tissue integrity
3. Motor
   a. Gross coordination
   b. Crossing the midline
   c. Laterality
   d. Bilateral integration
   e. Motor control
   f. Praxis
   g. Fine coordination/dexterity
   h. Visual/motor integration
   i. Oral/motor control

Cognitive Integration and Cognitive Component

1. Level of arousal
2. Orientation
3. Recognition
4. Attention span
5. Initiation of activity
6. Termination of activity
7. Memory
8. Sequencing
9. Categorization
10. Concept formation
11. Spatial operations
12. Problem solving
13. Learning
14. Generalization

Psychosocial Skills Psychological Components

1. Psychological
   a. Values
   b. Interests
   c. Self-concept
2. Social
   a. Role performance
   b. Social conduct
   c. Interpersonal skills
   d. Self-expression
3. Self-management
   a. Coping
   b. Time management
   c. Self-control

Reprinted with permission of the American Occupational Therapy Association, Inc., from *Uniform Terminology for Occupational Therapy* (3rd ed.). Rockville, MD: Author.

to acquire skills in natural environments, the environment can provide cues for the behavior throughout the day.

Collaboration Is a Pertinent Method to Produce Functional Outcomes

Occupational therapists view individuals' needs in relation to what they want or need to do in their lives. The collaborative process of problem solving lends itself to this perspective. Other professionals and family members and the occupational therapist have complementary perspectives on a particular situation. Occupational therapists acknowledge the value of others' viewpoints as an important mechanism for creating an optimal intervention plan. Information provided by other persons enables the occupational therapist to create an intervention plan that fits into the individual's lifestyle and life environments. Collaboration enables the team to create interventions that incorporate all facets of the individual's needs into the life routines [Dunn, in press; Idol et al. 1987].

Services Provided in Various Settings

Service Provision Models

There are three primary service provision models in occupational therapy practice settings: direct service, monitoring, and consultation [Chandler et al. 1989; Dunn 1988; Dunn 1991]. These service provision models enable the occupational therapist to design a comprehensive program for an individual, taking into account person, context, task, and other support factors.

Direct Service

Direct service involves carrying out individualized intervention plans with one person or a small group of persons. The occupational therapist has immediate and ongoing contact with the individual and carries out specialized intervention techniques that can be implemented safely only by occupational therapists. Direct service is an important service provision model, because it gives individuals access to specialized interventions that other persons in the individual's life would have difficulty implementing safely. Occupational therapists employ direct service to introduce new behaviors, establish new behavioral schemes, or build tolerance for sustaining performance in activities.

Historically, direct service has been provided in clinical environments separated from the individual's life environments. There are times when this separation is necessary to the therapeutic process. For example, if the individual is distracted by events, objects, or persons in the context, separation enables the individual to focus on the therapeutic task. Some direct service intervention activities would be disruptive to the life environment, and so it is better to carry them out in a more private setting.

There have been recent shifts in the prevailing opinions about the appropriate setting for direct service activities [Dunn & Campbell 1991]. As more individuals who require occupational therapy services have been integrated into natural settings for school, work, daily living, and leisure activities, it has become clearer that many direct service techniques and strategies can be applied within these natural settings. There are many advantages to this method:

- First, the natural setting is comfortable and familiar for the individual, which can be more conducive to participation, especially when the individual has frustrations or anxiety about some aspects of intervention.

- Second, the environment provides stimuli that can be incorporated within the therapeutic activities.

- Third, there are naturally occurring cues or opportunities within the natural environment to perform desired tasks that have to be artificially created in isolated clinical settings.

- Fourth, the natural environment provides a rich source of reinforcement that can also support functional behavior.

Monitoring

Monitoring is sometimes called supervised therapy. Occupational therapists provide monitored services when they create intervention plans that other persons in the individual's environment implement for the therapist. Monitoring is a useful service provision option for activities that are a part of the individual's routine, because the occupational therapist cannot be available every time the task is performed. The occupational therapist can have a positive impact on life routines through monitored services. Eating, dressing, and personal hygiene programs are frequently targets of monitored intervention.

After designing the intervention strategies, the occupational therapist conducts a meeting with the person who will be carrying out the intervention on a regular basis. The occupational therapist teaches the person the techniques, observes the person performing the techniques, and addresses any behavioral signs that the techniques are failing or should be discontinued. The occupational therapist is responsible for the intervention being carried out in a safe and therapeutic manner. The monitored program is stopped and an alternative plan is created when these assurances cannot be made. When the occupational therapist is certain that the person will implement the program safely and that the person knows when to stop an intervention and call for assistance, the person can initiate the monitored program. The occupational therapist keeps in regular contact with the implementor (at least bimonthly) to review progress, update interventions, and address questions.

Monitoring extends the occupational therapist's expertise into the daily routines of the individual needing service. Family members, friends, aides, and other service providers can participate in monitored programs. The advantage for the individual receiving service is the opportunity to participate in the task in some way. There is an increased possibility for generalization of skills when therapeutic techniques are embedded into the naturally occurring routines. The advantage for the service or care providers is that they were carrying out these activities already and can now perform the activities in a therapeutic manner. This frequently makes the routines easier to complete as well. Occupational therapists have particular expertise at analyzing the components of daily life tasks and so are excellent resources for service providers. Monitoring provides a vehicle for this interaction.

Consultation

In recent years, many disciplines have discovered the value of providing consultation as a service provision option [Idol et al. 1987; West & Idol 1987]. The consultant provides expertise to enable others to meet their specified goals. Family members, other professionals, or other providers (e.g., baby-sitter) may identify the specific problems; the consultant works within the framework of this problem to gather additional information and to formulate possible recommendations.

The literature suggests that professionals prefer a collaborative style of consultation [Idol et al. 1987; Pryzwansky & White 1983]. The definition from Idol et al. [1987] is considered the benchmark for collaborative consultation: "Collaborative consultation is an interactive process that enables people with diverse expertise to generate creative solutions to mutually defined problems. The outcome is enhanced, altered, and produces solutions that are different from those that the individual team members would produce independently."

Interventions created within a collaborative consultation process embody a consolidation of expertise from several perspectives. Occupational therapists bring unique skills to the collaborative process, particularly in relation to the functional application of skills to the performance of necessary or desired life tasks.

The occupational therapy consultant meets with the consultee to define the problem. The occupational therapist uses active listening and careful interviewing skills to clarify the problem with the individual. Sometimes, the occupational therapist incorporates assessment data into the discussion as well. When the problem has been defined as clearly as possible, the collaborators explore alternatives to resolve the problem. For the occupational therapist, intervention options include designing strategies to remediate the problem; teaching the service provider a skill; adapting the tasks, materials, or environment to make the activity more "user friendly"; or adjusting postural or motor demands of the task. The occupational therapist maintains regular contact with the consultee to provide support.

Consultation extends the impact of the occupational therapy knowledge base into natural life environments. The core principle of occupational therapy is to facilitate the functional performance of life tasks [Dunn 1991]. When occupational therapists use a consultative model to facilitate naturally occurring opportunities to perform, the environment can cue and reinforce functional performance. The occupational therapist's ability to analyze tasks and create contextual modifications is well suited to the consultative model of service provision.

Service Provision Approaches

There are also several service provision approaches available to the occupational therapist. These approaches enable the occupational therapist to intervene at a variety of levels to achieve the best outcome for the individual served. Dunn et al. [1994] propose five approaches to service provision, which enable the occupational therapist to consider the person, the task, and the context for performance when designing interventions.

- **Establish/Restore.** These approaches have classically been called remedial interventions and are the most familiar to service providers. The professional identifies the deficits and creates strategies that remedy the problems. While many strategies exist to establish or restore a person's skills, most of them still require validation through systematic research.

- **Adapt.** As in remedial approaches, the therapist using an adaptive (or compensatory) approach also identifies the individual's strengths and deficits. Instead of trying to fix the problem, however, an occupational therapist employing an adaptive strategy attempts to work around the problem to enable performance. For example, decreasing the amount of writing for a student with fine motor problems is an adaptive strategy. Whenever tasks, materials, or environments are changed to accommodate a particular individual's needs, an adaptive approach has been used. Occupational therapists are particularly skilled at designing adaptations due to their knowledge of both the individual's abilities and characteristics of the environment.

- **Alter.** This approach to service provision involves assessing the individual and considering possible contexts that would provide the best match for the individual's performance. Sometimes individuals have problems with performance because they are in an environment that creates barriers for them. For example, some grocery stores have cluttered aisles with additional displays in them, providing the shopper with additional options. This type of store may be overwhelming for some individuals and could decrease its efficiency at shopping. Rather than expecting the grocery store to change their arrangements to accommodate these persons (an adaptive approach), an occupational therapist might search the community to find a less cluttered grocery store for an individual with this difficulty. The "alter" approach acknowledges the inherent skills and preferences of the individual and the inherent properties of particular environments and seeks to find the best match, rather than addressing personal weaknesses or environmental barriers as other intervention options might indicate.

- **Prevent.** Professionals also recognize that there are risk factors that might interfere with development in the future. In these situations, a prevention approach is selected; anticipating the possible outcome, the therapist intervenes to minimize the effects of the expected result. Professionals might select a prevention approach for a preschooler who is more active than other children and who avoids manipulative toys. If this trend continues in this child's play, eye/hand coordination skills might be affected. By providing an environment that is structured to persuade the child to interact with objects more frequently, visual/motor problems can be avoided or minimized.

- **Create.** This approach is used to foster the optimal evaluation of an individual's skills and abilities. A creation approach is used frequently in early intervention programs; families collaborate with professionals to provide an optimal developmental environment for their children. A creation approach is also used for designing community living environments for elders. There is not a presumption of a disability with a creation approach; environments are designed to take the greatest advantage of resources and knowledge about what makes places optimal for the diverse population that will use it.

The service provision models and approaches can be used in any combination to address individualized needs. Table 7 provides examples of various combinations of service provision approaches and models being used to address various problems.

Providing Services Within Community Settings

Occupational therapy services are provided to individuals with performance deficits across the life span and with both physical and mental health needs. There are a wide range of settings that serve individuals with special

Table 7. Examples of Service Provision Options When Considering Models and Approaches Together

Service Provision Models	Service Provision Approaches				
	Establish/ Restore (remediate)	Adapt (compensate)	Alter	Prevent	Create (promote)
Direct	Facilitate neck extensor muscles so child can look at friends when playing.	Fabricate a splint to enable the child to hold the cup at snack time.	Select a community preschool based on the level of noise the child can manage.	Facilitate weight bearing during infancy to prevent possible delays in walking.	Provide a play program for the community for all children to attend.
Monitoring	Supervise the teacher's aide to facilitate tone for reaching during a game.	Supervise a feeding program that minimizes the time for eating and enables socialization.	Work with parents to identify which community locations will be best for their family outings.	Create a "positions alternative" chart for the aides to prevent skin breakdowns.	Oversee the development of a morning preschool routine that optimizes early development possibilities.
Consultation	Teach classroom staff how to incorporate enhanced sensory input into play routines during free time.	Show teachers how to change the pieces of a game so all children can handle the pieces.	Provide the team with information from skilled observations that enable them to select the best play partner for a child.	Teach parents a range of motion sequence to prevent deformities.	Assist the day care provider to develop a comprehensive curriculum.

needs; occupational therapists are part of the teams in all of these settings. The service provision models and approaches described above can all be applied to every setting. The ultimate objective is for the individual to accomplish necessary and desired life tasks; this objective is met a little differently within these various settings.

Early Intervention Programs

Increasingly, more early intervention programs are developing as P. L. 99-457 is implemented. Occupational therapists address most frequently the regulation of the infant's state, functional caregiving strategies, socialization, and play, with this population. The family is the central focus of the services, with team members interacting at a high level to intertwine various frames of reference to the best benefit of the family and the child. Although some direct service is warranted with this age group, it is much more useful for the therapist to employ monitoring and consultation to help the family be better prepared to care for their family member. Prevention and promotion approaches are prevalent schemes for all team members.

Medical Settings: Hospitals, Clinics, and Communities

These settings primarily address the needs of individuals during more acute phases of their illness or disability. Therefore, individuals in these settings are more limited due to medical precautions, lower tolerance for activities, and reduced capacities in general. Occupational therapists assess the impact of the current problem on the individual's ability to perform within life demands. Frequently, intervention is direct and remedial in nature initially, in an attempt to correct the new problems that have arisen. As medical status improves, the occupational therapist combines compensatory strategies with other techniques to enable the individual to perform daily life tasks, such as bathing, dressing, and eating (e.g., adding velcro to shirts to minimize fine motor control needed for buttoning).

Residential Programs for Children and Youth

Occupational therapists who serve in residential programs focus their attention on the care staff. When the care staff understand the reasons for particular recommendations, they are more likely to carry out the recommendations consistently. For example, when a child has increased extensor tone, the body arches back and the child is difficult to position in sitting for subsequent tasks, such as toileting. Simple handling and carrying techniques can minimize the power of extensor tone, enable the care staff to keep the child in a more flexed position when being carried, and therefore make toileting easier to accomplish. The occupational therapist provides individual supervision (e.g., monitored therapy programs) and in-service training for the staff. Individualized programs are written by the therapist and carried out within the daily routines. Direct service is a small part of the professional activities in these settings.

Community Services for Persons with Disabilities

These settings are well suited to the expertise of the occupational therapist, but unfortunately, few occupational therapists work in such community settings as supervised living, transitional placement, and employment. When individuals wish to live or work within the community, they can profit from the functional and adaptive approach of the occupational therapist. Remediation is emphasized less; resource management and adaptation assume prominent roles. Occupational therapists investigate areas that are barriers to independence (e.g., inability to carry out meal planning), and consider alternatives that tap individual strengths, provide adequate cues, or make the task easier to perform. These recommendations are embedded into the individual's life routine so the environment (including the people) can support functional performance.

Programs for the Elderly

Caregivers play a central role with the elderly and so require support from professionals to ensure the best possible situation for the individual served. The occupational therapist addresses successful ways to support independent and assisted activities of daily living performance. Elders frequently are aware of their decreasing abilities and this causes frustration. When the occupational therapist can adapt the tasks, materials, and the environment (e.g., organizing the counter around the sink; attaching a toothpaste holder) to make the task more achievable, both the caregiver and the individual are less frustrated. The performance of families' routines is organizing and comforting; the individual has a sense of accomplishment and then remains motivated through the next task, which might be more difficult. The longer an elderly family member can participate in daily life tasks, the more manageable the family life situation can be.

Relationship to Other Disciplines

Occupational therapy emphasizes individual's functional abilities as they attempt to perform desired and necessary life tasks. This emphasis complements other disciplines, highlighting the importance of the interdisciplinary team. Table 8 summarizes the overlap between occupational therapy and other disciplines and provides an example of strategies that can be used to coordinate services. This is not meant to represent a comprehensive analysis, but only to provide a sample of key areas of interest as these professions collaborate on teams [Dunn 1992].

Key Issues Regarding Participation in Teams

Interdisciplinary team members face several challenges as they serve individuals with disabilities as a unit, rather than a single discipline.

Team members must **value the diversity of viewpoints** that interdisciplinary team members provide. This is sometimes difficult for us to embrace, since most professionals learned their disciplines in isolation from other disciplines. Higher educational policy changes are necessary to enable professionals to be trained together, thus instilling the value of multiple points of view from the start.

When the team struggles to create the best solution for an individual and family, **the team negotiation is an all-winner or all-loser proposition.** Everyone is a winner when the solution fits the family's lifestyle and the individual's learning or work preferences, and when it addresses key functional needs and desires. Everyone loses when one discipline dominates unnecessarily, causing the solution to have the appearance of that discipline, rather than the family or the individual's lifestyle.

Team members must value the individual's needs more than any discipline-specific agenda. Sometimes, one discipline needs to recognize that a recommendation is not in the overall best interest of the individual served. For example, the occupational therapist may identify serious oral motor problems that will interfere with talking. Intervention for this problem would not be appropriate in relation to talking, however, if the team determined that an augmentative communication device was a better op-

Table 8. Relationship Between Occupational Therapy and Other Disciplines (strategies for coordinating services)

Discipline	Overlap with Occupational Therapy	Strategies for Coordination of Services
Physical Therapy	Understanding the human body and its function and capacities; Understanding the developmental process across the life span.	PT can provide preparatory work to increase tolerance/capacity for activity; OT can apply the capacities to the desired functional task.
Social Work	Recognition of the importance of individuals living and working in the community; understanding the importance of family supports.	SW can provide specific links to the community for the family and can facilitate movement through the systems to obtain desired resources and placements when needed; OT prepared the child and family to function within desired settings.
Special Education	Understanding the cognitive aspects of performance; understanding task analysis.	SPED can provide the cognitive tasks that are appropriate for the child; OT considers the sensorimotor, cognitive, and psychosocial aspects of the particular cognitive tasks; they collaborate to create a single intervention.
Psychology	Understanding the psychosocial aspects of performance.	PSY can provide in-depth background regarding the psychosocial aspects and their context within the family; OT supports these endeavors through skilled observation about how these difficulties interfere with functional skill performance.
Speech/Language Pathology	Knowledge of the oral motor structures; knowledge of the swallow patterns; knowledge of the nonverbal aspects of communication.	S/LP can provide swallowing intervention; OT can address food acquisition and oral motor control. S/LP can provide expertise regarding the selection of the proper augmentative communication device; OT addresses functional aspects of communication; e.g., access to augmentative communication device.

Reprinted with permission of author from W. Dunn. (1992). Occupational therapy evaluation. From F. R. Brown, E. H. Aylward, & B. K. Keogh (Eds.), *Diagnosis and management of learning disabilities: An interdisciplinary/lifestyle* (2nd ed.). San Diego, CA: Singular Publishing Group, Inc.

tion. The occupational therapist might refocus attention to the reaching and pointing skills needed to gain access to the device.

It is critical for **interdisciplinary team members to be equal collaborators in the program planning process.** Flexible group leadership enables team members to take advantage of members" strengths for each case. It becomes important to team members to have other team members present (not just their reports); more flexible scheduling ensures that critical points of view are represented.

Team members must clearly understand the target outcome. Teams have emphasized independence for so long, that individuals with developmental disabilities become "rejects" of the system, because they can never achieve this elusive goal. However, teams continue to select a remedial approach to intervention. In reality, all of us are dependent for some aspects of our life task performance; we know how to manage the resources around us to get our tasks completed. For example, poor cooks go to fast-food or take-out restaurants; some people hire a service to clean the house. These resourceful choices do not make us less capable members of society; they demonstrate our abilities to use resources to obtain the same desired functional outcome as individuals who do these tasks themselves. Persons with disabilities have this same right to demonstrate their ability to manage resources to get their life tasks performed. Team members ought to support an individual's endeavors to manage resources as rigorously as they have historically supported remediation techniques.

Professional training typically focuses on the individual receiving service. This leads us to learn how to recognize our success only via individuals with disabilities: the professional can observe as the person acquires a new skill. Teamwork requires a new focus on other adult professionals who don't provide this same direct, concrete feedback.

Team members must learn how to provide each other reinforcement for work well done. Many of these issues are related to our lack of knowledge about collaboration and how to operationalize it within our teams. Idol et al. [1987] provide a benchmark discussion of the principles of collaborative consultation and provide methods for developing these skills.

Levels of Training, Certification, and Licensure

Educational Preparation

There are two levels of practice in occupational therapy. Individuals can become occupational therapists or occupational therapy assistants.

Individuals become occupational therapists via two types of accredited educational curricula. The most common mode of entry into the profession is through completion of a baccalaureate program. An individual with a previous bachelor's degree in another field can enter a professional degree program in Occupational Therapy at the graduate level; this individual generally receives a Master of Occupational Therapy degree. Both types of programs address the *Essentials for Accredited Programs in Occupational Therapy*, a document created by the American Occupational Therapy Association. In the past, the Committee on Allied Health Education Accreditation (CAHEA), a branch of the American Medical Association, accredited occupational therapy curricula to establish minimum standards for these programs. The CAHEA has disbanded, and now an accrediting body has developed to accredit occupational therapy programs exclusively: the American Certification of Occupational Therapy Education programs (ACOTE).

Individuals also can choose to become occupational therapy assistants. These individuals obtain an associate degree, usually from a community college, and can practice under the supervision of an occupational therapist. The primary emphasis in the preparation of occupational therapy assistants is on intervention; they do not receive the same level of science or theoretical background as occupational therapists. The occupational therapy assistant carries out intervention programs designed by the occupational therapist. This relationship is extremely beneficial in many community settings, because it is a cost-effective way to extend occupational therapy services.

Individuals generally complete prerequisite coursework prior to entry into occupational therapy programs. A few universities incorporate necessary learning from other disciplines into a full four-year curriculum, interspersing occupational therapy coursework with these other courses. Background knowledge from other disciplines include general university requirements, such as English, math, and humanities, as well as specialized knowledge in the biological and social sciences. Both the biological and social sciences are important because occupational therapists address sensorimotor, cognitive, and psychosocial aspects of the individual's life.

Occupational therapy curricula contain both academic and clinical experiences. The academic curricula emphasize several areas of learning. Additional emphasis is placed on the biological and social sciences so that students have in-depth knowledge about how the human organism operates from all perspectives. Since occupational therapy is a life span profession, developmental issues from fetal development to the aging process are also emphasized. Another important aspect of occupational therapy knowledge is the ability to analyze the components of a task or environment; students learn how to do this through both didactic and laboratory experiences. Specific theories of occupational therapy, intervention practices, and service provision strategies are also addressed in the academic program. Students also learn about management, documentation, and the research process during their academic programs.

The configuration of fieldwork experiences varies greatly across the programs in the country, but they all contain certain essential components. Students participate in shorter supervised experiences during the academic preparation, and then spend six to nine months in full-time work with other occupational therapists in at least two different settings. Again, since occupational therapy is a life span profession, the student generally completes fieldwork in two quite different settings (e.g., an acute care hospital and a community mental health center).

After students complete the academic and fieldwork requirements, they are eligible to sit for the national certification examination administered through the American Occupational Therapy Certification Board (AOTCB). They must pass this examination to be eligible to practice occupational therapy.

Credentialing

In addition to the AOTCB certification examination, most states have some form of credentialing required to practice within that state. A minimal requirement of state credentialing is graduation from an accredited school in occupational therapy, a passing score on the AOTCB certification examination, and payment of a fee for processing. Some states also require annual activities, such as continuing education experiences, to renew the credential. Many states have licensure laws, other states have registration or trademark protection; the differences are related to the disposition of the state. Most of these activities are carried out through a state board of healing arts, which keeps a record of credentialed professionals in the state.

Professional Organizations and Leading Journals

Professional Organizations

The **American Occupational Therapy Association (AOTA)** is the primary national professional organization for occupational therapists. State associations are also strong and are encouraged to be active on behalf of their constituents. The legislative body is called the Representative Assembly, and members elect representatives based on geographic population. This group addresses the issues of the profession in a formal way and charges other groups within the organization to respond to mandates created through the legislative process. Official documents of AOTA are approved through the Representative Assembly.

The AOTA has several divisions. The Practice Division deals with members who have concerns or questions as they provide occupational therapy services. The Education Division deals with educational programs and their specific needs, including educational standards and recruitment. Each of these divisions has a corresponding Commission made up of occupational therapists from the national community who volunteer to serve. The Commissions serve as advisors, liaisons, and experts on issues related to practice and education. They frequently act on charges from the Representative Assembly on behalf of the membership. The Commission structure is important, because it keeps AOTA focused on its role to serve the members; volunteers from the community are addressing issues, rather than paid staff members.

The AOTA also has divisions for Government Affairs, Membership, Publication, Public Affairs, Continuing Education, Research Information and Evaluation, Financial Management, Accreditation, Information Systems, Marketing, Conferences and Meetings, and Administrative Services. These divisions address issues that arise related to their area of expertise. Their priority is to serve the needs of the membership, and so each division has a mechanism in place to keep in communication with members across the country. The staff in these divisions also have strong relationships with other professional organizations so that collaborative efforts can be activated when appropriate.

The **American Occupational Therapy Foundation (AOTF)** is an organization that supports research efforts in occupational therapy. As a foundation, the AOTF obtains funds from various sources and has an ongoing grants program to disburse the monies to occupational therapy researchers. In addition to prioritizing research, the AOTF stimulates new researchers, facilitates the development of clinicians to participate in research, and provides research-oriented educational experiences for occupational therapists.

The **American Occupational Therapy Certification Board (AOTCB)** serves the certification needs of the profession. The AOTCB oversees the registration, administration, and cataloging of the certification examination. The AOTCB also addresses inquiries and complaints about individuals who may not be following ethical standards of practice in the profession by conducting investigations and taking action against the individual when necessary.

Professional Journals

Several journals serve the occupational therapy community. In recent years, these journals have begun to broaden their scope of topics so that they contain information that is also useful to other professionals.

The *American Journal of Occupational Therapy (AJOT)* is the official publication of the AOTA and is available to all members. Occupational therapists are responsible for information published in this journal as part of their performance of best practices. The *AJOT* is published monthly and contains a variety of types of articles, which are submitted and reviewed by the editorial board to determine acceptability for the journal. Data-based articles have become more common in the journal in the last several years; this trend is representative of the movement in the profession toward more systematic data collection. The *AJOT* also publishes theoretical articles and articles that summarize literature and create hypotheses for discussion. The official documents of the AOTA are published in an archival issue each year

(December issue). The *AJOT* also publishes the Eleanor Clark Slagle Lectureship, a lecture given at the annual AOTA National Conference. This lectureship is the highest teaching honor in the profession and is awarded to individuals for lifetime contributions to the profession through teaching.

The *Occupational Therapy Journal of Research (OTJR)* is the publication of the AOTF and is published six times a year. As the name implies, this journal publishes research studies and articles about research topics. Some of the articles are followed by a commentary by an invited respondent, with an opportunity for rebuttal from the original authors as a means to initiate scholarly interactions. All articles are juried by the editorial board and not all articles are accepted for publication.

There are also a number of other, more specialized journals, such as *Occupational Therapy in Mental Health, Occupational Therapy in Health Care,* and *Physical and Occupational Therapy in Pediatrics.* Each of these journals serves a specific purpose for the field. They usually have a small number of subscribers and are available in libraries as resources. They are helpful within the field, because these journals can address current and specific information that might take a longer time to get published in the other journals. They provide a mechanism for dialogue within specialty areas. These journals publish a wide variety of articles, including practice articles, data-based articles, and opinion pieces. They also publish book reviews to assist their readership in selecting appropriate new books for their libraries. They accept contributors from other disciplines readily and have multiple disciplines represented on their editorial board. They have an editorial process and do not accept all submissions as appropriate for publication in the respective journals.

Standards of Ethics

The *Occupational Therapy Code of Ethics* was approved by the Representative Assembly of the American Occupational Therapy Association in April 1988. There are six principles delineated in the Code of Ethics (see Appendix A). Principles 2 and 5 specifically address the necessity for occupational therapists to function as members of teams.

The fourth specification of Principle 2 states that "The individual shall refer clients to other service providers or consult with other service providers when additional knowledge and expertise is needed." Occupational therapists are expected to recognized the behaviors that indicate needs, whether or not those needs can be met by occupational therapy services. The actions taken to address the individual's needs acknowledge the wide range of expertise represented by all professionals on the team. Sometimes this also includes referrals to other occupational therapists with specialized skills (e.g., to a therapist who has expertise in designing and constructing splints).

Principle 5 addresses professional relationships directly. This principle addresses the occupational therapist's obligation to interact with colleagues for the benefit of the individual, to expect quality and ethical performance from them in professional activities, and to participate with them in the same manner. Occupational therapists must also respect their relationships with team members and consider this area of performance a reflection of ethical behavior.

Summary

Occupational therapy is a key profession on the interdisciplinary team. Occupational therapy addresses the needs and desires of individuals to participate in activities that are meaningful in their lives. They address this goal of participation by considering the individual's sensorimotor, cognitive, and psychosocial skills and deficits; the features of the tasks the individual wishes to perform; and the characteristics of the environment within which the task occurs. Occupational therapists are particularly skilled at creating adaptations that make tasks and environments more user friendly.

Because occupational therapists employ a contextual view of the individual's performance, they have many complementary skills with other disciplines. Occupational therapists value the collaboration among other colleagues and families, because multiple points of view create a more complete picture of performance and expand intervention possibilities.

References

Chandler, B. E., Dunn, W., & Rourk, J. D. (1989). *Guidelines for occupational therapy services in school systems* (2nd ed.). Rockville, MD: American Occupational Therapy Association.

Dunn, W. (in press). How, when, and why. In C. B. Royeen (Ed.), *AOTA self study series: Lesson 5*. Rockville, MD: American Occupational Therapy Association.

Dunn, W. (1988). Models of occupational therapy service provision in the school system. *American Journal of Occupational Therapy, 42*, 718-723.

Dunn, W. (1990). Assessing function. In C. B. Royeen (Ed.), *AOTA self study series: Lesson 11. Clinical case workbook 1*. Rockville, MD: American Occupational Therapy Association.

Dunn, W. (1991). *Pediatric occupational therapy: Facilitating effective service provision*. Thorofare, NJ: Slack.

Dunn, W. (1992). Occupational therapy evaluation. In F. Brown, E. Aylward, & B. Keogh (Eds.), *Diagnosis and management of learning disabilities*. San Diego, CA: Singular Press.

Dunn, W., Brown, C., & McGuigan, A. (1994). The ecology of human performance: A framework for considering the effect of context. *American Journal of Occupational Therapy 48*, 595-607.

Dunn, W., & Campbell, P. (1991). Designing pediatric service provisions. In W. Dunn (Ed.), *Pediatric occupational therapy: Facilitating effective service provision*. Thorofare, NJ: Slack.

Dunn, W., Campbell, P., Oetter, P., Hall, S., & Berger, E. (1989). *Guidelines for occupational therapy services in early intervention and preschool services*. Rockville, MD: American Occupational Therapy Association.

Idol, L., Paolucci-Whitcomb, P., & Nevin, A. (1987). *Collaborative consultation*. Austin, TX: PRO-ED, Inc.

Pryzwansky, W. B., & White, G. W. (1983). The influence of consultee characteristics on preferences for consultation approaches. *Professional Psychology Research and Practices, 14*, 457-461.

West, J. F., & Idol, L. (1987). School consultation (Part I): An interdisciplinary perspective on theory, models, and research. *Journal of Learning Disabilities, 20*, 388-408.

Willard, H. S., & Spackman, C. S. (1978). *Occupational therapy* (2nd ed.). Philadelphia, PA: Lippincott.

Special Education

By Charles Heuchert & Donald Roe

A Brief History of Special Education

In the western world, special education can be traced to the middle ages in Europe, when religious orders in Switzerland began to provide and chronicle assistance to persons with physical handicaps [Juul 1981]. Prior to the Christian era in Europe, persons with handicaps were considered misfits and were typically rejected, mistreated, and sometimes put to death. With the emergent Christian philosophy, however, churches began to protect and shelter persons with handicaps. At about the same time, the establishment of a public hospital in France in 1260 for individuals who were blind represented a dramatic change in the way individuals with disabilities were treated by the laity. For the first time in recorded European history, the population saw a need to provide some form of care to less able persons. However, for centuries little was done or known about how to make these individuals contributing members of society. It was not until the 18th and 19th centuries that specific programs were developed to help persons with disabilities. Even then, best practice at the time meant isolating these persons in asylums, hospitals, or separate educational facilities.

If a particular event could be linked to the beginning of formal special education, it would be Itard's work with Victor, the wild boy of Aveyron, in the early 1800s [Itard 1962]. A physician by profession, Itard documented his attempts at educating the young boy, who displayed behaviors that today might be diagnosed as a pervasive developmental disorder. This was the first documented effort to educate a child with severe disabilities.

Other influential European researchers working about the same time included Edouard Seguin, who worked with individuals with mental retar-

Charles Heuchert, Ph.D., is Associate Dean of the Curry School of Education at the University of Virginia. Donald Roe, Ph.D., is Program Director at the DeJarnette Center, a public psychiatric hospital for children and adolescents in Staunton, Virginia.

dation; Alfred Binet, who developed a method for assessing intelligence; Louis Braille, who developed a tactile representation of language through a series of raised dots on paper; Maria Montessori, an innovator in the education of young children; and Alfred Strauss, who worked with individuals who were brain injured.

Americans, too, were engaged in research efforts that greatly influenced the genesis of special education in the United States. Thomas Hopkins Gallaudet observed French instruction of deaf students in sign language and brought the method to America; Samuel Gridley Howe, a social and political reformer, founded the Perkins School for the Blind and organized the establishment of an experimental school for children with mental retardation in Massachusetts; Alexander Graham Bell worked with amplified speech in order to facilitate communication with people with hearing impairments; and Dorothea Dix lobbied government officials for better facilities for people who were labeled poor, idiotic, epileptic, and insane [Knoblock 1987]. These professionals brought new direction and hope to persons at one time considered to be disabled or handicapped.

The efforts of such people have provided the framework from which current thinking in special education emerges. What is realized today in special education resulted from several additional contributing factors [Knoblock 1987]:

- First, parents of children with specific disabilities organized to form strong local, state, and national organizations to advocate aggressively for their children's rights.

- Second, exposés by Dorothea Dix, Burton Blatt, and others brought to light the horrendous conditions in some residential institutions maintained for the purpose of meeting the needs of persons with handicaps.

- Third, in contrast to the medical and psychological positions espoused by early advocates of services for persons with disabilities which focused on people's defects and deficiencies, social scientists in the 1950s and 1960s helped broaden perspectives in the field of special education by focusing on the ways society treats individuals with disabilities.

- Fourth, litigation that began in the 1950s and continues today has given individuals with disabilities victories in their fight for equal access and opportunity.

- Fifth, court decisions upholding the rights of people with disabilities have directly influenced the federal government's definition of national policy on behalf of children and adults with disabilities.

In the 1960s and 1970s, federal legislation and funding had a dramatic impact on the development and expansion of special education services. Schools across the country began to provide, through systematic processes, special education services to children in need in the least restrictive environment possible. Federal monies were appropriated for research and development of exemplary programs in special education; teacher training programs in special education grew in number; early intervention for children from birth to 6 years of age was emphasized; and young children with handicaps were included in the Head Start program. Recently, professionals dealing with children have begun to focus on the alarmingly high rate of school dropout among students with disabilities and have emphasized the development of programs to enhance transition from school to employment.

Current Demographic Data

The U.S. Department of Education [1992] reported that, in the 1990-91 academic school year, more than 4.75 million children received special education services. The number of special education teachers employed during this time exceeded 300,417 and more than 30,000 additional teachers were needed. In addition, more than 255,000 personnel other than teachers were employed to serve students with disabilities ages 3-21, including psychologists, paraprofessionals, social workers, occupational therapists, audiologists, physical therapists, nurses, psychiatrists, and pupil transportation personnel [U. S. Department of Education 1992].

The trend since the 1970s has been toward educating as many students with disabilities as possible in the mainstream of regular public education. Two-thirds of all children with handicaps receive at least part of their education in regular classrooms with nonhandicapped peers [Heward & Orlansky 1988]. The majority of the students in the two largest special education groups spend most the school day in regular classrooms, including 77% of children with learning disabilities and 93% of children with speech or language impairments. Only 13% of children who are deaf/blind and 14% of children with multiple handicaps are placed in the regular classrooms; however, this represents an increase over previous years.

Current Philosophies of Treatment and Services

During the 1980s and 1990s, the dominant theme in special education continues to be the assurance that persons with handicaps are given opportunities to live, learn, and work in schools and communities. While few would disagree with those objectives, professionals involved in service provision do not agree on how society is to meet the needs of those persons. Debate ranges from the opinions of those who maintain that for many children, special education services are best provided in self-contained classrooms and separate programs, to those who advocate for total elimination of special education labels and services and promote the inclusion of all children in regular classrooms. An overview of regulations is necessary to adequately discuss issues of philosophy and service provision in special education.

Three pieces of federal legislation have had significant impact on the provision of special education services:

- P.L. 94-142, the Individuals with Disabilities Education Act (IDEA), which provides the basis for special education services nationwide;

- Section 504 of P.L. 93-112, the Rehabilitation Act of 1973, which sets forth the civil rights of persons with handicaps and prohibits discrimination on the basis of handicap in any program or activity receiving federal funding; and

- P.L. 99-457, which extends the provisions of P.L. 94-142 to preschool children from birth through 60 months.

The Impact of Public Law 94-142 on the Provision of Services

To date, the most significant legislation has been Public Law 94-142, the Individuals with Disabilities Education Act (formerly the Education for

All Handicapped Children Act), passed in 1975. P.L. 94-142 has four major purposes:

- To guarantee the availability of free appropriate public education to children and youth with handicaps;

- To assure fair and appropriate decision making regarding special education services;

- To establish guidelines for managing and auditing requirements and procedures regarding special education at local, state, and federal levels of government; and

- To provide financial assistance to state and local governments in implementing the programs.

Inherent in the law is the participation and empowerment of parents in the processes of evaluation, placement, and program planning for their children.

In order to achieve the purposes for which it was intended, P.L. 94-142 includes four major provisions: the development of an **individualized education program**, placement of the child in the **least restrictive environment**, **zero reject**, and the use of **multidisciplinary teams** in the referral of children for special education services.

The **individualized education program** (IEP) is a written framework developed to meet the needs of each student receiving special education services. The IEP must include the following components:

- A statement of the child's present level of performance, to include academics, self-help skills, social adequacy, prevocational and vocational skills, and psychomotor skills;

- A statement of annual goals for the child to achieve;

- A list of short-term instructional goals expressed in measurable terms;

- A list of all special education and related services required to meet the goals;

- The amount of time that the child will spend in special and regular education classes;

- The planned dates for beginning and ending the special education services;

- An annual review of the short-term objectives; and

- A list of the professionals responsible for delivering the services outlined in the IEP.

The intent of federal legislation in developing the concept of the **least restrictive environment** was to create the impetus for including children with disabilities in environments with nondisabled peers to the maximum extent possible. Regardless of placement, children must be given a chance to participate with nonhandicapped students in nonacademic and extracurricular activities. To this end, the special education eligibility committee must not determine that a child should be placed in special classes or separate schools unless education in regular classes with aids and services cannot be achieved satisfactorily. Some see this as a directive to fully integrate all children with disabilities into regular classrooms in public schools.

The concept of **zero reject** holds that all children with handicaps are to be given a free and appropriate education in the public schools. There are to be no exceptions to this provision. Although the concept has been challenged in court, the principle stands firm; there can be no rejection of services regardless of the severity of the handicapping condition [Zirkel 1990]. This concept was upheld in the *Timothy W. v. Rochester School District* [1989] ruling which recognized that education for students with severe handicaps is to be broadly defined to include basic functional life skills as well as academic skill development [Snell 1991]. The three judges ruling on the *Timothy W. v. Rochester School District* [1989] concluded:

> The law explicitly recognizes that education for the severely handicapped is to be broadly defined, to include not only traditional academic skills, but also basic functional life skills, and that educational methodologies in these areas are not static, but are constantly evolving and improving. It is the school district's responsibility to avail itself of these new approaches in providing an education program geared to each child's individual needs.

P.L. 94-142 mandates that **multidisciplinary teams** be established to evaluate students referred for special education services and their placement. Friend and Cook [1992] observed, however, that "(s)tates interpreted the federal law differently and mandated different composition requirements and operational procedures for teams." The law did not prescribe the composition of the team nor the specific procedures the team would follow; therefore, it is left to the individual states to establish guidelines for team composition and role.

Public Law 99-457 and Early Intervention

Another trend indicative of the present movement in special education includes the identification of children who need special services at birth, or as soon as possible thereafter, to provide them with necessary professional attention and support. Current thought holds that the earlier such children are helped, the greater will be the success of the intervention [Bricker 1986]. Through the efforts of "child-find" programs in most school districts (usually involving education professionals as well as transdisciplinary team members such as social service workers, pediatricians, nurses, and other medical personnel), many children have been identified as being at risk or disabled at an early age and have been referred for special services.

Public Law 99-457, signed in 1986, extended the age range for eligibility for services to children with disabilities. While states had programs in place for preschool children prior to P.L. 99-457, federal money was not available for service to children too young for regular public school education except for money provided through special grants. Beginning with the 1990-91 school year, all rights and protections of P.L. 94-142 (IDEA, Part B) were extended to include children with handicaps from age 3 and older. This law also encourages the development of programs for infants with disabilities [Hallahan & Kauffman 1991]. States are not required to report children by disability category, thereby allowing localities the opportunity to avoid placing stigmatizing labels on very young children. P.L. 99-457 incorporates family services in the preschool programs, and preschoolers' IEPs now include instructions for parents.

Section 504 of the Rehabilitation Act of 1973

Section 504 of the Rehabilitation Act of 1973 covers discrimination against persons with handicaps in many areas, including education. If a school division receives federal funds, a free appropriate public education must be provided to qualified handicapped persons. Under Section 504, a handicapped child is one who has a physical or mental impairment that substantially limits one or more daily activities, has a history of such an impairment, or is regarded as having such an impairment. In order to qualify for services under Section 504, the child with the disability must either (a) be the same age as nonhandicapped children receiving services, (b) be an age that the state is required by law to serve, or (c) be qualified for a free appropriate public education under Public Law 94-142.

Services Provided in Various Settings

For the past two decades, special educators have debated what Deno [1970] and others [Dunn 1973; Gallagher 1972] refer to as a cascade of services. This hierarchical structure actually shows the continuum of educational placements (not necessarily services) that are available in special education. The placements range from a regular classroom (with or without support-ive services) to a segregated residential school or institution. Within this structure, professionals in the field have established several approaches for working with students and professionals in these placements. These ap-proaches, termed "mainstreaming," "collaboration and consultation," "re-source classroom," and "special education classroom," follow the continuum of placements described by special educators in the early 1970s [Deno 1970; Dunn 1973].

Mainstreaming and the Least Restrictive Environment

At the close of the 20th century, there is a significant drive for total integration of children with disabilities into the mainstream of school and society [Reynolds et al. 1987; Stainback et al. 1989; Will 1986]. This is primarily due to the emphasis in P.L. 94-142 on the concept of least restric-tive environment. Some professionals refer to this movement as the Regular Education Initiative (REI) [Will 1986] or full inclusion [Stainback & Stainback 1992]. Supporters of the REI hold that children do not benefit from being segregated in special education programs or from being taken out of the regular classroom periodically for related services. Furthermore, REI and inclusion proponents maintain that the stigma attached to being classified as a "special education" student is detrimental to a child's self-esteem [Reynolds 1991].

While the REI and full inclusion advocates have found a broad base of support, there are professionals who harbor serious reservations about the impact of total integration of students with disabilities into the mainstream public school classroom [Carnine & Kameenui 1990; Kauffman 1989; Kauffman et al. 1988]. Link [1991] observed the following:

> Yet there is a population of students—those with severe retardation and multiple disabilities—who, despite any currently popular intervention, will not be capable of functioning in the regular classroom, will not be completely self-sufficient, and will not live independently within our society. The forced exodus of these students from special education schools for the purpose of encouraging "normalization" merely provides statistics for state and federally funded programs. It does not provide the most appropriate educational setting for these students.

The issue of definition and application of least restrictive environment is longstanding. It is believed that most professionals in special education feel integration of students in regular classrooms is the ideal toward which all should strive.

Collaboration and Consultation

Another outgrowth of the move toward mainstreaming is the emphasis on teacher consultation. In this model, teachers assume roles that promote the greatest levels of communication between special education teachers and regular education teachers who work with children with special needs. Systems utilizing this approach attempt to maintain students with disabilities in regular classrooms while providing regular classroom teachers with assistance in specialized educational planning. Usually, this assistance is given by a specialized educational consultant, special education teacher, school psychologist, or resource teacher [Dettmer et al. 1993; Friend 1988; Idol-Maestas 1983].

Resource Classroom

In the resource model, students eligible for special education services are placed for most of the school day in the regular classroom. They receive specialized instruction from a special education teacher in a separate resource classroom; the amount of time spent in such a setting is prescribed by the multidisciplinary team and outlined in the IEP. After separate special education classrooms, resource models are the most commonly used approaches to educating students with disabilities [U. S. Department of Education 1992].

Self-Contained Special Education Classroom

At one time, the most common educational placement for students with disabilities is the separate classroom setting. This setting, however, has become a controversial one in recent years [Hallahan & Kauffman 1994]. Generally, such a setting is required by law to contain from 4 to 15 students, depending upon their disabilities, and may have one or more paraprofessionals working with the special education teacher. Students placed in such settings are often mainstreamed into regular classrooms whenever possible and usually participate in physical education, arts instruction, and lunch with their same-age peers.

Current Special Education Instructional Models

Prior to the 1950s, special education services were provided primarily to persons with obvious handicaps, including speech disorders, physical and sensory disabilities, and intellectual impairments. These services most often took the form of remedial instruction that was based on some type of teacher assessment of academic skills. Educational programs in the 1960s and 1970s were significantly expanded to include persons with emotional disturbance, severe mental retardation, and learning disabilities. With this expansion, educators began to consider other approaches for working with students in special and regular education classrooms and began working to involve other professionals outside the classroom. The following presents a few of the most commonly used approaches in special education.

Remedial Instruction

Typically, special education teachers prepare remedial lessons for their students. These lessons are based on needs of the individual as shown through assessment of the individual's academic skills and deficits (see Table 9 for testing instruments used to assess academic abilities). The teacher chooses to work with students individually or in groups depending on the subject

Table 9. Tests Most Often Used in Assessing Special Educational Needs

Test of Nonverbal Intelligence
Slosson Intelligence Test
Peabody Picture Vocabulary Test-Revised
Developmental Test of Visual Motor Integration
Piers-Harris Children's Self Concept Scale
Motor-free Visual Perception Test
Wide Range Achievement Test-Revised
Peabody Individual Achievement Test-Revised
Key Math-Revised
Brigance Diagnostic Inventory of Basic Skills
Gates-McKillop-Horowitz Reading Diagnostic Test
Test of Written Language
Test of Language Development-Primary
Test of Language Development-Intermediate

matter and the abilities of the students in her classroom. A curriculum-based assessment program is typical of the formal way teachers might approach remediation instruction in the classroom [Howell & Morehead 1987].

Cooperative Learning

Cooperative learning reduces the amount of academic competition in classroom. Students work in groups and assist one another toward completion of projects and assignments. The classroom teacher becomes the organizer and facilitator of the learning process. Student are active participants in learning. Although research does not yet show gains in academic achievement with use of this approach, there have been noted improvements in attitudes toward student partners when teams consist of students with and without disabilities [Johnson & Johnson 1986]. Some teachers gain new perspectives on their students' abilities in the classroom [Nowacek 1992]. For more information regarding this approach see Slavin [1988] and Johnson and Johnson [1986].

Direct Instruction

A teacher-directed procedure, direct instruction is a highly routinized program of stimulus cues and responses. Teachers usually select such an academic instructional approach when other methods have not been successful. The **DISTAR** reading, language, and mathematics programs are the most widely used direct instruction programs. For information on this approach see Engelmann et al. [1988] and Silbert et al. [1981].

Peer Tutoring

Although research on peer tutoring is inconclusive [Gerber & Kauffman 1981], this approach gained wide acceptance during the 1980s. In peer tutoring, students with disabilities serve as tutor and tutee. Generally, nondisabled students tutor students with disabilities. Sometimes, the student with disabilities becomes the tutor for younger children. Lipsky and Gartner [1991] discussed the positive outcomes of peer tutoring. Hallahan and Kauffman [1991] noted that research on the effectiveness of peer tutoring is mixed. For a more detailed account of this approach, see Jenkins and Jenkins [1987].

Transition and Vocational Education

Recent research has shown that the dropout rate among students with disabilities is alarmingly high [Hendrick et al. 1989]. Students with emotional or behavioral disorders are especially vulnerable to transition failure [Walker & Bullis 1991]. Even though it is mandated that special education services must be made available to students up to 22 years of age unless the student has graduated from special education before then, many students with disabilities have difficulty remaining in school. During the 1980s, both vocational and career education options were developed within special education. These have emphasized successful transitioning of special education students into adulthood and the work world. Career education began in the early 1970s. According to Gloeckler and Simpson [1988], students receive educational services in the public school through career awareness programs in grades K to 6, career orientation in grades 7 and 8, and career exploration in grades 9 and 10. Within the public school and agency setting, the student receives preprofessional education, vocational education, or general education in grades 11 and 12. In the postsecondary years, the student either moves into college, vocational or technical training, or directly into the community where the public school leaves the picture and the agency supports the person in employment and community living.

Relationship to Other Disciplines

In the past, special educators often worked in isolation from their counterparts in general education. Just as persons who were placed in institutions had difficulty being discharged, children placed in self-contained special education classrooms and programs seemed doomed to stay in their placements. An attitude of regular educators was that once a child was placed in special education, he or she no longer was their concern. Special educators, on the other hand, often accepted, and sometimes promoted, this attitude. It was felt that special educators could "do it better" than regular educators; they believed that their "special students" were not ready to return to the "polluted mainstream." This attitude has changed. The "we against them" mentality has been significantly reduced. To achieve integration in the least restrictive environment, special education professionals now work closely with their regular education counterparts and the related services personnel.

Current Responsibilities of Special Education Teachers

Hallahan and Kauffman [1991] outlined some specific responsibilities of special educators. The following guidelines show how these responsibilities can enhance the role of special education teachers who work with transdisciplinary teams:

- Special education teachers should have knowledge of assigned students' learning needs that is derived from a variety of academic assessment instruments.

- They should have knowledge of different instructional methods in order to suggest successful teaching approaches for working with specific students.

- They must be able to consult and collaborate with parents, teachers, and other professionals working with assigned students and have knowledge of current educational progress including academics and social skills.

- They should have knowledge of and skills for managing serious problem behaviors and be cognizant of the various approaches to classroom discipline such as behavior modification, reality therapy [Glasser 1986], positive classroom discipline techniques, and other accepted approaches that might be best utilized with specific students.

- They should have awareness of most current practice and research in academic instruction for students in special education so that technological advances can be incorporated into instructional programs as appropriate.

- They should have knowledge of special education law and be able to communicate legal issues that may relate to team decision making.

Transdisciplinary Teams

Teachers may use the terms multidisciplinary, interdisciplinary, and transdisciplinary teams synonymously. Since P.L. 94-142 mandates the use of multidisciplinary teams in eligibility and placement decision making, most educators may define the team as consisting of educators, school psychologists, and other school administrative personnel. It might need to be clarified that the transdisciplinary team can involve members from several professions outside school settings, including parents, nurses, occupational therapists, physical therapists, speech and language pathologists, psychologists, physicians, and social workers.

In this model, each person is released from his/her defined role and assumes the role of service coordinator representing the transdisciplinary team when implementing a plan for the child. The transdisciplinary team's service plan for a child is implemented through the service coordinator's efforts and in consultation with the team members. For example, a nurse may engage in some physical therapy positioning, aid the student in learning tasks, and instruct the parents in using effective interventions. (For a more detailed account of the transdisciplinary team, refer to Chapter 2.)

Special Education Teachers as Team Members

It is incumbent on professionals representing their own constituencies that they work with the other disciplines to formulate, monitor, and evaluate the most effective intervention programs for children with disabilities. Paul [1981] stated that:

> [T]he problems of handicapped children are interdisciplinary in nature. It is reasonable to expect an educational understanding of the mentally retarded, the emotionally disturbed, or the learning-disabled child, for example, to prevail in an educational setting, a psychiatric understanding to prevail in a mental health setting, or a social work perspective to prevail in a social welfare setting.

P.L. 94-142 mandates that a multidisciplinary team composed of professionals and parents must plan and implement appropriate educational programs and related services for children with disabilities. Related services are those required to assist a handicapped child to benefit from special education. Team members are trained in a variety of professions including psychology, social work, counseling, physical therapy, language therapy, adaptive physical education, medical services required for diagnosis and evaluation, occupational therapy, vocational rehabilitation, juvenile court counseling, law, and psychiatry (although the provision of medical treatment, per se, is not a related service). The more severe the student's handicapping condition, the more likely the team will be expanded in membership to include a more diverse representation of professional disciplines, and engage in a greater intensity of involvement among team members.

There are several different team structures in special education; much of the structure will depend on the setting. For instance, if the team is based in the public school, it is likely that the school system's director of special education or a designee will be the team leader. However, in a psychiatric hospital, a psychiatrist or clinical psychologist will most likely be the team leader. Furthermore, the setting often will determine the type of intervention. In a psychiatric setting, the emphasis will be on psychotherapy and psychological testing. Education, occupational therapy, and activities therapy may be viewed as important but not the most critical parts of the intervention program. Conversely, in a school setting, the emphasis will be on structuring the child's learning environment so that other disciplines are utilized as support services to accomplish the psychosocial and educational goals.

Teamwork in Special Education

When a child is referred to be evaluated for special education services, interdisciplinary teamwork is set in motion. For example, a visiting teacher or the school social worker may make a home visit and gather valuable information regarding the child's life outside the school and bring it to the eligibility meetings. The psychologist will conduct tests and observe the child to determine intelligence and achievement levels and to assess the child's emotional life. The regular classroom teacher presents educational testing results and classroom anecdotal information. The principal brings a comprehensive school perspective. The school nurse provides medical information. If community social service agencies have been involved with the child and/or the family, their reports are included. Depending on the nature of the child's problems, juvenile court officers and law enforcement agents may be asked to add their information and recommendations.

A cornerstone of the interdisciplinary team approach is assessment of the student's skills. In the early days of special education, testing was done with an aim to exclude the child from education due to low intelligence, inability to hear or see, or extreme physical and health disabilities. Today, however, the focus has changed. Rather than trying to find a basis to exclude, the purpose of assessment is to learn where the child is functioning so the best possible plan for inclusion can be made. (For a partial list of assessment instruments used in special education, see Table 9.)

In addition to standardized tests, special education teachers make informal assessments in the major subject areas, including reading, handwriting, spelling, and mathematics. Behavior observation and vocational assessments are often a part of the assessment as well.

P.L. 94-142 requires that a wide array of assessment tools be used before decisions are made regarding the placement or the continuation of a child in special education services. Assessments must be made of the child's present level of functioning and the degree of the deficit in such areas as hearing, behavior, vision, speech, and communication. Assessments must be free of racial and cultural bias. There is a move away from relying solely on standardized tests that yield statistics to including structured naturalistic observations [McLaughlin & Lewis 1990].

With input from the various disciplines, the team is able to construct the IEP best suited to the student's specific needs.

Key Issues Regarding Participation in Teams

Most teams strive to work smoothly and efficiently; at times, however, barriers may be present which weaken or inhibit the effectiveness of the interdisciplinary process. Friend and Cook [1992] reviewed the research regarding the many problems that multidisciplinary teams experience and identified seven main problem areas:

- Use of unsystematic approaches to collecting and analyzing diagnostic information,

- Minimal parent or regular educator participation on the teams,

- Use of a loosely construed decision-making/planning process,

- Lack of interdisciplinary collaboration and trust,

- Territoriality,

- Ambiguous role definition and accountability, and

- Lack of experience and training for professionals to work together.

Furthermore, professionals voiced concerns of parents about feeling left out of the process because of the intimidation they suffer when, as the only nonprofessionals at the meeting, they hear psychological and educational jargon that is foreign to them. In addition, parents may believe that placement decisions have been made prior to their being involved in the IEP process. As a result, the special education teacher may become the advocate for the parents, creating tension among the team, the parents, and the teacher. Another serious accusation leveled at multidisciplinary teams is that related services believed to be crucial for the student are sometimes deleted or dramatically altered because the service did not exist.

To ensure that interdisciplinary teams function at the optimal level, Golin and Ducanis [1981] suggest that competent professionals be trained to function as part of a team. Based on suggestions made by Giangreco et al. [1991], the following may enable transdisciplinary teams to facilitate the delivery of services to children with disabilities:

- Evaluations should be made by related services staff whose summary reports would include descriptive student information that is based on discipline-specific assessments and observations of the student. Summary reports of related services personnel should be discipline-specific and describe the student's strengths and weaknesses only as they pertain to educational outcomes.

- The team should write a single set of discipline-free goals that reflect priorities shared by all team members.

- Related service delivery recommendations should be made by consensus.

- The team should make related service delivery decisions only after it has reached consensus regarding student learning needs.

- The educational placement decision should be based only on the student's learning needs. Additional services to support the student's access to educational opportunities should then be determined by the team.

The more severe a learner's handicap, the more his or her education will be planned by professionals outside the regular school personnel. When students have more severe disabilities, there are usually multiple problems that affect all aspects of the child's life. Some children may come from dysfunctional homes, where parental involvement is minimal, or where emotional, physical, and/or sexual abuse is evident. As a result, normal public school education may be negatively influenced. The effects of alcoholism and drug abuse on the very young are becoming increasingly apparent in the classroom. Babies born to mothers who abuse drugs and mothers with AIDS present a whole new array of symptomatology. Educators must be kept updated in order to recognize students with needs brought about by substance abuse and to adapt effective teaching techniques to meet special learning needs.

Levels of Training, Licensure, and Certification

Members of teams should expect the special educators to possess appropriate credentials for their profession. There are several ways in which persons may be certified as a special education teacher. The primary procedure to obtain teacher certification with an endorsement in special education is through state-approved teacher preparation programs. (Most of these programs offer baccalaureate and master's degrees in categorical areas of special education.) Many states have alternative certification programs that allow persons to become certified without having had the benefit of a state-approved teacher preparation program. The alternative route to certification comprises a minimal number of college courses and practicum experiences. Many beginning teachers are awarded provisional certification. After three to five years of teaching experience, depending upon individual states' procedures, teachers are then awarded permanent or professional certification.

Most college programs that prepare special education teachers require students to obtain certification in a specific field of special education. Some programs provide cross-categorical or dual certifications. Teacher education programs provide both initial certification and specialized endorsements in special education. The National Council on the Accreditation of Teacher Education (NCATE) accredits teacher education programs throughout the country. Vlaanderen [1980] reports that "...certification is virtually assured if a teacher candidate has been awarded a baccalaureate degree from an institution whose teacher preparation program has been accredited."

In recent years, some states have mandated that special education teachers hold a baccalaureate in a liberal arts field and a master's degree or endorsement in a specific special education area. Endorsements may be obtained in one or more areas of special education:

Emotional/Behavioral Disorders	Orthopedic Impairments
Gifted and Talented	Preschool Handicaps
Hearing Impairments	Severe/Profound Handicaps
Learning Disabilities	Speech & Language Disorders
Mental Retardation	Visual Impairments
Mild Handicaps	Multiple Handicaps

Each state may have variations in the terminology used to describe the endorsement area; for example, "emotional disturbance" may be referred to as "emotional impairment or maladjustment" or "behavioral disorders." (Not surprisingly, the titles of teams also vary widely from state to state: child study team, school assessment team, placement team, planning team, and multidisciplinary team are among the names used.) Each state has their own standards for obtaining a teaching certificate and an endorsement in special education.

As of 1990, 31 states and the District of Columbia have become members of the Interstate Certification Contract (ICC) and have outlined procedures whereby teachers can move from state to state within the ICC. The manual *Movement of Teachers Across State Lines* [1990], which is an addendum to Section I of the 1988 National Association of State Directors of Teacher Education and Certification Manual on Certification and Preparation of Educational Personnel in the United States, lists the procedures for seeking provisional and permanent certification in those states and the District of Columbia.

Although the National Teachers Examination (NTE) has been developed, successful completion of the examination is required for certification in only 15 states [Goddard 1991]. Other states use either a combination of the NTE and a state-specific examination, or a state examination only. The NTE consists of a core battery of general knowledge and subsections of specialty areas. The *NTE Bulletin of Information* (1991-92) lists the following specialty tests in special education: mental retardation, special education (general), speech communication, speech-language pathology, emotional disturbance, learning disabilities, teaching speech to persons with language impairments, orthopedic impairments, physical and mental handicaps, and visual handicaps. In addition to the national and state tests, local school divisions may require additional testing.

In some states, the permanent teaching certificate may require no additional updating. In other states, teachers may be required to update their certificates by periodically enhancing their professional development through college coursework or other professional activities, such as attending conferences and workshops, serving on education advisory committees, and publishing reports, articles, and books.

In the wake of a pressing need for teachers and a shrinking pool of applicants from which to draw, some states have enacted programs that require preservice teachers to take a minimum of formal education courses. Such minimal coursework may suffice for emergency, temporary, provisional, or even permanent teaching certificates, depending on states' policies.

Licensure in education has been addressed in the past few years [McNergney et al. 1988]. Presently, the only area requiring licensure is speech pathology and audiology. Forty states require licensure in this area. However, there is a lack of homogeneity in standards. The American Speech, Language and Hearing Association (ASHA) offers the Certificate of Clinical Competence-Speech Pathology or Audiology (CCC-SP or CCC-A) and is considered the professional licensure in this specialty area. Persons holding a CCC have master's degrees or the equivalent, have undergone a minimum of 300 practicum clinical hours during training, have completed one-year clinical fellowships beyond graduation, and have successfully completed the national board examination administered by the Educational Testing Service. Persons beginning training programs after 1992 will not be eligible for the CCC if they did not graduate from an ASHA-approved program. Other areas of special education are just beginning to develop standardized licensure procedures.

Professional Organizations and Leading Journals

A broad spectrum of professional organizations and journals are dedicated to and reflective of the research, technology, learning and teaching strategies, current issues, and future directions in the field of special education. The edited listing of organizations and journals in Table 10 are representative of a considerably longer inventory.

Standards of Ethics

The Code of Ethics established by the members of the Council for Exceptional Children (CEC) is included in Appendix A. While the Code is specific to the members of CEC, it is applicable to all professionals working in special education. To date, the Code reflects the opinion of the CEC related to professional behavior. It is not binding and is rarely part of teacher per-

Table 10. Professional Special Education Organizations and Journals

Professional Organizations	Professional Journals
Attention Deficit Disorder Association	American Journal on Mental Retardation
Alexander Graham Bell Association for the Deaf	ASHA, American Speech and Hearing Association Journal
American Foundation for the Blind	Augmentative and Alternative Communication
American Speech-Language-Hearing Association (ASHA)	Behavioral Disorders
Association for Retarded Citizens	Beyond Behavior
Council for Exceptional Children*	Canadian Journal of Special Education
Muscular Dystrophy Association	Career Development for Exceptional Individuals
National Association for Gifted Children	Deaf American
National Association of the Deaf	Diagnostique
National Association of Private Schools for Exceptional Children	Education and Training in Mental Retardation
National Information Center Clearinghouse	Exceptional Children
Spina Bifida Association	Focus on Exceptional Children
The Association for Persons with Severe Handicaps (TASH)	Gifted Child Quarterly
The United Cerebral Palsy Association	Intervention in School and Clinic
	Journal of the Association for Persons with Severe Handicaps
	Journal of Autism & Developmental Disorders
	Journal of Childhood Communication Disorders
	Journal for the Education of the Gifted
	Journal of Learning Disabilities
	Journal of Rehabilitation
	Journal of Special Education
	Journal of Special Education Technology
	Journal of Speech & Hearing Research
	Journal for Vocational Special Needs Education
	Language Speech & Hearing Services in Schools
	Learning Disabilities Research and Practice
	Parents Voice
	Preventing School Failure
	Remedial and Special Education
	TEACHING Exceptional Children

*Note: The premier professional special education organization is the Council for Exceptional Children, founded in 1922. It is the only professional organization in the world dedicated to advancing the quality of education for all exceptional children (gifted and handicapped) and improving the conditions under which special educators work. CEC currently has 18 subdivisions that deal with a wide range of disabilities such as physical disabilities, mental retardation, behavioral disorders, learning disabilities, communication disorders, and visual disorders.

formance ratings. However, over the past five years, the CEC has taken a more active role in upholding and advancing the principles of the Code among all special educators.

Summary

Special education is an evolving field with an extensive past. Throughout contemporary history, special educators have been in the forefront of issues pertaining to individuals with disabilities by serving as mentors, friends, service providers, and advocates. In addition, parents of children with disabilities have been a driving force in expanding the quality and quantity of special education services. These efforts have resulted in several important federal laws that assure equal access and educational opportunities. Federal mandates have allowed for the expansion of services and growth of knowledge in the field.

Professionals in special education continue to seek the best approaches for educating students with disabilities in the most inclusive environments possible. As members of transdisciplinary teams, they are able to assist in the development of sound client goals by contributing information on learning needs, social skill abilities, and legal issues related to federal laws in special education.

References

Bricker, D. D. (1986). An analysis of early intervention programs: Attendant issues and future directions. In R. J. Morris & B. Blatt (Eds.), *Special education: Research and trends* (pp. 28-65). New York: Pergamon Press.

Carnine, D., & Kameenui, E. J. (1990). The regular education initiative and children with special needs: A false dilemma in the face of true problems. *Journal of Learning Disabilities, 23*, 141-144.

Deno, E. (1970). Special education as developmental capital. *Exceptional Children, 37*, 229-237.

Dettmer, P., Thruston, L. P., & Dyck, N. (1993). *Consultation, collaboration, and teamwork for students with special needs.* Boston: Allyn & Bacon.

Dunn, L. M. (Ed.). (1973). *Exceptional children in the schools: Special education in transition.* New York: Holt, Rinehart and Winston.

Engelmann, S., Carnine, D., Johnson, G., & Meyers,L. (1988). *Corrective reading: Decoding.* Chicago: Science Research Associates.

Friend, M. (1988). Putting consultation into context: Historical and contemporary perspectives. *Remedial and Special Education, 9,* 7-13.

Friend, M., & Cook, L. (1992). *Interactions: Collaboration skills for school professionals.* White Plains, NY: Longman Publishing Group.

Gallagher, J. (1972). The special education contract for mildly handicapped children. *Exceptional Children, 38,* 527-535.

Gerber, M. M., & Kauffman, J. M. (1981). Peer tutoring in academic settings. In P. S. Strain (Ed.), *The utilization of classroom peers as behavior change agents* (pp. 155-187). New York: Plenum.

Giangreco, M. F., Edleman, S., & Dennis, R. (1991). Common professional practices that interfere with the integrated delivery of related services. *Remedial and Special Education, 12,* 16-23.

Glasser, W. (1986). *Control theory in the classroom.* New York: Harper and Row.

Gloeckler, T., & Simpson, C. (1988). *Exceptional students in regular classrooms.* Mountain View, CA: Mayfield Publishing Co.

Goddard, R. E. (1991). *Teacher certification requirements in all fifty states: How and where to get a teaching certificate in all fifty states* (9th ed.). Sebring, FL: Teacher Certification Publications.

Golin, A. K., & Ducanis, A.J. (1981). *The interdisciplinary team: A handbook for the education of exceptional children.* Rockville, MD: Aspen Systems.

Hallahan, D. P., & Kauffman, J. M. (1991). *Exceptional children: Introduction to special education* (5th ed.). Englewood Cliffs, NJ: Prentice-Hall.

Hallahan, D. P., & Kauffman, J. M. (1994). *Exceptional Children: Introduction to special education* (6th ed.). Englewood Cliffs, NJ: Prentice-Hall.

Hendrick, I. G., MacMillan, D. L., & Balow, I. H. (1989). *Early school leaving in America: A review of the literature.* Riverside, CA: California Educational Research Cooperative.

Heward, W. L., & Orlansky, M. D. (1988). *Exceptional children: An introductory survey of special education* (3rd ed.). Columbus, OH: Merrill.

Howell, K. W., & Morehead, M. K. (1987). *Curriculum-based evaluation for special and remedial education.* Columbus, OH: Merrill.

Idol-Maestas, L. (1983). *Special educator's consultation handbook.* Rockville, MD: Aspen Systems.

Itard, J. M. G. (1962). *The wild boy of Aveyron.* (Trans. George & Muriel Humphrey). Englewood Cliffs, NJ: Prentice-Hall.

Jenkins, J. R., & Jenkins, L. M. (1987). Making peer tutoring work. *Educational Leadership, 44,* 64-68.

Johnson, D. W., & Johnson, R. (1986). Mainstreaming and cooperative learning strategies. *Exceptional Children, 52,* 553-561.

Juul, K. D. (1981). Special education in Europe. In J. M. Kauffman & D. P. Hallahan (Eds.), *Handbook of special education* (pp. 24-46). Englewood Cliffs, NJ: Prentice-Hall.

Kauffman, J. M. (1989). The regular education initiative as Reagan-Bush education policy: A trickle-down theory of education of the hard-to-teach. *Journal of Special Education, 23,* 256-278.

Kauffman, J. M., Gerber, M. M., & Semmel, M. I. (1988). Arguable assumptions underlying the regular education initiative. *Journal of Learning Disabilities, 21,* 6-11.

Knoblock, P. (1987). *Understanding exceptional children and youth.* Boston: Little, Brown & Company.

Link, M. P. (1991). Is integration really the least restrictive environment? *Teaching Exceptional Children, 23,* 63-64.

Lipsky, D. K., & Gartner, A. (1991). Restructuring for quality. In J. W. Lloyd, N. N. Singh, & A. C. Repp (Eds.), *The regular education initiative: Alternative perspectives on concepts, issues, and models,* (pp. 43-56). Sycamore, IL: Sycamore Publishing Company.

McLaughlin, J. A., & Lewis, R. B. (1990). *Assessing special students* (3rd ed.). Columbus, OH: Merrill.

McNergney, R. F., Medley, D. M., & Caldwell, M. S. (1988). Making and implementing policy on teacher licensure. *Journal of Teacher Education, 39,* 38-44.

National Association of State Directors of Teacher Education and Certification. (1990). *Movement of teachers across state lines.* Seattle, WA: Author.

Nowacek, E. J. (1992). Professionals talking about teaching together: Interviews with five collaborating teachers. *Interventions in School and Clinic, 27,* 262-276.

Educational Testing Service. (1991-1992). *NTE Program Bulletin of Information.* Princeton, NJ: Author.

Paul, J. L. (1981). Service delivery models for special education. In J. M. Kauffman & D. P. Hallahan (Eds), *Handbook of special education* (pp. 291-310). Englewood Cliffs, NJ: Prentice-Hall.

Reynolds, M. C. (1991). Classification and labeling. In J. W. Lloyd, N. N. Singh, & A. C. Repp (Eds.), *The regular education initiative: Alternative perspectives on concepts, issues, and models* (pp. 29-41). Sycamore, IL: Sycamore Publishing Company.

Reynolds, M. C., Wang, M. C., & Walberg, H. J. (1987). The necessary restructuring of special and regular education. *Exceptional Children, 47,* 302-304.

Silbert, J., Carnine, D., & Stein, M. (1981). *Direct instruction mathematics.* Columbus, OH: Merrill.

Slavin, R. E. (1988). Cooperative learning and student achievement. *Educational Leadership, 46,* 31-33.

Snell, M. E. (1991). Schools are for all kids: The importance of integration for students with severe disabilities and their peers. In J. W. Lloyd, N. N. Singh, & A. C. Repp (Eds.), *The regular education initiative: Alternative perspectives on concepts, issues, and models* (pp. 133-148). Sycamore, IL: Sycamore Publishing Company.

Stainback, S., Stainback, W., & Forrest, M. (Eds.). (1989). *Educating all students in the mainstream of regular education.* Baltimore: Paul H. Brookes.

Stainback, S., & Stainback, W. (1992). Schools as inclusive communities. In W. Stainback & S. Stainback (Eds.), *Controversial issues confronting special education: Divergent perspectives* (pp. 29-43). Boston: Allyn & Bacon.

Timothy W. v. Rochester, New Hampshire, School District, 875 F.2d 954 (1989).

U. S. Department of Education. (1992). *Fourteenth annual report to Congress on the implementation of the Education of the Handicapped Act.* Washington, DC: U. S. Government Printing Office.

Vlaanderen, R. (1980). Competency-based teacher certification. *Teacher Education and Special Education, 3,* 15-18.

Walker, H. M., & Bullis, M. (1991). Behavior disorders and the social context of regular class integration: A conceptual dilemma? In J. W. Lloyd, N. N. Singh, & A. C. Repp (Eds.), *The regular education initiative: Alternative perspectives on concepts, issues, and models* (pp. 75-93). Sycamore, IL: Sycamore Publishing Company.

Will, M. (1986). Educating children with learning problems: A shared responsibility. *Exceptional Children, 52,* 422-415.

Zirkel, P. A. (1990). Testing the limits. *Phi Delta Kappan, 70,* 490-492.

Social Work

By Margaret West

A Brief History of Social Work

"Social work is the professional activity of helping individuals, groups or communities to enhance or restore their capacity for social functioning and to create societal conditions favorable to their goals" [NASW 1973]. The profession of social work is based on scientific knowledge and skill in human relations aimed at assisting individuals, groups, or communities obtain social or personal satisfaction and independence and was first carried out under the auspices of either private or public agencies concerned with the poor or disadvantaged. Today, however, social work includes services provided by private practitioners and various other types of counseling and service agencies and serves many groups of individuals with a broad range of needs [Friedlander & Apote 1980].

The history of social work in the United States is linked to the same charity and mutual aid societies that began to grow in Europe during the Middle Ages. The church in European countries had played a major role in establishing institutions for people who were poor, homeless, sick, orphaned, old, and handicapped. With the movement for separation of church and state in the 16th century, the community's legal responsibility for the poor began to gain recognition. The Elizabethan Poor Laws of 1601 set the pattern of public relief in Great Britain for the next 300 years. They required local communities to organize and finance poor relief for their residents and provide sustenance to the unemployable and children as well as work for the able-bodied. These laws, which contained features of both repression and disdain for the destitute while accepting obligation for the aid of people who could not provide for themselves, became a key element in the

Margaret West, Ph.D., is Regional Program Consultant for the Health Resources and Services Administration, within the U.S. Department of Health and Human Services, at the Seattle, Washington, Field Office.

present concepts guiding American public assistance and social legislation [Friedlander & Apote 1980].

Social work as a profession has therefore evolved within the social welfare context. Siporin [1975] has identified the following four basic functions of social work.

- To develop, maintain, and strengthen the social welfare system so that it can meet basic human needs,

- To assure adequate standards of subsistence, health, and welfare for all, and

- To enable people to function optimally within their social institutional roles and statutes.

- To support and improve the social order and institutional structure of society.

History of Social Work and Teams

For many years, social workers have been attuned to working as team members in interdisciplinary settings. Some early examples of social work participation in teams and interdisciplinary practice can be seen in social work in schools and in the history of the Children's Bureau in the U.S. Department of Health and Human Services and Title V or Maternal and Child Health Programs. The first five chiefs of the Children's Bureau were social workers: Julia Lathrop (1912-1921); Grace Abbott (1921-1934); Katherine Lenroot (1934-1951); Martha May Eliot (1951-1957), who was a social worker as well as a physician; and Katherine Oettinger (1957-1968) [Hutchins 1985]. The Children's Bureau focused on the need for cooperation among professionals to address the interrelated problems of child health, dependency, delinquency, and child labor. This emphasis on collaboration led to the development of teams consisting of experts in several fields, including medicine, law, administration, and social work. It was hoped this approach would "give a more scientific appraisal than was possible when only one aspect of child life was considered" [Hutchins 1985].

Julia Lathrop and Grace Abbott provided leadership for the development of programs that used teams to improve the welfare of children and child life with special emphasis on infant mortality and birth rates. When

Title V of the Social Security Act was enacted in 1935, Martha May Eliot provided leadership for the development of maternal and child health services, services for "crippled children," and child welfare services for children with other special needs [West et al. 1989].

The first school social workers, often referred to as "visiting teachers," were hired in New York City in 1907 in the recognition that conditions outside of the school might prevent youths from receiving their mandated education. It was also thought that social workers might act as liaisons to groups of students who might not otherwise participate in school. At the same time school social work positions were created in Boston and in Hartford, Connecticut, to bring about greater cooperation and better understanding between the home and the school [Hancock 1982]. These early school social workers were teamed with educators in furthering the mandate of schools to prepare young people to meet the requirements of adult roles in occupational training, character and emotional development, and preparation for responsible citizenship [National Association of Social Workers 1978].

Mary Richmond's writings during the early 20th century reveal that she used teams in her work. These teams often combined the work of a paid social worker with volunteers. In the 1960s, a shortage of social work personnel power provided an impetus for the development of social work teams as a useful means of incorporating persons without professional education into social service programs [Brieland et al. 1973].

Research conducted in the early 1960s by the University of Chicago's School of Social Service Administration on the use of teams concluded that the efficiency and effectiveness of services to clients improved more with the team approach than with the conventional case method of service [Barker & Briggs 1968; Schwartz & Sample 1972]. Another event marking the development of social work teams was the Illinois Beach conference of 1966 on "Differential Use of Manpower." This conference led to several agencies implementing the team approach [Brieland et al. 1973]. These teams were basically social work teams; that is, they were groups of social welfare personnel who had mutual responsibility for providing appropriate social services to a common clientele. They grew out of a need for more professionals and used personnel and volunteers without professional social work training to increase the range and quality of service offered to the clients of an agency [Brieland et al. 1973].

Current Philosophies of Treatment and Services

Social work does not limit its concern to the problems of poverty. Social workers focus on concerns that affect all social classes. Over the past 100 years, social work has also benefitted from and contributed to the knowledge acquired by the behavioral, social, and natural sciences [Friedlander & Apote 1980]. Hepworth and Larsen [1990] have described social work as the profession "that serves as the nation's conscience." There is no single basic philosophy of social work treatment. Rather a set of principles has evolved for guiding practice. These principles generally have as the central focus the individual within the context of his or her situation, or the person-in-the situation [Monkman 1978].

Hepworth and Larsen [1990], in the text, *Direct Social Work Practice*, have set forth 17 principles of direct social work practice. These principles include recognizing that people need to make their own choices, emphasizing that people are capable of learning new behaviors, and understanding that many problems need to be addressed by working toward societal and environmental change.

In the development of social work as a profession, social workers have participated in two types of teams:

- Interdisciplinary teams, where the expertise of work with clients is broadened by the collaboration of professionals from a number of different professional backgrounds; and

- Teams in which nonprofessional workers and volunteers work collaboratively with social workers to enhance the efficiency and effectiveness of the services of a particular agency.

In applying the philosophies outlined by Hepworth and Larsen [1990], social workers bring a focus to teamwork that assures a broad, ecological focus, often including factors that would not be brought in by other disciplines. For example, the social worker on the team may be the only professional who has information about the role of extended family members or community groups in the lives of the clients being served. This individual may also have access to specific information about the ethnic or cultural uniqueness of the clients.

Services Provided in Various Settings

Social work practitioners perform a variety of roles. These can be viewed within the context of five areas: direct provision of services, system linkage roles, system maintenance and enhancement, researcher/research consumer, and system development [Hepworth & Larsen 1990].

The setting in which social workers are employed may determine the services they provide. These settings include mental health programs; health care settings; juvenile courts and youth services; child protective and child welfare agencies; family counseling programs; schools and day care settings; aging and senior service programs; developmental disability programs; rehabilitation and vocational programs; federal, state, city, and community human services planning and administration; and behavioral and medical research programs. Each setting has its own set of values, mandates, and established practices. These may include policies set by federal and state laws and codes, professional association standards, agency history and practice, as well as preferences of individuals working within the setting. There is often a complicated web of agency requirements that emerge from the funding bases of social service programs, making programs accountable to multiple sources. For example, the move of the federal government to revenue-sharing through block grants has allowed for a closer relationship between government and voluntary social service agencies, as local and state health and welfare agencies have increasingly moved toward contracting with voluntary agencies for specialized services [Friedlander & Apote 1980].

Roles of Direct Social Work Practitioners

Listed in Table 11 are the roles and activities carried out by social workers in direct practice [Hepworth & Larsen 1990]. These include focus on the client, organization, and community and a wide range of activities ranging from individual counseling to research regarding practice and program efficacy. The roles carried out by each individual social worker are determined by a combination of agency policy and individual practitioner initiative.

The first two areas, direct provision of services and system linkage roles, are where social workers on interdisciplinary teams most often focus. Here the social worker may be responsible for individual, marital, or group counseling for the identified client or may serve as a coordinator or broker for direct services provided by others. In some cases they may be referred to as

Table 11. Roles of Direct Social Work Practitioners

Role	Activities
Direct service provision	Individual counseling
	Family, marital therapy
	Group work
	Educator, information provider
System linkage roles	Broker
	Case manager or coordinator
	Mediator/arbitrator
	Advocate
System enhancement/maintenance	Organizational diagnostician
	Facilitator
	Team participant
Research investigator/consumer	Evaluation of intervention or
	program effectiveness
	Review of research in areas of practice
System development	Program developer
	Program planner
	Development of policies and procedures
	Advocate

case managers or care coordinators. The approaches to carrying out these activities may vary from one practitioner to another in accordance with the individual's background and training. For example, some social workers are trained in approaches that emphasize behavioral techniques, while others have had training that emphasizes use of psychodynamic approaches to work with individuals. Direct services may include a preventive focus as well as a problem-solving or remedial one.

In addition to direct work with individual clients, social workers are often involved in program and policy development and planning. This might include revising or developing new agency programs or practices designed to improve services provided to clients. In these activities, the social worker may be working either individually or as a member of a team. For example, social workers may be members of interdisciplinary task forces that review existing programs and that develop plans and policies for new programs and services.

Relationship to Other Disciplines

In examining the roles that social workers take on, it is apparent that participation in interdisciplinary teams is often an important part of carrying out these roles. In many instances, completion of these activities is shared by one or more disciplines. For example, the social worker on an interdisciplinary team serving children with disabilities and their families is frequently the facilitator and advocate for the child and his or her family. The social worker might also act as a consultant or a partner to professionals in other disciplines in carrying out their work with families [West 1977].

Determining where overlap exists and establishing coordination with other team members is an ongoing task of most teams. This requires commitment and attention to this process by the team members and to the tasks of the client and/or agency. Conflict and overlap often emerge on teams between social workers and nurses. In some settings, they may have such closely intertwined responsibilities that they provide backup or coverage for one another. Some examples of other areas that challenge social workers in the coordination of roles on teams and activities are discussed in the next section. Social workers may be able to play a leadership role in the resolution of these conflicts as their training often includes study of human dynamics and group process.

Key Issues Regarding Participation in Teams

There are many possible formats for teams in which social workers participate. They may take on varying roles, including member, leader, and consultant [Abramson 1989]. Clinical teams that collaborate in assessment and treatment of client problems are found in many settings in which social workers are employees; i.e., health, mental health, schools, or child welfare. Social workers often contribute knowledge related to family dynamics and take responsibility for therapeutic work with family members. In addition, they often bring specific knowledge about community resources needed for community reentry for persons who have been in hospitals or residential treatment settings [Hepworth & Larsen 1990].

The social worker on the team may also take on the role of client advocate. "Social work frequently finds itself in a position to influence the interdisciplinary team toward change when the team recommendations make unnecessary demands on the client. Professionals who espouse middle class values, for instance, can be influenced to react in a receptive manner to values of a different class. The social worker's optimistic dedication to the capacity of man to change can be particularly refreshing to a team when working with a seemingly immutable client" [Hersey 1977].

The teams in which social workers participate may consist of members from a range of professional backgrounds depending on the agency or practice setting. The role of the social worker on the team may also vary across settings and may in some instances be designated by state laws or administrative code. In addition, the configuration of the team may include the following:

- Multiple professionals with multiple agency representation,

- Multiple professionals with a single agency, or

- A combination of the two.

The social worker may participate in many different types of teams, both formal and informal. The two most common formal types of teams are those that conduct assessments of client and community issues and those that are convened for treatment planning, coordination, review, and consultation. The composition of these teams varies with the setting and type of clients involved. For example, the social worker who is working in an early childhood special education program may participate in an interdisciplinary team composed of the social worker, classroom teacher, teacher's aide, occupational therapist, physical therapist, communication disorders specialist, psychologist, and the parents. This same team may carry out initial assessment and monitoring of the individual family service plan by which progress is monitored. In another situation, such as one involving a child protection agency, the social worker may participate in a team comprising professionals from many different community agencies, including a children's hospital, public health nurse, school representative, and community physician. Such a team might focus on problem solving, ongoing treatment planning, and case management. In this latter example, challenges often arise from both overlaps and gaps that exist between the mandates of the various agencies the professionals represent as well as from individual and professional differences.

Social workers who are members of interdisciplinary teams may find themselves working in settings where the philosophical base and authority of the agency are derived from another discipline. This is the case in hospitals, mental health clinics, health clinics, criminal justice programs, schools, and day care centers. These differences may lead to conflicts and difficulties in building positive team efforts. When the formal power structure of an agency defines professional roles and possibilities in a way that conflicts with the views of individual team members, conflicts may arise between members of the team in carrying out their team responsibilities. There may also be situations when discrepancies between overt and covert expectations of team members exist, as George Orwell illustrated in his book, *Animal Farm*: "All disciplines are equal with some more equal than others" [1954]. Problems arise from stereotypes that other team members hold about social workers, such as their being "handmaidens," "bleeding hearts," do-gooders," "go-fers," "crisis fixers," or "finance fixers." If these problems emerge in the team, it is crucial that the social worker be able to use professional skills to develop a strategy to deal with them. One of the most difficult roles for the social worker on a team is advocacy. This is a role that other team members often expect the social worker to take, but one that may put the social worker in the uncomfortable position of disagreeing with other team members [Hersey 1977].

Many issues have been identified as arising from social workers' participation with teams. Role blurring with others has often been identified as a concern in health settings [Davidson 1990]. A specific example of a particular concern is the cooperation or role conflict between nurses and social workers [Church 1956; Fessler & Adams 1985; King & Fasso 1962; Kulys & Davis 1987].

"Being a team member requires an understanding of the interrelatedness of roles and functioning and the ability to break down interprofessional rivalries. Communication is the essential ingredient in the team approach. Social work or nursing cannot do teamwork alone; but by joining forces have a better chance for success. Working together as a dyad or triad may be the most effective and realistic method of delivery care" [Lowe & Herranen 1981].

Sands et al. [1990] have suggested that these conflicts may be most difficult when team members see themselves more as discipline representatives than team members. He suggests that developing a common value base, language, and conceptual framework can be helpful in avoiding and resolving these conflicts.

Levels of Training, Licensure, and Certification

There are three levels of formal preservice training for social workers: the baccalaureate, master's, and doctoral training in social work. The courses of study required to earn degrees in each of these programs is established by the university that awards the degree, based on the requirements established by the Council on Social Work Education. Accreditation review of social work programs is conducted every seven years to determine if a program is in compliance with the standards of the Council on Social Work Education [Bardhill & Hurn 1988]. In 1993, there were 394 baccalaureate programs and 111 graduate programs accredited by the Council on Social Work Education. In addition, there were 53 doctoral programs in social work. In 1993, 10,288 baccalaureate; 12,583 master's; and 229 doctoral degrees were awarded in social work. [Statistics on Social Work Education in the United States 1993].

In most instances it is expected that social work professionals will have completed a master's degree (M.S.W.) at an accredited school of social work. In many settings, such as child protective services, public welfare, and some public health settings, however, persons in social work positions have bachelor's degrees. It is important to distinguish social workers from the broader field of social welfare, which refers to a field of service that includes the system of social services and employs many individuals who do not have professional training in social work.

Social work education programs began to develop in the early 1900s. Some of these early programs were connected with such schools as Columbia University and the University of Chicago, while others were independent institutes that had close affiliations with private social work agencies. It was not until 1935 that the debate over which model of educational program should be accepted was resolved. At that time, the American Association of Schools of Social Work established the requirement that schools be linked with institutions of higher education in order to receive accreditation [Friedlander & Apote 1980].

Master's programs in social work include both classroom and agency practice experience. The length of the program varies from one university to another, but generally lasts from one and one-half to two years of full-time study. Part-time program options may take three or more years to complete. The course of study includes direct practice in human services, community and organizational services, and research methodology. Objectives include intensive preparation in one area of social work practice; facilitation of the acquisition and critical analysis of substantive knowledge about selected social problems and groups where social work practice is conducted; sensitization to broad issues, trends, and dilemmas in the field of social welfare; and reinforcement of a sense of social responsibility and awareness of the role of social work in constructive social change [School of Social Work Bulletin, University of Washington 1985].

As the number of social workers with master's degrees was insufficient to meet the growing national demand for social workers, it began to be recognized that many social worker functions did not require graduate-level training. By the 1960s, there was an increase in the undergraduate programs in social work. Some of these programs were linked with graduate schools of social work, while others were established as independent programs in colleges and universities or incorporated into other departments such as sociology or family studies. These programs included associate degrees, as well as baccalaureate degrees [Friedlander & Apote 1980].

The professional association (NASW) maintains a voluntary certification system. A professional social worker may be admitted to the Academy of Certified Social Workers (ACSW) after two years of supervised practice and having passed a written examination. All states, including the Virgin Islands and Puerto Rico, now have licensure or certification for social work practice [Whiting 1991]. This most often requires at least two years of supervised practice and passing a written and in some instances, an oral examination. In many states the requirement for licensure or certification applies only to social workers in private practice or those who "accept a fee for service." This has allowed many state agencies to continue with their practices of filling social service positions with persons who have a variety of backgrounds and who do not meet professional requirements described in this chapter. Thus, many individuals whose positions refer to them as social workers in state agencies may have little or no training in social work. Current changes in many states that are in the process of increasing managed health and managed mental health care during the last several years have lead to additional requirements for social workers in direct practice. Many managed care groups have established guidelines for provision of mental health services that include requirements for credentials of providers and approaches for intervention. For example, a managed care company may establish rules regarding which providers it will reimburse for services and for how many visits at what intervals. Social workers are often included as approved providers by managed care but may be required to submit credentials to and sign a contract with each managed care company they receive reimbursement through. This has led to increased requirements of paperwork and confusion for many in practice who are now required to keep up with rapid market changes in health care.

Professional Organizations and Leading Journals

The National Association of Social Workers (NASW) is the largest professional organization in the United States representing social workers. It establishes standards to define and describe professional social work practice, provides certification for professional practitioners through ACSW and publishes a number of professional social work journals.

Other professional organizations include the Council on Social Work Education (CSWE), which sets accreditation standards for higher education in social work, and clinical societies and associations for social work practice. There are also many professional organizations associated with a field of specialized practice within social work, including the Child Welfare League of America, Association of Public Welfare Administrators, and the Association of Perinatal Social Workers. Many social workers participate in professional organizations that include membership of professionals from a number of disciplines (e.g., American Association on Mental Retardation and the American Public Health Association).

Since social work is a profession with a broad base of practice, social workers read a wide range of journals. These journals are associated with various disciplines, including psychology, education, medicine, sociology, and other behavioral sciences. *An Author's Guide to Social Work Journals* [Mendelsohn 1987] lists more than 100 journals. Seventeen journals have a circulation of more than 3,000 [Mendelsohn 1987]. The journal with the widest circulation (more than 100,000) is *Social Work*. This journal is published six times a year by the National Association of Social Workers and is sent to all NASW members. Its focus is on "new insights into established practices, evaluation of new techniques and research, examination of current social problems and critical analysis of problems of the profession itself" [Mendelsohn 1987]. The other journals with wide circulation are *Journal of Orthopsychiatry, Child Welfare, Children Today, Clinical Social Work, Health and Social Work, Public Administration Review,* and *Social Casework.*

Standards of Ethics

The Code of Ethics for social work has been established by the National Association of Social Workers (NASW). It provides a guide for social workers in the various roles and relationships across various levels of responsibility in which they function [Hepworth & Larsen 1990]. (See Appendix A).

Summary

Since social work is a profession that includes focus on many fields of practice in many different settings with a diverse client population, there are infinitely more variations of how social workers work on teams than can be addressed in this chapter. It is important for social work practitioners to develop their own variation of team participation in their practices. Because social workers have training in human relations and group process, they often are in a position to provide formal or informal leadership to the teams they are on to improve team process and to resolve conflicts and disputes that emerge among the various team participants.

Some of the newest challenges affecting social work direct practice come from rapid changes at the present time in federal, state, and local government reform that is directly impacting the types and amounts of services that will be provided. In addition the expanding changes in health and mental health managed care will continue to bring many changes to provision of direct services.

References

Abramson, J. S. (1989). Making teams work. *Social Work with Groups, 12,* 45-63.

Bardhill, D. R., & Hurn, J. (1988). The accreditation site visit process: The site visited and site visitor. *Journal of Independent Social Work, 3,* 61-72.

Barker, R. L., & Briggs, T. L. (1968). *Differential use of social work manpower.* New York: National Association of Social Workers.

Brieland, D., Briggs, T., & Leuenberger, P. (1973). *The team model of social work practice.* Syracuse, NY: Syracuse University.

Church, G. M. (1956). Understanding each other to achieve a common goal. *The American Journal of Nursing, 52*(2), 201-204.

Czirr, R., & Rapport, M. (1984). Tool kit for teams: Annotated bibliography on interdisciplinary teams. *Clinical Gerontologist, 2*(3), 47-53.

Davidson, K. W. (1990). Role blurring and the hospital social worker's search for a clear domain. *Health and Social Work, 15*(3), 228-234.

Fessler, S. R., & Adams, C. G. (1985). Nurse/social worker role conflict in home health care. *Journal of Gerontological Social Work, 9*(1), 113-123.

Friedlander, W. A., & Apote, R. Z. (1980). *Introduction to social welfare.* Englewood Cliffs, NJ: Prentice Hall Inc.

Hancock, B. L.(1982). *School social work.* Englewood Cliffs, NJ:Prentice Hall Inc.

Hepworth, D.H., & Larsen, J. (1990). *Direct social work practice, theory and skills.* Belmont, CA: Wadsworth Publishing Company.

Hersey Jr., W. J. (1977). Social work. In P. J. Valletutti, & F. Christoplos (Ed.), *Interdisciplinary approaches to human services* (pp. 373-386). Baltimore: University Park Press.

Hutchins, V. L. (1985). Celebrating a partnership: Social work and maternal and child health. In A. Gitterman, R. B. Black, & F. Stein (Eds.), *Public health social work in maternal and child health* (pp. 3-12). New York: Columbia University.

Iles, P., & Asuluck, R. (1990). Team building, interagency team development and social work practice. *The British Journal of Social Work, 20*(2), 151-64.

King, E. S., & Fasso, T. E. (1962). How nursing and social work dovetail. *The American Journal of Nursing, 62*(4), 89-90.

Kulys, R., & Davis, M. A. (1987, Spring). Nurses and social workers: Rivals in the provision of social services? *Health & Social Work,* 101-112.

Lennon, T. M. (1993). *Statistics on Social Work Education in U.S., 1993,* Alexandria, VA: Council on Social Work Education.

Lowe, J., & Herranen, M. (1978). Conflict in teamwork: Understanding roles and relationships. *Social Work in Health Care, 3*(3), 323-329.

Lowe, J., & Herranen, M. (1981). Understanding teamwork: Another look at the concepts. *Social Work in Health Care, 7*(2), 1-11.

Mendelsohn, H. N. (1987). *An author's guide to social work journals.* Silver Spring, MD: National Association of Social Workers.

Monkman, M. (1978). A broader more comprehensive view of school social work practice. *School Social Work Journal, 2*(2), 89-96.

National Association of Social Workers. (1973). *Standards for social service manpower.* New York: Author.

National Association of Social Workers. (1978). *NASW standards for social services in schools.* Silver Spring, MD: Author.

National Association of Social Workers. (1980). NASW code of ethics. *NASW News, 25,* 24-25.

National Association of Social Workers. (1982). *NASW standards for social work in health care settings.* Silver Spring, MD: Author.

O'Hara, D. (1978). An overview of training for social work. In Y. H. Appel (Ed.), *The incorporation of maternal and child health content into health concentrations in schools of social work* (pp. 7-14). New Brunswick, NJ: Rutgers.

Orwell, G. (1954). *Animal farm.* New York: Harcourt, Brace.

Sands, R. (1989). The social worker joins the team: A look at the socialization process. *Social Work in Health Care, 14*(2), 1-14.

Sands, R. G., Stafford, J., & McClelland, M. (1990). I beg to differ: A conflict in the interdisciplinary team. *Social Worker in Health Care, 14*(3), 55-72.

School of Social Work Bulletin. (1985). Seattle, WA: University of Washington.

Schwartz, E. E., & Sample, W. C. (1972). *The Midway office: An experiment in the organization of work groups.* New York: National Association of Social Workers.

Siporin, M. (1975). *Introduction to social work practice,* New York: Macmillan.

West, M. A. (1978). The social worker specializing in handicapped children. In K. E. Allen, V. A. Holm, & R. L. Schiefelbusch (Eds.), *Early intervention: A team approach* (pp. 269-286). Baltimore, MD: University Park Press.

West, M. A., Stuart, S., & Carlin, E. (1989) *Training for social work leadership in maternal and child health.* Seattle, WA: University of Washington.

Whiting, L. (1991). *State comparison of laws regulating social work.* Silver Spring, MD: National Association of Social Workers.

Speech-Language Pathology

By Lissa Power-deFur

A Brief History of Speech-Language Pathology

The profession of speech-language pathology had its origins in the 1920s. Prior to this time, there was no single recognized profession that provided services to persons with communication impairments. The field of medicine encompassed the treatment of speech disorders. Early in the 20th century, public schools hired speech correctionists to improve the articulation and elocution of students. In the 1920s, the University of Wisconsin and the University of Iowa developed the first doctoral programs with an emphasis on speech disorders. Groups of professionals also created a professional association and established scholarly journals focusing on speech disorders. Significant expansion of the field occurred following World War II, when veterans returned to the states with various speech and language deficits acquired during the War.

The next major expansion occurred with the increase of public school services offered to all students with disabilities. Historically, many students with disabilities had not received access to public education. Parents began advocating for services, with a resultant growth in the demand for special education services, including speech-language services. Federal funds supported training of speech-language pathologists in master's programs in the late 1960s and throughout the 1970s. Congress passed the Education for All Handicapped Children Act (P.L. 94-142) in 1975, establishing the standards that direct special education for students with disabilities.

Significant growth in the knowledge base of the profession also occurred during this period—the scope of practice was expanded to include language. In the 1980s, the field further advanced into the area of swallow-

Lissa Power-deFur, Ph.D., CCC-SLPA, is Associate Director, Office of Special Education and Student Services, at the Virginia Department of Education in Richmond.

ing disorders as speech-language pathologists, schooled in working with persons with impairments involving the mouth and throat, recognized how this expertise could be of assistance to persons with swallowing impairments.

Professional nomenclature has changed with the change in the scope of the profession. In early years, professionals were called **speech correction teachers** or **speech correctionists**. **Speech therapist** and **speech clinician** emerged as titles as the field moved beyond a focus on elocution and articulation. In recognition of the autonomy of the profession, the ability to provide services independent of the direction of a physician, the title **speech pathologist** emerged. As language became an increasingly important component of the profession, the title became **speech-language pathologist**. Speech-language pathology is the nomenclature recognized by national certification, licensure in more than 40 states, and most third-party reimbursers. However, despite the transformation of the professional title, many public school children keep it simple and call their speech-language pathologist their "speech teacher."

Current Philosophies of Treatment and Services

Speech-language pathologists strive to improve the skills of persons with speech, language, hearing, or swallowing disorders. Focusing on the provision of the highest quality services, speech-language pathologists assume primary responsibility for evaluating and treating children and adults with speech, language, communication, and swallowing impairments.

Scope of Practice and Preferred Practice Patterns

The scope of practice has grown from addressing articulation and stuttering disorders in children and adults to one that encompasses both developmental and acquired disorders in persons throughout the life span. Speech-language pathology services are provided to persons with impairments in any of the following areas:

- Speech: articulation, fluency (stuttering), voice (including respiration for vocalization, voice production, and speech resonance);

- Language: oral, written, manual, or graphic language; cognitive-language communication; social-language; or

- Swallowing.

The etiology of the speech and language disorder may be organic or neurological (e.g., hearing loss, neurological disorder, motor disorder) or a functional or developmental deficit (e.g., certain articulation and language disorders).

Surveys completed by the American Speech-Language-Hearing Association indicate that language impairments account for over half of the caseloads of speech-language pathologists [American Speech-Language-Hearing Association 1994b]. Language impairments encompass both childhood language problems and language impairments that result from acquired neurological impairment, such as aphasia and acquired cognitive language impairments. Articulation impairments account for approximately one-third of caseloads, with a small incidence of voice and fluency impairments (less than 5% each). Persons with disorders of swallowing (dysphagia) account for approximately 10% of caseloads. Caseload demographics have shifted since the early years of the profession. There has been a reduction in the proportion of persons with articulation, voice, and fluency impairments, and an increase in the number of persons with language and swallowing disorders.

Speech-language pathologists diagnose the communication or swallowing disorder and assess the nature of the disorder. They provide intervention services to improve the individual's communication or swallowing skills. This improvement occurs through restoration or attainment of normal function or reduction of, or compensation for, the deficit. In addition to therapy focusing on improved articulation, language, fluency or voice skills, the speech-language pathologist develops augmentative and alternative communication techniques, aids, and devices. Augmentative and alternative communication maximizes the individual's communication ability through use of supplementary aids or devices. The speech-language pathologist's role is to identify the appropriate augmentative and alternative communication techniques and to provide support services to persons using a communication prosthesis.

Speech-language pathologists provide other services not directly related to diagnosis or intervention. Clinicians work with family members and other persons to support the client's development of improved communication. They counsel individuals with the communication disorder and pertinent family members and caregivers, as necessary, to support the intervention. They may provide services to enhance speech and language proficiency and communication effectiveness for persons who do not have an impairment. These services include accent reduction, communication instruction for speakers with limited English proficiency, speech-language instruction, and professional voice production.

Speech-language pathologists regularly refer to other professionals when appropriate, or provide consultation to other professionals. They provide services in a manner that is sensitive to race and ethnicity, culture and language, gender, age, religion, national origin, sexual orientation, and disability.

The American Speech-Language-Hearing Association (ASHA) adopted a Scope of Practice for the profession of speech-language pathology [American Speech-Language-Hearing Association 1995e]. The purpose of the policy statement is to delineate services and supports provided by speech-language pathologists and to ensure the appropriateness and quality of speech-language services and support to persons across the life span. The level of experience, skill, and proficiency will vary among individual speech-language pathologists, based on their particular area(s) of practice.

ASHA also adopted the Preferred Practice Patterns [American Speech-Language-Hearing Association 1993]. These describe the fundamental components of service delivery that should apply regardless of the client, the clinician, or the setting (e.g., record keeping, universal health precautions). The Preferred Practice Patterns also address the specific parameters of screening, prevention, and counseling, and assessment and intervention for each area of speech-language and swallowing disorders. Specific sections address augmentative-alternative communication, speech-language instruction, and communication instruction.

Services Provided in Various Settings

Traditionally, speech-language pathologists serve individuals directly, in a clinical environment. This is the predominant model used in health care settings: the speech-language pathologist works with one client at a time. In the schools, the direct service model is a "pull-out" model—services are provided outside the classroom setting, frequently in small groups. New models emerged in the 1980s, as educators recognized the relationship between a student's communication skills and his or her classroom performance.

Speech-language pathologists in school settings are increasingly working in the classroom. In some cases, the speech-language pathologist serves as the primary classroom teacher, responsible for academic instruction as well as speech-language remediation. Other times, the speech-language pathologist works with a small group of students in the classroom or team-teaches with the classroom teacher.

Speech-language pathologists in all settings collaborate with other professionals. Working as a team, speech-language pathologists, parents, clients, and others determine and provide the most appropriate intervention. Often the parent, educator, or other professional is the primary service provider, with the speech-language pathologist, providing support as a consultant. This model is most frequently used for clients whose articulation and language impairments are developmental in nature—these errors are common as children develop their articulation and language skills—or for persons with acquired impairments who have reached a plateau in their rehabilitation. The age of the individuals receiving speech-language services influences the types of work settings for speech-language pathologists. The majority (42%) of persons receiving speech-language services are school-age children (6 to 17 years), followed by preschoolers, infants, and toddlers (29%). Adults of all ages (18 through 85+) account for only 30% of caseloads [American Speech-Language-Hearing Association 1994]. As a result, schools are the most common employment setting. According to data maintained by the American Speech-Language-Hearing Association [Spahr 1995], most speech-language pathologists who are members of the Association are employed in schools—public, private, preschool, or residential settings (53%). Another 40% of the ASHA speech-language pathologists work in health care settings—hospitals, nursing homes, rehabilitation facilities, and home health care. Other speech-language pathologists work in administrative, college or university, or research settings.

Educational Settings

The role of a specialist in the development of proper enunciation habits in the public schools has long been recognized. However, the implementation of special education resulted in a significant increase in services in the schools. The Education of all Handicapped Children Act (P.L. 94-142) provided that all children with disabilities receive a **free and appropriate public education** (FAPE). Congress renamed the Act as the Individuals with Disabilities Education Act, IDEA, during the 1990 reauthorization. The law currently provides for special education and related services for children from age 3 through age 21.

Students with speech-language impairments may be eligible for special education services, if their only disability is a speech-language impairment. The federal law defines speech-language impairment as "a communication disorder such as stuttering, impaired articulation, a language impairment, or a voice impairment that adversely affects a child's educational performance" (34 CFR 300.7 [b] [10]). In addition, students with other disabilities (e.g., learning disability, mental retardation) who also have a speech-language impairment may receive speech-language services. These services are considered "related services," defined in federal regulations as "... developmental, corrective, and other supportive services as required to assist a child with a disability to benefit from special education, and includes speech pathology ..." (34 CFR 300.16[a]).

The federal definition does not encompass all children who can benefit from the services of a speech-language pathologist. Only children who have a speech-language impairment that adversely impacts their educational performance, or that hinders their ability to benefit from special education, are eligible for services under IDEA.

Private schools also hire speech-language pathologists. These include private day or residential special education schools that specialize in serving students with a particular disability (e.g., autism, serious emotional disturbance, specific learning disabilities) and private collegiate schools serving all students. Speech-language pathologists also work in state facilities for persons with mental retardation.

Health Care Settings

The aging of the American population has resulted in increased numbers of persons with acquired communication and swallowing disorders. These include aphasia (language impairment), dysarthria and apraxia (motor speech disorders), dysphagia (swallowing disorder), and cognitive communication impairments. Employment opportunities in hospitals, rehabilitation centers, nursing homes, and home health care settings have grown to meet the need. Speech-language pathologists in hospitals provide both in-patient and outpatient services. The reduction in the length of hospital stays is increasing the proportion of outpatient services. Some speech-language pathologists work in state facilities for persons with mental illness or in private psychiatric hospitals.

Early Intervention Settings

Intervention during the years when articulation and language are de-veloped is critical, and speech-language pathologists have worked in early intervention settings for decades. The amendments to the Education for all Handicapped Children Act in 1986 (known as "Part H") vastly expanded the availability of services to infants, toddlers, and preschoolers, with a re-sultant increase in the number of speech-language pathologists working in early intervention (birth through age 2) and preschool (ages 3 through 5) settings. Early intervention services are offered by professionals working in a variety of settings—community agencies (e.g., community mental retar-dation and mental health service boards), public schools, or hospital set-tings. Public schools provide preschool programs for students eligible for special education. Preschool services may also be offered through private preschools, or community speech and hearing or outpatient health care facilities.

Private Practice Settings

A small percentage of speech-language pathologists are self-employed, either running their own private practice or as an independent contractor. Recent shifts in the reimbursement practices of health insurance, Medicare, and Medicaid may make it easier for a private practitioner to work as an independent contractor than as a solo practitioner.

Other Settings

Undergraduate and graduate college and university programs hire speech-language pathologists as faculty or as clinical supervisors for their speech and hearing clinics. Speech-language pathologists may also work in community speech and hearing clinics; in federal, state, and local govern-ment agencies (health departments, state education agencies, veterans ad-ministration facilities); or exclusively in research settings.

Relationships to Other Disciplines

The development of effective communication skills cannot be completed in isolation. Speech-language pathologists work with parents and a variety of health care and educational professionals to assure that the communication skills their clients are learning are used in "real-life" settings. Table 12 lists the types of professionals with whom speech-language pathologists are most likely to work.

Key Issues Regarding Participation in Teams

Speech-language pathologists, like other education and health care professionals, face many challenges in serving effectively as a team member rather than a specialist. There are, however, several current issues unique to speech-language pathologists that influence their role and involvement on interdisciplinary teams.

In recent years, a **shortage of qualified speech-language pathologists** has emerged in all settings. The shortage in public schools is, perhaps, more problematic, as services identified on a student's IEP must be provided, and public schools are often put in the position of having students requiring services under federal law but lacking an available speech-language pathologist to hire. Schools may contract with a speech-language pathologist who is not part of the school faculty or may hire clinicians on a provisional status while they are completing their education. Speech-language pathologists in public schools often have high **caseloads** (generally at least 50 students, perhaps as high as 100). They often have difficulty finding time for all children eligible for services. In addition, many speech-language pathologists provide services to more than one school, resulting in loss of time due to travel. The speech-language pathologist has primary (and often total) responsibility for meeting the special education requirements for identification, eligibility determination, and development of the IEP for each student on the caseload.

Both the personnel shortage and caseload issues challenge the speech-language pathologist's ability to serve as an effective team member in public

Table 12. Disciplines with Whom Speech-Language Pathologists Collaborate

Education Settings	Health Care Settings
Special education teacher	Physician (e.g., pediatrician,
Regular education teacher	family practitioner, otolaryngolo-
Principal	gist, oncologist, neurologist,
Guidance counselor	radiologist, psychiatrist)
Occupational therapist	Occupational therapist
Physical therapist	Physical therapist
Vocational education teacher	Psychologist
Transition specialist	Dietician
Employment counselor	Nurse
School psychologist	Nurse's aide
Teacher's aide	Rehabilitation engineer

schools. Some speech-language pathologists are significantly constrained by time and energy, whereas others may not have the work and educational background to be an effective team member.

However, creativity on the part of both the speech-language pathologist and the educator can maximize the role of the speech-language pathologist as a team player. The expansion in the use of collaborative consultation and classroom-based services has enabled many speech-language pathologists to increase their involvement with other educators, while maintaining the requirements of their caseload.

A final issue concerns education and health care eligibility policies. In public school settings, the eligibility requirements for special education and related services may limit a speech-language pathologist's ability to work with students with developmental articulation and language impairments. **Reimbursement policies** focus on intervention for an impairment that is attributable to an injury, disease, or disorder, limiting coverage for developmental or functional disorders, or for impairments secondary to mental retardation or specific learning disabilities. The unfortunate result may be that some persons requiring speech-language pathology services may not receive them, since the services will not be reimbursed.

Levels of Educational Preparation and Credentialing

Speech-Language Pathologist Preparation

Speech-language pathology is a master's degree field. Graduate programs are accredited by the Council on Academic Accreditation in Audiology and Speech-Language Pathology of the American Speech-Language-Hearing Association.* During their undergraduate program, students complete liberal arts and science courses, such as psychology, learning theory, biology, linguistics, and statistics. Programs include some preprofessional preparation. Introductory courses include anatomy and physiology, acoustics, phonetics (the science of production and perception of speech sounds), the normal development of communication, and an overview of assessment and treatment of communication disorders.

Graduate coursework provides advanced information on diagnostic, treatment, and scientific information about each of the various disorders of communication (articulation, language, voice, fluency, hearing impairment), and of swallowing. Other courses provide advanced information in anatomy and physiology, development of communication skills, and requirements associated with specific work settings (e.g., special education, health care). Speech-language pathologists also take coursework in audiology.

Students must complete clinical practicum requirements as part of the master's program. Standards specify a minimum number of hours of direct services to persons with communication impairment (currently 375 hours). Standards further specify minimum hours for each type of communication disorder, for persons of different age groups, and for different clinical settings. The standards also specify the requirements for direct supervision by a certified speech-language pathologist.

Speech-Language Pathologist Credentialing

The standard for credentialing speech-language pathologists is the Certificate of Clinical Competence (CCC), granted by the American Speech-Language-Hearing Association. The CCC requirements include comple-

---

* In 1994, accreditation became the responsibility of this newly created board, replacing the Educational Standards Board that had accredited programs for decades.

tion of the master's degree and the clinical practicum requirements, a passing score on a nationally administered comprehensive examination in speech-language pathology, and completion of a clinical fellowship year. The Educational Testing Services administers the examination as part of the national teacher's examination program. The clinical fellowship year is a nine-month paid, full-time professional experience (or the equivalent part-time experience), under supervision of a certified speech-language pathologist. There is no requirement for continuing education following attainment of the Certificate of Clinical Competence. However, more than 80% of ASHA members participate in continuing education and maintain a record with ASHA.

In addition to national certification by the American Speech-Language-Hearing Association, speech-language pathologists must meet the requirements of the state where they wish to work. A professional organization issues the Certificate of Clinical Competence, demonstrating that the person has met the standards set by that profession. State licensure or certification requirements carry the force of law within that state. States do not permit persons who do not hold the state license or certification to practice the profession of speech-language pathology.

Depending upon the state, there may be either one or two credentialing standards. The State Department of Education has certification (or licensure) requirements for persons working in the public schools. Each state has its own standards, which may or may not be equivalent to ASHA certification requirements. Some states require additional coursework in education (e.g., education methods and practices) to be credentialed. Certificates (or licenses) issued by state departments of education are specific to that state's public school settings.

Licensure boards offer a second state credentialing standard. As of 1994, 43 states licensed speech-language pathologists working in nonpublic school settings. Third-party reimbursers generally require evidence that the professional holds a valid license to practice. The Certificate of Clinical Competence serves as the basis for most licensure requirements. A board administers the license, a board that generally includes speech-language pathologists, audiologists, and consumers.

Support Personnel

There is no recognized standard for support personnel in the field of speech-language pathology. In certain settings, speech-language pathologists may have assistance, ranging from clerical support personnel to instructional or health care aides. The American Speech-Language-Hearing Association recognizes that support personnel may be used to perform activities adjunct to the primary clinical efforts of speech-language pathologists [American Speech-Language-Hearing Association 1995d]. However, currently there are no national standards for credentialing of support personnel. In some states, departments of education or licensure boards may have standards for both credentialing and using support personnel.

Professional Organizations and Leading Journals

American Speech-Language and Hearing Association

The American Speech-Language-Hearing Association represents more 81,000 speech-language pathologists, audiologists, and speech and hearing scientists. (This number does not represent all of the speech-language pathologists working in the United States.) ASHA is a national scientific and professional organization located in the Washington, DC metropolitan area. Speech-language pathologists, audiologists, and speech and hearing scientists who hold the master's degree or equivalent with major emphasis in speech-language pathology or audiology, or in speech, language, and hearing science are members.

ASHA was established as the American Academy of Speech Correction in 1925. It has had several name changes over the years (American Society for the Study of Speech Disorders, 1927; American Speech Correction Association, 1934; American Speech and Hearing Association, 1947). The current name was approved in 1974, recognizing the importance of language. The acronym, ASHA, developed in 1947, was retained. ASHA has several goals:

- Encourage basic scientific study of the processes of individual human communication,

- Promote appropriate academic and clinical preparation of individuals in the disciplines of human communication sciences and disorders,

- Promote investigation and prevention of disorders of human communication,

- Foster improvement of clinical services and procedures,

- Stimulate exchange of information among persons and organizations, and

- Advocate for the rights and interests of persons with communication disorders.

ASHA is governed by two bodies: the Legislative Council and the Executive Board. The Legislative Council has 150 members who are representatives of each state, elected by the ASHA members in that state. The Executive Board has 11 members, elected by the Association as a whole. National office staff provides support to these policy bodies and to committees, board and task forces, and the general membership.

ASHA supports the needs of consumers through its Helpline (which responded to more than 22,000 consumer inquiries in 1994) and through publications sent to consumers. It also provides information for persons considering a career in speech-language pathology, audiology, or speech and hearing science. The **American Speech-Language-Hearing Foundation** (ASHF) is a private, nonprofit foundation, created in 1946 and dedicated to innovation and new horizons in communication sciences and disorders. It is funded, in part, by the tax-deductible contributions of individuals, corporations, and organizations. ASHF furthers education, supports research, and identifies and facilitates new directions in the field through support of conferences, publications, and other activities [American Speech-Language-Hearing Association 1995a]. The **National Student Speech-Language-Hearing Association** is an organization of students in undergraduate and graduate education programs in the field of human communication sciences and disorders. Chapters are located at universities offering programs in the communication sciences and disorders.

The **American Speech-Language-Hearing Association Political Action Committee** (ASHA-PAC) is a nonprofit, unincorporated, and bipartisan committee of speech-language pathologists and audiologists. The purpose of the ASHA-PAC is to support candidates for Congress whose records and policy positions demonstrate support for ASHA positions on health care, education, and disability issues [American Speech-Language-Hearing Association 1995c].

State Associations

Each state has its own professional association to support speech-language pathologists and audiologists. These associations are organized separately from ASHA and have their own membership requirements. State associations may have associated foundations and political action committees.

Leading Journals

The official journal of the American Speech-Language-Hearing Association is ASHA, a monthly publication for members. It is available to nonmembers through subscription. This journal provides members with up-to-date information on key topics, ranging from federal and state government action, to activities of the national office, committees, and boards. Research articles with broad appeal are also included.

ASHA produces a number of other refereed journals that focus on research in the field. The *Journal of Speech and Hearing Research* is a forum for basic research and clinical practice in the fields of speech-language pathology and audiology. *Language, Speech and Hearing Services in the Schools* is a journal focusing on clinical research of particular interest to school-based speech-language pathologists and audiologists. The two newest journals, the *American Journal of Speech-Language Pathology* and the *American Journal of Audiology*, were created to provide a focus on clinically relevant research for each profession.

Standards of Ethics

The ASHA Code of Ethics is binding on ASHA members and certificate holders [American Speech-Language-Hearing Association 1995b]. The Code is approved by the Legislative Council. The Code contains four Principles of Ethics that are both aspirational and inspirational in nature and form the underlying moral basis for the Code. Rules of Ethics are specific statements of minimally acceptable professional conduct or of prohibitions. Listed below are the four Principles:

- Individuals shall honor their responsibility to hold paramount the welfare of persons they serve professionally.

- Individuals shall honor their responsibility to achieve and maintain the highest level of professional competence.

- Individuals shall honor their responsibility to the public by promoting public understanding of the professions, by supporting the development of services designed to fulfill the unmet needs of the public, and by providing accurate information in all communications involving any aspect of the professions.

- Individuals shall honor their responsibilities, to the professions and their relationships with colleagues, students and members of allied professions. Individuals shall uphold the dignity and autonomy of the professions, maintain harmonious interprofessional and intraprofessional relationships, and accept the professions' self-imposed standards.

Summary

Speech-language pathology is a dynamic profession. It continues to evolve in response to the growth of research and knowledge regarding speech, language, hearing, and swallowing disorders and their treatment. New areas of practice may continue to emerge as a result of technological and scientific advances. Shortages in some employment settings may influence the development of the support personnel in speech-language pathology. Changes in federal and state education and health care policy have the potential for impacting the availability of services. However, despite the expected changes of the future, the goal of the speech-language pathologist will continue to be the provision of the highest quality treatment and other services, in partnership with the consumer of these services.

References

American Speech-Language-Hearing Association. (1993). Preferred practice patterns for the professions of speech-language pathology and audiology. *ASHA, 35* (3 Suppl. 11), 1 - 100.

American Speech-Language-Hearing Association. (1994a). *By-Laws of the American Speech-Language-Hearing Association.* Rockville, MD: Author.

American Speech-Language-Hearing Association. (1994b). *Omnibus Survey Materials.* Rockville, MD: Author.

American Speech-Language-Hearing Association. (1995a). American Speech-Language-Hearing Foundation. *ASHA, 37* (2), 74 - 75.

American Speech-Language-Hearing Association. (1995b). Code of Ethics 1995. *ASHA, 37* (2), 74 - 75.

American Speech-Language-Hearing Association. (1995c). Political Action Committee. *ASHA, 37* (2), 76 - 77.

American Speech-Language-Hearing Association. (1995d). Position statement for the training, credentialing, use and supervision of support personnel in speech-language pathology. *ASHA, 37* (Suppl. 14), 21.

American Speech-Language-Hearing Association. (1995e). *Scope of practice in speech-language pathology.* Rockville, MD: Author.

Individuals with Disabilities Education Act, Part B Regulations (34 C.F.R. Parts 300 and 301).

Spahr, F. (1995). ASHA in 1994: On your behalf ... *ASHA, 37* (2), 18 - 26.

Psychology

By Maria Sopasakis & Ian M. Evans

A Brief History of Psychology

"Psychology has a long past, but a short history" [Boring 1950]. Questions about human nature—our feelings, thoughts, and actions—have fascinated people from time immemorial. Philosophers, scientists, and theologians have long speculated about the mind, and yet the formal empirical study of "mental" processes did not begin until the middle of the 19th century. At that time, particularly in Germany, rapid advances were being made in the physiology of the nervous system. The application of the experimental techniques to the traditional philosophical questions regarding conscious experience, created a new discipline: experimental psychology. Wilhelm Wundt established the first formal psychological laboratory at the University of Leipzig in 1879 and was the first to explicitly identify himself as a psychologist.

The kinds of phenomena that Wundt investigated were the everyday mental events of the typical adult—perception, memory, attention, and learning. Dry as some of the early studies may now seem, the enterprise became enormously popular, and scholars, many with backgrounds in medicine or philosophy, flocked to Wundt's laboratory to study this new science. Those returning to America immediately set up comparable laboratories in the leading graduate universities.

From the outset, however, American psychology had a different flavor. While Wundt and his colleagues were mostly interested in the structure of consciousness, American psychologists were more fascinated by the function of mental processes and the nature of personality. The *Zeitgeist* of late

Maria Sopasakis. M.A., is finishing her doctoral internship in the Department of Psychology at the State University of New York in Binghamton. Ian M. Evans, Ph.D., is Professor in the Department of Psychology at the University of Waikato, Hamilton, New Zealand. This chapter was prepared while Ms. Sopasakis was a predoctoral fellow under a National Institute of Mental Health Training Grant in child clinical psychology. This support is acknowledged with thanks.

19th-century America encouraged the pragmatic application of knowledge. American psychologists quickly became interested in the adaptive significance of phenomena, such as learning, as well as in expanding the range of topics for investigation. William James [1890], for example, included in his textbook of psychology discussions of child development, of habit, of emotion, of language. Darwin's discoveries also had a great impact on psychology, because they demonstrated the biological continuity between humans and other animal species, thus stimulating research on animal behavior and leading to the inevitable white rat studies experienced by every psychology major today.

Applying Psychology

By the beginning of this century, psychology as a scientific discipline was in full swing—the American Psychological Association was organized in 1892, scholarly journals had been founded, and psychology departments in universities, originally just subsections of philosophy, were becoming larger and independent programs. The first systematic *application* of the new science was in the area of "mental testing" [Cattell 1890]. Some of the first tests, in which one person's performance on some task was compared to average performance, were designed by Francis Galton, Darwin's half-cousin. Galton was fascinated by measurement, and he developed simple questionnaires for vividness of imagery, tests of sensory acuity, and measures of various skills. The first really practical tests, however, were devised by a French psychologist, Alfred Binet, who was recruited by the Paris school system to help determine which children might be intellectually handicapped and thus benefit from specialized education. Eventually Binet's tests became the basis for so-called intelligence tests, and an elaborate statistical and measurement methodology called psychometrics emerged. Today, the use of tests to measure such constructs as intellectual ability, personality, and aptitude has become a major part of applied psychology [Anastasi 1982].

The earliest attempts to devise programs for individuals experiencing psychological problems evolved from the application of experimental methodology to the individual case. The measures developed in the laboratory to study, for example, visual perception or learning rates, could be extended to individuals to explore such problems as why a child might be failing at school. Thus, psychological *clinics* were established (the first, founded by

Witmer, was at the University of Pennsylvania), initially oriented toward childhood problems like reading difficulties, delinquency, and "inappropriate habits."

Ironically, the two world wars had a profound influence on applied psychology. During World War I, American and British psychologists organized to support the war effort by developing tests of recruits' suitability for different occupations, improving training methods, and finding ways to rehabilitate the enormous number of service personnel experiencing physical and mental trauma. After World War II, there was a particular demand for such services for returning troops, many of whom had brain injuries, rehabilitation needs, and emotional disorders. The Veterans Administration encouraged the training of applied psychologists by setting up paid predoctoral internships for graduate students being trained in academic programs [Reisman 1991].

Psychology and Mental Illness

For many people, psychology and psychotherapy are more or less synonymous. However, Sigmund Freud, who developed the first "talking cure" for persons with severe neurotic disorders, was a physician, not a psychologist [Fancher 1979]. People exhibiting severely aberrant behavior were, by the end of the 19th century, typically treated by neurologists in large sanitaria, or hospitals. It was assumed that "nervous" diseases caused these major dysfunctions, and hence the term mental "illness." Freud was one of the first to demonstrate that disruptions of normal personality, even physical symptoms, could be caused by *psychological* trauma.

The theory of personality development and functioning that Freud cultivated based on his study of patients did, naturally, have enormous influence on psychology. There emerged a renewed concern for unconscious processes, particularly defense mechanisms, not merely the conscious experiences that subjects could introspectively describe. There was interest in the effects of early experience, in motivation, in instincts, and in *abnormal* individuals, rather than the typical. However, Freud's theories were also criticized—they lacked rigor and were not easily subject to laboratory test. The behavioristic perspective, first articulated by Watson [1924], began to dominate American psychology, and such areas of psychological study as developmental, personality, and social—all based on empirical research— drew on psychoanalytic concepts but did not embrace them uncritically.

Current Status

As many modern undergraduate psychology majors discover to their dismay, contemporary psychology is not, therefore, about dreams, love, penis envy, or Leo Buscaglia. Psychology is an experimental science, a pivotal discipline between the natural and the social sciences. Although psychology might investigate unusual human experiences, it is essentially concerned with normal, everyday processes like emotion, learning, memory, perception, motivation, and social interactions. As such, it provides the foundation for knowledge that would be pertinent to understanding psychological deviance.

Current Philosophies of Treatment and Services

As can be readily imagined, psychologists interested in clinical problems quickly discovered that basic experimental psychology was of little relevance to the everyday concerns of clients. Thus, there was a tendency for practitioners to develop their own body of insights and methods derived from experience. Unstandardized tests that did not have a strong psychometric foundation, such as "projective" tests like the Thematic Apperception Test and the Rorschach Inkblot Test, became popular clinical tools. Consequently, practicing psychologists began to move further and further away from the parent discipline of experimental psychology. Many espoused Freudian and other psychodynamic theories that were at odds with the tenets of scientific psychology. There was little application of scientific method in clinical context, and in many instances, since psychotherapy was almost exclusively psychoanalysis and practiced by physicians (psychiatrists), psychologists began gradually to have the more limited role of testers in the human service arena.

Two developments radically changed this picture in the last 30 years. The first of these has been the reaffirmation that professional practice should be based on the scientific discipline of psychology. This view was articulated at a conference held in Boulder, Colorado, in 1947, on the training of clinical psychologists [Shakow 1947]. The training model endorsed was that of the "scientist-practitioner": psychologists should be trained in both research foundations and the skills necessary for practice, such as psychotherapy, clinical judgment, assessment, relating to patients, and interacting with other professionals. Thus, it was decided, applied psychologists would continue to be trained in academic departments of psychology (generally in graduate programs of Arts and Sciences, but increasingly in Schools of Education, medical schools, and today in free-standing Schools of Professional Psychology).

A major problem with this model was that there was little overlap or integration between research psychology and professional application [Frank 1984]. Since the practice arena was dominated by psychoanalytic ideas that, if anything, eschewed scientific evidence, psychologists were caught in an uncomfortable split, often described as "doing science in the morning and practice in the afternoon." What changed this, and the second large influence on practice, was the steady increase in *psychological* principles and knowledge to guide practice.

There are many good examples of these trends. For instance, Carl Roger's [1951] counseling principles were derived from psychological concepts regarding relationships and the nature of the change process, and systematic research began to explore what it was about the relationship between client and therapist that produced the major benefits [Truax & Carkhuff 1967]. Another example was the realization that psychoanalysis was not effective [Eysenck 1952] and that there were many clients for whom intensive, verbal therapy was not helpful, such as elderly persons, young children, or individuals who were severely disturbed or psychotic. Behavioral principles of learning and conditioning derived from the laboratory began to be applied to client populations [Ullmann & Krasner 1965]. Early efforts, now known as behavior therapy, suggested that these applications could be quite effective, particularly for persons not considered good candidates for psychoanalysis, such as those with mental retardation or autism [Franks 1969].

Today, there are many features of modern scientific psychology that have found application. Perhaps the most obvious is the "cognitive revolution" in which concepts from cognitive psychology (sometimes referred to as information processing) have been extended into practice. Some examples might include the following:

- Trying to understand the thought processes of persons with schizophrenia using psycholinguistic analysis,

- Examining the logical errors in reasoning made by persons with depression, and

- Teaching impulsive or overactive children to regulate their own behavior by self-talk and other covert strategies [Beck 1976; Meichenbaum 1977].

Professional Roles

Given the diversity within the discipline, it is not surprising that psychologists have developed a variety of generic roles, as well as specialized functions within each one. The first clinic in psychology tended to focus on children's school-related problems. In 1915, the Connecticut State Board of Education gave Arnold Gesell the official title of *school psychologist*. Predictably, the need for schools to have professionals able to administer psychological tests and provide consultation on children's social and emotional development has resulted in school psychology becoming a major area of application [Reynolds & Gutkin 1982].

The immediate connection between research psychology and the understanding and treatment of sever psychological disorders—people who become sufficiently dysfunctional that they may need specialized treatment in some clinical (i.e., hospital) facility—resulted in mental health applications generally being referred to as clinical psychology. But individuals need services in a broader context than a psychiatric hospital or mental health setting. People have difficulties with relationship, with career choices, within families, in adjusting to college, and so on; thus a separate area, known as counseling psychology, has emerged [Brown & Lent 1984]. There is often considerable overlap across the research, areas of practice, and knowledge base of school, counseling, and clinical psychologists, but different training programs, professional identifies, and professional networks [Psyzwansky & Wendt 1987].

Specialized subgroups, usually under one or the other of these three categories, include such areas as forensic psychology, neuropsychology, family therapy, rehabilitation psychology, and health care (behavioral medicine). And to add one final confusion, psychological principles can be applied in nonhelping professional contexts as well. The best examples are psychology applied to business and industry (industrial/organizational psychology), the military, and to all the areas where humans perform—in operating equipment (human factors) and in sports.

Service Philosophies

Psychologists share broad general commitments to client care, as we will discuss later under ethical principles. Psychologists have come to practice in every type of organization and setting, particularly mental health facilities (psychiatric hospital, community mental health clinic), schools, prisons, general medical/surgical facilities, health maintenance organizations, preschools, community centers, nursing homes, and many others. Psychologists are also likely to be found in independent practice, seeing private patients, families, and groups, generally for psychotherapy, assessment, and other psychological services for which health insurance typically provides coverage. In all these different settings, there are standards of practice and of concern for clients that are well articulated in the field [APA 1974]. With the diversity of the human condition, psychologists are particularly interested in combating racism and sexism; practicing psychologists are trained to be sensitive to multicultural issues and to respect different lifestyles and sexual orientation [Myers et al. 1991].

Services Provided in Various Settings

Due to the variety of settings where psychologists may practice, the services that they typically perform can be quite varied. In this section, we will briefly outline and define the types of service most commonly provided.

Assessment

Historically, assessment and testing have been the primary activities of practicing psychologists [Walsh & Betz 1990]. Although this has changed considerably over time so that the roles that psychologists fill have expanded and diversified, assessment has remained an important endeavor. Whether one is referring to psychologists in schools, counseling centers, private clinics, or research laboratories, all are involved in the basic collection of information from a variety of sources to make intervention decisions. These sources of information may include direct observation, interviews, and psychological tests, as well as reports made by schools, families, physicians, or police records. Administering such "intelligence" tests as the Stanford-Binet or the Wechsler Intelligence Scales is still one of the most common activities of psychologists. However, the overreliance on these instruments that caused such controversy in the past [Gould 1981] is less prevalent [Evans 1991].

Once all available information has been gathered and interpreted, a conceptualization is made that reflects what course of action the psychologist believes needs to be taken. In clinical psychology, diagnoses are often made according to the fourth edition of the *Diagnostic and Statistical Manual of Mental Disorders* (DSM-IV) [American Psychiatric Association 1994], which is a descriptive list of the various syndromes recognized in psychiatry. DSM-IV diagnoses are based on five "axes": major mental disorders, personality disorders, medical diagnoses, level of psychosocial functioning, and adaptiveness. Any given diagnosis is made according to how well a client's symptoms and behaviors meet the specified criteria, which are often vague and poorly defined. The diagnosis leads to further action (therapy, hospitalization) that is tailored to meet the client's needs. For this reason, the reliability and validity of testing instruments are crucial, since incorrect assessment may lead to inappropriate treatment.

Psychotherapy

Perhaps the most frequent activity of professional psychologists, particularly those in private practice, is psychotherapy. Although the nature of the interaction between psychologist and client is generally verbal, within the context of meaningful, one-to-one relationship, there are various exceptions, such as using play rather than conversation with children, or working with clients in a group. Psychotherapy involves applying psychological principles to help individuals, families, or groups identify and address their problems in adjusting, coping, and psychological well-being [Corsini-Wedding 1989].

While the techniques of psychotherapy are extremely varied, the different approaches fall roughly into three major divisions:

- In *psychodynamic* therapies, the general goal is to resolve unconscious conflicts based on past traumatic experiences. Usually the therapy is grounded in the theories of one of the major psychoanalysts. The role of the therapist is, through dream interpretation, careful listening, pointing out blocks in thinking and development, to break down defense mechanisms and give the individual new insights into unconscious needs and feelings.

- In *humanistic* therapies, the focus is much more strongly on the relationship between the therapist and client. By providing an uncritical, empathic relationship, the therapist assists clients to understand themselves better, appraise their own feelings more accurately, and make lifestyle adjustments in the relatively safe context of a warm, genuine relationship with another person, the therapist.

- In *behavioral* or learning-based therapies, the focus is on arranging conditions so that the client can learn new skills and new ways of coping, or extinguish maladaptive habits. Sometimes, as in behavior modification, these learning situations are quite structured and involve explicit reward or negative feedback. In cognitive therapies, however, the change takes place through verbal reasoning and argument in an attempt to modify irrational behavior.

Obviously, elements of all three approaches may be found in almost all psychotherapy, regardless of what it is called. For example, behavior therapists might try to reduce the anxiety that is causing some undesired behavior, such as a compulsive ritual, and psychoanalysts and humanists will both recognize the value of new experiences in shaping more adaptive behavior. There are also certain principles of therapy that seem generic, and the value of a trusting relationship that permits the client to attempt new activities is universally accepted. More debatable, however, is the effectiveness of different approaches to different types of problems. Only in fairly recent years has there been a systematic attempt to evaluate the outcomes of different psychotherapeutic procedures [Garfield & Bergin 1986].

Program Design and Administration

Programs in psychology tend to be a logical extension of principles of psychotherapy. If the mechanisms of healthy personality development are understood, or if the principles of behavior change can be specified, then it follows that these can be built into programs that are actually carried out by others. Such programs extend all the way from teaching sound parenting skills, to designing rehabilitation for individuals with the most socially deviant behaviors. In program design, the assumption is that others, not the psychologist, will actually be responsible for behavior change. An example of this can be found in a program such as a ward in a psychiatric hospital being conducted according to principles of reinforcement: when patients engage in appropriate behavior, direct care staff would be expected to reward them with social attention. Another kind of program might be a two-week intensive period of self-discovery for people with a history of alcohol abuse, with nonprofessional staff conducting the day-to-day activities of the program.

It is quite interesting to note that many of the well-known programs nationally were *not*, in fact, initiated by psychologists, despite their apparent basis in psychological principles. Programs such as Head Start, community residence for persons with mental retardation (deinstitutionalization), or educational efforts to reduce drug use, have generally been initiated at a much more grassroots level, often by parents, consumer groups, or advocacy organizations. Psychology has played a significant role in the refinement of such programs, but has not taken the radical lead in their initiation, to the regret of many [Albee 1986]. Psychologists interested in changing environments and social agencies to promote more adaptive development are called community psychologists [Rose & Black 1985].

Consultation

Because psychological principles are so fundamental for most of the human service areas, the role of the psychologist as consultant is complex. In this role, the psychologist provides input in a broader, more general process in which psychological knowledge represents only one component of program design or decision making. Usually, psychologists are involved in consultation on the basis of a particular area of specialization. It is common, for example, for psychologists to be asked to consult with a school program over the question of a student's behavior, because the psychologist is seen as the expert in behavior management rather than, say, learning in general.

As psychologists have developed various subspecialties, this role has expanded. A good example might be neuropsychology, in which interest is on brain/behavior relationships. Neuropsychologists serve as consultants to neurology departments in medical settings in order to assist in providing clues as to the patient's neurological problems by studying deficits in behavior. In forensic psychology, consultants might be asked to assess the dangerousness of a convicted criminal or testify in court to provide insights concerning an individual's motivation for committing a crime. Since social psychologists have studied the ways jury members make decisions, consultant psychologists often work for large law firms to assist in such matters as jury selection or the presentation of testimony to match jury members' attitudes. Social psychologists are also active in opinion polling and market research.

In the arena of health care, psychologists have become increasingly involved in such important areas as changing lifestyles to improve health, in stress reduction programs, in the prevention of unsafe sexual practices (AIDS prevention), in pain management, and in methods that prepare patients better for invasive medical procedures or which increase compliance with medical treatments [Taylor 1991]. In military, industrial, and corporate settings, psychologists serve major consultative roles in personnel selection, improving decision making, improving work performance and motivation, and in the design of equipment and machines to enable their more effective use by human operators.

Research and Evaluation

Because most psychologists are trained at the doctoral level, and since this involves a significant exposure to research methodology and statistics, psychologists generally consider their ability to design and implement research as a major feature of the profession and one that differentiates them from all other mental health and social service providers. Psychologists will often conceptualize applied work as an opportunity to gather additional information and knowledge and may suggest the design of a study to monitor the results of an intervention more carefully.

There is a great deal of interest in single case studies, since these designs present research opportunities for practicing psychologists. Behavior modification and therapy has been a particularly forceful influence in favor of single-subject research designs. Generally, such designs involve monitoring a client or student before some intervention is implemented, initiating the intervention and evaluating the resultant behavior change, and then temporarily removing the intervention to see whether it was truly responsible for the noted improvement. Since removing an effective intervention could be unethical in many applied situations, variations in the standard single-subject design have been developed to allow the research clinician to infer causal influence of the treatment [Barlow et al. 1984].

Program evaluation is one of the most neglected areas in human services and education. There literally thousands of programs designed to remedy human problems that seem like good ideas, but that have never been subjected to objective scrutiny. Psychologists, with their strong empirical background, have played a major role in encouraging the development of evaluative models that will allow practitioners to be able to demonstrate the effectiveness of their efforts. This involves defining and measuring the meaningful outcomes desired.

Relationship to Other Disciplines

Because psychology is both a basic scientific discipline and an area of professional practice, the knowledge domain of psychology is extensive. Psychologists are likely to have at least some knowledge of such areas as child development, learning, language and communication, sensory processes such as vision and hearing, and basic physiological mechanisms of behavior. This means that there will be a degree of overlap with the core knowledge bases of various other areas of practice, such as early childhood and special education, teaching, speech and language therapy, occupational and physical therapy. This can create certain tensions in practical situations. For example, many of the text instruments routinely used in speech pathology or in occupational therapy are similar to, or derived from, tests developed and used in psychology. Unless psychologists are sensitive to the degree to which their knowledge in these domains is likely to be general rather than specific and clinical, resentments can occur if it seems that psychologists are making pronouncements and recommendations that related to another professional's area of specialized expertise.

In the mental health arena, there is some disciplinary overlap regarding the practice of psychotherapy. Psychiatrists and social workers are also extensively trained in psychotherapy and may also offer these services privately to patients for a fee. The slightly more generic activity of "counseling" is widely used by many different mental health team members, including alcohol and drug rehabilitation counselors, psychiatric nurses, pastoral counselors (specially trained ministers of religion), and vocational and guidance counselors in schools and colleges. Grassroots support services also offer counseling services: self-help groups such as Alcoholics Anonymous, groups for battered spouses, survivors of incest, and many other examples, offer support from other experienced group members and lay volunteers. Individuals in this situation are usually careful to define their services cautiously and not to imply that they are offering psychotherapy. Only in areas where fees may be charged and reimbursed by third-party payers do the professional rivalries become intense. For example, social workers or psychiatrists cannot advertise their services under the heading of "psychological" services or treatment; under the topic of "marriage and family counseling," however, as will be seen from any telephone book's Yellow Pages, social workers, psychologists, psychiatrists, and doubtless other professions as well, all list themselves equally.

The major rivalry that occurs in the profession of psychology is with psychiatry. The typical lay person has a difficult time defining the difference between these two professions, and although most people may be able to state that psychiatrists have medical training, few realize that psychiatrists have had little formal exposure to psychology as a discipline [Breggin 1991]. Thus, in the media psychiatrists are often asked to give their opinion on some matter relating to psychological knowledge, like whether children's reports of sexual abuse are likely to be reliable, why children experience stress at times of national crisis, how to reduce drug abuse, or the causes of crime. Psychologists tend to be resentful of pronouncements on such topics, largely because psychology, with its strong scientific foundation, takes a conservative and often overly elaborate theoretical position regarding their complexity.

Because psychiatrists are first trained as medical doctors and then specialize in psychiatry, psychiatrists work predominantly in medical settings such as psychiatric hospitals, the acute care psychiatry wards of general hospitals, and mental health clinics. Psychiatrists have privileges in these settings, such as being able to admit patients, see their patients after admission and write orders for others (e.g., nurses) to follow, and prescribe medication and other physical or organic treatments. Psychologists have fought long and hard to have similar privileges as ancillary health care providers. Hospital admitting and other privileges have now generally been acquired by psychologists, usually through legislative action.

Twenty years ago the differences in power structure among these professions was much more apparent. Most older psychologists will remember team meetings and case discussions in which the psychiatrist or medical doctor was seen as the most important, the most busy, and the most authoritative member, usually acting as chair of meetings and making final decisions. This strict hierarchy has changed considerably in more recent years, and much greater respect for the professional contribution of other disciplines is now apparent in educational and mental health settings.

Key Issues Regarding Participation in Teams

In professional team contexts, dominance by one profession's feelings of superiority seems to be in sharp decline. That does not mean, however, that team interactions are always going to be constructive and democratic. Social psychologists have studied the processes involved when individuals interact in groups, and some of these findings might be helpful to understanding how teams work [Brehm & Kassin 1990]. Groups form when individuals share a goal that can only be accomplished by uniting their efforts, resources, and knowledge. When combined efforts are reinforced with success, morale improves and further group goals and planning will develop and be maintained. Note, however, that although simple tasks are performed better when one is around others (the social facilitation effect), difficult tasks are performed better when alone. Team meetings are not necessarily effective settings for completing complex tasks, such as writing reports or designing the details of an intervention.

Social Roles

Once the group begins stabilizing into a more long-term unit, role differentiation occurs and a power structure within the group may develop. The role is the particular social identify that each individual fills within the group, which is separate from, although not in conflict with, the overall identity of the group. That is, while each member will interact uniquely within the group, the group as a whole will also develop a set of norms for behavior and attitudes that will become the defining features of the group as a single entity. A psychologist may attend team meetings of professionals who work together in other contexts, such as the nursing staff of an inpatient psychiatry ward, or the direct care staff of a group home. In this setting, the psychologists will be an outsider, relatively speaking, and may find it difficult to influence group decisions. It is also possible that the group will elicit conformity, so that the individual's behaviors and attitudes will be swayed by subtle group pressure. Thus, the psychologist's recommendations regarding a client, based on objective assessment data, may be influenced by the team's perspective.

Group Pressure

There are two particularly important group phenomena that have implications for teaming. By recognizing these, the psychologist might be able to devise strategies to reduce their negative impact. First, group polarization refers to the well-established tendency for a group as a whole to take a more extreme position on a particular issue than would the individual members alone. This can be problematic, for instance, if the team is recommending an intrusive intervention for a child with disruptive behavior. One way to avoid this is to follow formal decision rules that ensure the least restrictive or intrusive strategy is explored first [Evans & Meyer 1985].

A second phenomenon is known as "groupthink"; this is the tendency to "preserve group harmony by going along uncritically with whatever consensus seems to be emerging" [Janis 1989]. Signs that the group might be susceptible to this influence are when individual members keep their doubts to themselves, when dissent is discouraged, or questioners are accused of delaying progress, and when the group feels uniquely important or powerful in some way. There are various strategies to encourage more critical group thinking:

- The group leader should not state his or her preferences early in discussion;

- Team members should be allowed to discuss issues with people outside the group having possible different opinions (this is especially important in obtaining a variety of impressions of a client, such as talking to a teacher who is not a member of the IEP team about a certain student); and

- Some team members should be assigned to be "devil's advocates" and argue persuasively for another perspective.

Psychologists need to be especially aware of the influence of the group on the client. At IEP meetings, for instance, a parent may be the only individual not part of the team. Even the parent advocate will have worked with the team on numerous other occasions. In these situations, it is critical to avoid compliance on the part of the outside person, since the team usually is seen as having authority and power.

Cooperation and Conflict

Within the group, the status of individuals will form the basis for determining the distribution of power. Depending upon how cooperative or competitive an orientation each member decides to hold, the group can become more or less effective in attaining its goals. One strategy for developing cooperation in group members is to use a cooperative reward system, where completion of tasks requires joint participation of all members (task interdependence) and rewards or payoffs to members are equally or fairly distributed. A psychologist accustomed to always writing his or her own independent reports, for instance, will impede cooperative behavior and the sharing of information regarding the client. Team collaboration can be enhanced by rotating key roles within the group, such as the team leader (chair), the recorder of decisions reached, and the individual responsible for summarizing and presenting data on the client.

The distinctive orientations of professionals from different disciplines can exacerbate conflict. Although generalizations are always dubious, it can be argued that psychologists will have the following biases:

- They will be unlikely to blame the client, stressing instead family and other social influences;

- They will tend to avoid generalizations based on labels and prefer to look for patterns of behavior;

- They will presume that a client's behavior is not fixed, but varies according to the situation; and

- They will be prone to look for underlying causes to problems (such as defense mechanisms, early traumas, and other emotional stressors).

Some conflict within a team is not all bad; in fact, constructive disagreement is necessary to reduce the group conformity phenomenon already described. To assist in nonaggressive conflict and its resolution, it is necessary to have a win-win approach in which both parties can gain by cooperation. For instance, if the success of one team member's idea means another person's fails, this is the win-lose situation characteristic of most competitive sports or business situations. Psychologists in groups can help reduce conflict by recognizing the interpersonal factors that tend to discourage compromise strategies. One of these negative influences is issue proliferation, in which team members bring up controversial topics that were not part of the original discussion. Another is the use of threats, such as saying that one will complain to a more senior official if the other team member does not agree to a decision. A third problem is when someone in the group makes attributions about the other members' motives. For example, it is easy to feel that another professional is less concerned about a client's welfare than oneself. As a basic strategy, conflict resolution should involve an understanding of one's own needs and intentions, recognition of hidden agendas, practice in listening to others, and avoidance of mixed messages that develop feelings of mistrust.

Psychologists in Distress

While an understanding of social processes can assist a group in functioning effectively together, no amount of care can correct for the isolated individual in the group who has serious personal problems. Obviously, professionals who are themselves in need of psychological therapy represent a special problem for all human service fields, and the issue of psychologists who are manifesting the symptoms of severe behavioral or emotional problems is a complex one.

Recognizing this fact, psychologists have developed a variety of sources of information for psychologists who may be experiencing their own personal difficulties to the extent that they interfere with their professional performance. Professional associations urge psychologists to recognize that helping others can be stressful and emotionally draining. Psychologists are encouraged to identify the signs of depression, drug abuse, and other problems in colleagues and to confront them in a constructive way of these issues. Psychologists frequently seek personal therapy from respected and well-established colleagues in their community.

Levels of Training, Licensure, and Certification

The major vehicle available to prevent entry into the profession of those people whose own emotional difficulties render them unsuitable for the helping role is that of training. For these reasons, training programs evaluate their products far beyond the basic issue of whether they have acquired the requisite knowledge base. The ethical, personal, and professional values of students in psychology training programs are carefully evaluated. To maintain the highest standards, various accreditation and certification procedures have been developed. In this section, we will provide a brief overview of these.

To pursue a career in psychology, one must begin at the undergraduate level, where requirements for a bachelor's degree in psychology are completed. Basic courses in the areas of experimental, social, developmental, and physiological psychology are combined with at least one research laboratory course. This undergraduate degree is meant to give students a general knowledge within psychology and therefore does not prepare one to practice in any area.

Graduate training is needed for practice in all specialties of psychology, but specific requirements vary with specialty chosen. Until recently, the master's degree was acceptable for practice in school psychology; in many states, however, this is changing. The Ph.D. or Psy.D. degrees are increasingly becoming the requirements set by individual states for practice in school, counseling, and clinical psychology. Moreover, many programs no longer offer terminal master's degrees and therefore only accept students who wish to complete a doctorate.

The Ph.D. in psychology takes approximately four to six years to complete, depending on the program. It is a research-rich degree geared for students requiring training in empirical methods within their area of specialty. Students who wish to hold administrative, academic, or research positions, or to practice psychology according to a scientist-practitioner model, require training in such a program.

The Psy.D. degree was first introduced in 1966; it takes three to five years to complete, depending on the specific program. It focuses less on research than a Ph.D. program, and is most suitable for those who wish to be trained in the practice of psychology but do not want rigorous exposure to basic experimental methods and research design. The Psy.D. degree is geared more toward applied issues than theoretical.

Regardless of type of degree, training programs will require students to participate in field placements during their years of didactic training. These are carefully supervised positions held in community organizations that are relevant to the type of psychology program. For example, placement for a clinical psychology graduate student may be in a local mental health outpatient clinic. Once all basic course requirements have been completed, programs require a one-year, full-time internship in an institution not directly affiliated with the school in which the student has been trained.

Training programs and internships in the areas of clinical, counseling, and school psychology are evaluated by a three-person review team from the American Psychological Association (APA) every five years. This evaluation investigates how well the programs are meeting their own training goals, as well as how well they meet the standards that APA has established. These standards include a broad curriculum, a focus on diversity and multicultural sensitivity, appropriate practicum, laboratory, and library resources, and a committed, productive faculty. Accreditation is one way in which a standardized minimum level of training can be assured nationwide.

Certification and Licensure

Requirements for certification and licensure are determined by individual states. They require an evaluation of the applicant's qualifications, regardless of whether he or she has already completed an APA-accredited training program. The purpose of certification is to protect the public by controlling use of the title "psychologist." States usually only specify the type of degree or level of training as a requirement for certification. Licensure requirements are more restrictive, usually specifying the type of degree necessary, one or two years of experience, as well as passing a state-administered national examination. Licensure laws specify the exact activities and services that a psychologist is authorized to carry out professionally. State licensure signifies at least a minimal level of competence.

The American Board of Professional Psychologists (AMPP) also certifies the professional competence of psychologists. A diploma can be earned in any of four areas: clinical, school, counseling, or industrial psychology. The qualifications for an ABPP include an earned doctorate, five years of experience, as well as a test that evaluates knowledge in the areas of assessment, therapy, research, theory, and ethics of psychological practice in the specific area in which the diploma is granted. Since the requirements that an ABPP diplomate must meet are more rigorous than those set by states for licensure, the diploma is often considered a more prestigious recognition of professional expertise.

To make it easier for certified and licensed psychologists to receive third-party payments from insurance companies, the *National Register of Health Service Providers in Psychology* was created. This register, which is updated annually, lists all psychologists who are legally authorized to provide mental health services and who have paid to have their names listed in this volume. The register does not in any way evaluate the competence of the individuals listed, but helps third-party payers ensure that a given provider does have the minimum necessary qualifications.

Professional Organizations and Leading Journals

The APA is the major organization representing psychology in the United States. It is dedicated to "the advancement of psychology as a science, a profession, and as a means of promoting human welfare." Currently, APA is the world's largest association of psychologists, with more than 70,000 members. (It is estimated, incidentally, that there are about 500,000 psychologists worldwide.) APA is organized into 45 different divisions to serve the diverse interests of its membership.

In addition to carrying out evaluation and accreditation of training and internship programs, giving awards, and influencing public policy, APA publishes 20 primary journals (the *American Psychologist* is the official journal of the association) and a number of books that are widely circulated and cited. Its *Publication Manual,* which is a guide to authors of technical papers, is widely recognized throughout the social sciences as the chief authority on matters of style and publication formats.

Many other well-known international publishers also produce scientific journals of great repute in the field—the sophisticated college library will probably have more than 200 scholarly periodicals that are primarily psychological in content. APA also publishes and enforces ethical guidelines for research and practice of psychology. Their annual convention and continuing education programs serve to bring together and inform thousands of psychologists on the latest advances in their fields.

During the 1980s, the APA underwent a period of turmoil. There has been an internal struggle over whether APA should become a conglomeration of semi-autonomous societies, or maintain its centralized governance structure. With increasingly larger numbers of clinical practitioners joining APA, many scientists and academicians felt their needs were no longer being met. Traditionally, state associations, affiliated with APA, had been primarily responsible for promoting the profession by state legislation, but this political effort of organized psychology has become more centralized at the national level.

It was argued that autonomy was needed so as to permit all groups to deal with their own issues without unwanted interference from others. In 1988, the American Psychological Society was founded, consisting mostly of scientists and academicians who were discontented with APA's apparent drift toward becoming a professional organization devoted to improving the professional practice opportunities of its members. It is too early to see whether a true split will develop within the field, or whether scientific standards and goals can coexist with interest in social and economic policies that will benefit the profession as well as society.

Several more specialized associations represent the interests of subgroups of psychologists. Although not limited to psychologists, many clinical psychologists with strong scientific interests belong to the Association for Advancement of Behavior Therapy. The National Association of School Psychologists (NASP) is a major organization that allows master's-level psychologists to have a voice that is essentially denied them in APA. NASP has developed special standards for competence and ethical principles that relate specifically to the practice of school psychology. There are also prominent organizations in behavioral medicine (Society of Behavioral Medicine), child development (Society for Research in Child Development), and basic research (Psychonomic Society).

Standards of Ethics

Ethical principles are based on the fact that the professional helper is sometimes in a state of conflict between the desire to help the client and the desire to advance the welfare or needs of the individual practitioner. APA has developed ethical principles for psychologists that guide the professional behavior of psychologists in the following areas:

- Responsibility,

- Competence,

- Moral and legal standards,

- Public statements,

- Confidentiality,

- Welfare of the consumer,

- Professional relationships,

- Assessment techniques,

- Research with human participants, and

- Care and use of animals [APA 1981].

The ethical code relates directly to professional activities and therefore is not enforced for complaints regarding the personal lives of psychologists. Furthermore, nowhere in the "Ethical Principles of Psychologists" does APA discuss the philosophical issues of what is "right" and "wrong." Rather, the principles reflect the attitudes and norms of American culture and are therefore subject to change as society evolves technologically and sociologically.

The ethical principles can be most simply thought of as rules of conduct governing professional activities, with APA carrying out law enforcement and judicial activities. The latter include referring transgressors to the respective state licensing boards that can then prohibit continued practice, as well as publicly dropping offenders from membership in the association. Accepting membership in APA assumes a commitment to these ethical standards of conduct and states require a similar affirmation for licensure. By enforcing the code, psychology maintains a high level of quality performance and earns the respect and confidence of other professionals, as well as of the public it serves [Keith-Spiegel & Koocher 1985].

The ten ethical principles touch upon a wide range of issues. With regard to psychologists participating in teams that include other professionals, the code is clear in placing the needs of the consumer as top priority and demanding full cooperation with others in meeting those needs. This requires that psychologists take the traditions and practices of other professional groups into account to act responsibly and effectively in their teamwork.

In many instances, two professionals will view a situation from different angles and therefore choose to treat a problem differently even if both are from the same field. The ethical code prevents one professional from offering services to a consumer who is already receiving similar services from another professional. Moreover, when a consumer who is already receiving services requests such further services, professionals are cautioned to proceed carefully and with sensitivity, as taking on such responsibility can seriously compromise therapeutic benefits for the consumer.

With regard to the client/therapist relationship, the ethical code supports the best welfare of the client. Dual relationships (treating family members, friends, or business associates) are particularly to be avoided and sexual and social liaisons with patients are proscribed. Dedication to client care demands that psychologists only offer services that they are qualified and trained to perform. Referral to other professionals is appropriate when one is not qualified or unable to provide effective treatment for a client. In addition, consultation with other professionals is common with unusual cases or difficult treatments.

The confidentiality of all matters discussed between a client and therapist is also protected by the ethical code. This principle is similar to the client privilege of confidentiality between a lawyer and a client. Both require strict confidentiality except with the written permission of the client or in cases where confidentiality may result in clear danger to the client or to someone else. Clients have the right to this type of privacy even in cases where they have agreed to allow information about themselves to be used for research purposes by their therapist. In this case, the researcher must make sure that all procedures used in the collection, storage, and publication of the research protects the client's anonymity. Competent, well-trained psychologists should neither treat any client as a "pathological case," nor judge any dysfunction as an issue of morality. Such attitudes are unprofessional, unscientific, and avoid the real issues that must be addressed to treat clients effectively.

Summary

Psychology is a highly complex field, since it involves both wide areas of scientific inquiry—every facet of human behavior—and the attempt to extend that knowledge base to assist individuals, groups, and societies deal with problems in living that arise from many sources: environmental, societal, economic, and cultural. Despite wide-scale differences in the degree to which individual psychologists may consider themselves to be trained or interested in the scientific nature of the field, a general respect for empirical knowledge, broadly defined, characterizes the field and distinguishes the professional psychologist from the nonpsychologist who might also have a store of knowledge about people but little formal training in theory and concepts. For example, a wise relative, neighbor, minister, politician, student of literature, writer, or film maker may have truly detailed understanding of people and the forces that affect development and personality, but they will not have a technical knowledge base from which this understanding is drawn. Their insights come more from personal experience, careful observation, reading, or, in some cases, guess work and speculation.

With access to the formal knowledge base of psychology comes professional responsibility, which is the origin of professional ethics. Ethics in the field of psychology have been developed from relatively simple principles to ensure that the technical understanding is promoted rigorously and is applied in the best interest of the individual consumer, not the psychologist. Procedures for improving training and other standards are all based on this concept. This does not mean that psychologists will never vary in their personal and political philosophies; however, in general it can be assured that psychologists will make efforts to promote understanding and perspectives that are as free from personal biases as possible.

Translating these standards into the role of the professional psychologist in providing services or working with others does not guarantee that every psychologist will be a competent and effective professional. Nevertheless, as a discipline, the factors that make us all less than perfect are themselves topics of investigation in psychology: the origins of attitudes, how our own needs influence our judgment; how our own learning histories distort our perceptions of others; and how aggression, bigotry, and bias in attitude is a function of individual experiences.

Training in these topics should enhance objectivity and professional integrity. Practicing psychologists, the professionals who will be the members of the interdisciplinary teams that this book is about, will today be applied scientists drawing heavily from the basic discipline of research psychology. This basic discipline is much broader than its origins in experimental studies of mental processes, and covers a vast domain of child development, personality, social, animal learning, and cognitive fields, as well as the rapidly developing area of neuroscience, or brain-behavior relationships.

Many practicing psychologists will describe themselves as eclectic in philosophical orientation and will often blend behavioral, cognitive, psychoanalytic, and humanistic constructs without feeling too much internal conflict. Many, too, will not see themselves as applied scientists and may base their practice on knowledge acquired through clinical experience, professional mentoring, or even everyday living. And yet, in general, what will distinguish a psychologist in the mental health or direct service fields, will be a disciplinary connection to research and scientific method. Psychologists will generally be interested in measurement, in testing hypotheses, and in applying psychological principles that have been validated in more basic research.

References

Albee, G. W. (1986). Toward a just society: Lessons from observations on the primary prevention of psychopathology. *American Psychologist, 41*, pp. 891-898.

American Psychiatric Association. (1994). *Diagnostic and statistical manual of mental health disorders* (4th ed.). Washington, DC: Author.

American Psychological Association. (1974). *Standards for providers of psychological services.* Washington, DC: Author.

American Psychological Association. (1981). Ethical principles of psychologists. *American Psychologist, 36*, 633-638.

Anastasi, A. (1982). *Psychological testing* (5th ed.). New York: Macmillan.

Barlow, D. H., Hayes, S. C., & Nelson, R. O. (1984). *The scientists practitioner: Research and accountability in clinical and educational settings.* New York: Pergamon.

Beck, A. T. (1976). *Cognitive therapy and the emotional disorders.* New York: International Universities Press.

Boring, E. G. (1950). *A history of experimental psychology.* New York: Appleton-Century-Crofts.

Breggin, P. R. (1991). *Toxic psychiatry.* New York: St. Martin's Press.

Brehm, S. S., & Kassin, S. M. (1990). *Social psychology.* Boston: Houghton Mifflin.

Brown, S. D., & Lent, R. W. (Eds.). (1984). *The handbook of counseling psychology.* New York: Wiley.

Cattell, J. M. (1890). Mental tests and measurements. *Mind, 15,* 373-381.

Corsini, R. J., & Wedding, D. (1989). *Current psychotherapies* (4th ed.). Itasca, IL: Peacock.

Evans, I. M. (1991). Testing and diagnosis: A review and evaluation. In L. H. Meyer, C. A. Peck, & L. Brown (Eds.), *Critical issues in the lives of people with severe disabilities* (pp. 25-44). Baltimore, MD: Paul H. Brookes.

Evans, I. M., & Meyer, L. H. (1985). *An educative approach to behavior problems: A practical decision model for interventions with severely handicapped learners.* Baltimore, MD: Paul H. Brookes.

Eysenck, H. J. (1952). The effects of psychotherapy: An evaluation. *Journal of Consulting Psychology, 16,* 319-324.

Fancher, R. E. (1979). *Pioneers of psychology.* New York: Norton.

Frank, G. (1984). The Boulder model: History, rationale, and critique. *Professional Psychology: Research and Practice, 15,* 417-435.

Franks, C. M. (Ed.). (1969). *Behavior therapy: Appraisal and status.* New York: McGraw-Hill.

Garfield, S. L., & Bergin, A. E. (Eds.). (1986). *Handbook of psychotherapy and behavior change* (3rd ed.). New York: Wiley.

Gould, S. J. (1981). *The mismeasure of man.* New York: Norton.

James, W. (1890). *Principles of psychology.* New York: Holt.

Janis, I. L. (1989). *Crucial decisions: Leadership in policy making and crisis management.* New York: Free Press.

Keith-Spiegel, P., & Koocher, G. P. (1985). *Ethics in psychology: Professional standards and cases.* Hillsdale, NJ: Erlbaum.

Meichenbaum, D. (1977). *Cognitive behavior modification.* New York: Plenum.

Myers, H. F., Wohlford, P., Guzman, L. P., & Echemendia, R. J. (Eds.). (1991). *Ethnic minority perspectives on clinical training and services in psychology.* Washington, DC: American Psychological Association.

Pryzwansky, W. B., & Wendt, R. N. (1987). *Psychology as a profession: Foundations of practice.* New York: Pergamon.

Reisman, J. M. (1991). *A history of clinical psychology.* New York: Hemisphere Publishing Corp.

Reynolds, C. R., & Gutkin, T. B. (Eds.). (1982). *The handbook of school psychology.* New York: Wiley.

Rogers, C. R. (1951). *Client-centered therapy.* Boston: Houghton Mifflin.

Rose, S. M., & Black, B. L. (1985). *Advocacy and empowerment: Mental health care in the community.* London: Routledge & Kegan Paul.

Shakow, D. (1947). *Recommended graduate training programs in clinical psychology.* Washington, DC: American Psychological Association.

Taylor, S. E. (1991). *Health psychology* (2nd ed.). New York: McGraw-Hill.

Truax, C. B., & Carkhuff, R. R. (1967). *Toward effective counseling and psychotherapy: Training and practice.* Chicago, IL: Aldine Publishing Co.

Ullmann, L. P., & Krasner, L. (Eds.). (1965). *Case studies in behavior modification.* New York: Holt.

Walsh, W. B., & Betz, N. E. (1990). *Tests and assessment* (2nd ed.). Englewood Cliffs, NJ: Prentice Hall.

Watson, J. B. (1924). *Behaviorism.* New York: Norton.

T E A M W O R K

Rehabilitation Counseling

By William E. Kiernan, Joseph Marrone, & Margaret VanGelder

The National Council on Rehabilitation [1944] defined rehabilitation as the restoration of people who are handicapped to the fullest physical, mental, social, vocational, and economic usefulness of which they are capable. Jacques [1970] defined it as a readaptation process following injury or a disorder. A more practical definition might be a process that persons with disabilities engage in to define individual or person specific goals, develop action steps to achieve those goals, and identify resources that can be accessed to meet those goals. Such resources may include those internal to the individual, those that naturally occur (such as friends at work), the use of appointment books or bells for crossing streets, and those provided by a paid support person, such as a rehabilitation counselor [Kiernan et al. 1991].

Rehabilitation counseling as a professional discipline is, in many ways, unique. While the provision of services to people with disabilities has a long history, the creation of the professional role of "rehabilitation counselor" followed the development of the service. The evolution of rehabilitation counseling reflects more a set of beliefs and values, rather than the development of a specific set of skills or competencies. In essence, the cornerstone of rehabilitation counseling is the belief that persons with disabilities will benefit from certain services and supports. Although there may be divergence of opinion as to approaches or environments within which services should be provided, there is seldom disagreement on the core concept; that is, assisting the individual with a disability in regaining or acquiring new skills and abilities that lead to greater independence and accomplishment.

William E. Kiernan, Ph.D., is Director of the Institute for Community Inclusion at the University Affiliated Program and Adjunct Professor in the Graduate College of Education at the University of Massachusetts, Boston. Joseph Marrone, Ed.M., is Coordinator of Training at the Institute for Community Inclusion, also in Boston. Margaret VanGelder, M.A., C.R.C., is Director of Employer Supports at the Massachusetts Department of Mental Retardation.

A Brief History of Rehabilitation

The English Poor Laws of 1601 formed the framework of Western society's commitment to assist those who could not fend for themselves. These laws are the basis for modern social policy legislation that often reflects governmental or public approaches to helping people with economic, social, educational, or medical problems. While these laws were primarily directed at indigent people, persons with disabilities ("the lame," "the crippled") were included in their purview [Wright 1980]. When Colonial America developed its own set of Poor Laws, these same groups were usually included. Such legislation was directed not at helping restore lost capacity or increasing levels of independence or productivity, but rather at taking care of those unable to care for themselves.

The 17th, 18th, and 19th centuries saw the development of Western European/American societal response to the problems of people with disabilities. Schools and programs were developed for persons who were deaf or blind, or who had emotional or mental illness or physical and cognitive disabilities [Cavalier 1986; Wright 1980].

But rehabilitation as a separate professional discipline (distinct from such related professions as medicine, social work, psychology, nursing, etc.) blossomed in the United States with the creation of the Federal-State Vocational Rehabilitation system [Kiernan 1979]. Because of the importance of this development, both to increased services available to people with disabilities over the last 70 years and to the subsequent genesis of the profession of rehabilitation counseling, this legislation is presented in greater detail in Table 13.

As can be seen from the evolution of the Vocational Rehabilitation legislation, the focus in rehabilitation has shifted from solely helping people with disabilities who were previously employed return to the labor market, to assisting those individuals with severe disabilities to enter employment for the first time. The emphasis of vocational rehabilitation until the last decade has been on the identification of skills and abilities and the development of strategies and approaches leading to employment for people with disabilities. The 1986 and 1992 changes in vocational rehabilitation legislation (P.L. 95-607 and P.L. 102-569) reflect the increased emphasis upon the empowerment of the individual, the active role of the person who is disabled in and throughout the rehabilitation process, and an expanded

Table 13. Legislative History of Vocational Rehabilitation

Title	Legislation Number	Date of Passage	Critical Features
Soldier Rehabilitation Smith-Sears Act	P.L. 65-178	1918	Genesis of what was to become the Federal-State Rehabilitation system.
Civilian Rehabilitation	P.L. 66-236	1920	Developed civilian counterpart to P.L. 65-178. Assist civilians with non-service-connected physical disabilities to receive job placement and retraining. An eligibility program that required clients to meet criteria that remain essentially unchanged to present day. Establishes disability as an impairment to work and expectation that, with services, an individual can return to work.
Vocational Rehabilitation Amendments or Barden-LaFollette Act	P.L. 78-113	1943	Expansion of VR services to people with mental illness and/or mental retardation. Inclusion of such services as medical/physical restoration in addition to vocational training and placement.
Vocational Rehabilitation Amendments or Hill-Burton Act	P.L. 83-565	1954	Authorized expenditures on training staff and creating the first graduate-level Rehabilitation Counseling programs.
Vocational Rehabilitation Amendments	P.L. 89-333	1965	Targeted rehabilitation services to those most in need. Established "extended evaluation" period (up to 18 months) before a determination of vocational feasibility rendered.
Rehabilitation Act of 1973	P.L. 93-112	1973	Created (Title V) protections in employment and in public accommodations, modeled after the Civil Rights legislation. Mandated VR services be targeted primarily to those labeled "most severely disabled." Requirement of significant client involvement in and throughout the VR process.
Rehabilitation, Comprehensive Services and Developmental Disabilities Amendment	P.L. 95-602	1978	For the first time, diverted a small amount of VR funding toward individuals who were presumed "too severely disabled" to work, but who could benefit from services in the arena of living more independently in the community. Established a functional definition of a developmental disability.

Table 13. Legislative History of Vocational Rehabilitation (continued)

Title	Legislation Number	Date of Passage	Critical Features
Vocational Rehabilitation Amendments	P.L. 99-506	1986	Created a new service category and attendant funding stream for "Supported Employment." Expanded service capacity to those unable to benefit from vocational services.
Americans with Disabilities Act	P.L. 100-336	1989	Full citizenship and rights for people with disabilities within our society (access to employment, housing, education, public areas, and transportation).
Vocational Rehabilitation Amendments	P.L. 102-569	1992	Preamble of values and beliefs. Presumption of employability. 60-day VR eligibility determination. Emphasis on the use of families and natural support systems. Emphasis on formal agreements to develop transition services from school-to-work.

interest in assisting persons with disabilities not only in entering employment but also in living independently in the community.

Current Philosophies of Treatment and Services

Rehabilitation is viewed as a range of services and supports that allow the individual who is disabled to be as independent and productive as possible in the community. Rehabilitation services are diverse and offered by a variety of professionals, including psychologists, social workers, physicians, nurses, physical therapists, occupational therapists, speech pathologists, and rehabilitation counselors. As noted in the previous section, the discipline of rehabilitation counseling reflects the early emphasis upon the need to assist individuals in returning to work. The role of the rehabilitation counselor has evolved over the past 50 years to reflect changes in legislative mandates and the growing body of literature regarding practices and services that can assist persons with disabilities to realize their full potential.

Rehabilitation counseling as a profession is eclectic in its service approaches, relying often on the support and assistance of many professionals in the development and implementation of a rehabilitation plan. As Barker [1988] noted, the training of rehabilitation counselors has often included theories borrowed from counseling psychology, medicine, applied behavior theory, and functional analysis/planning. Competencies in case management, individual and group counseling, career development, vocational assessment, work adjustment, job placement, training and support strategies on the job, and family supports represent only a few of the areas addressed in rehabilitation counselor training programs.

Beyond the development of competencies, practitioners have postulated clear philosophies and human values as key elements of a rehabilitation approach over the years. Core concepts and professional characteristics inherent in being a rehabilitation counselor—in fact all professionals involved in the provision of rehabilitative services—were offered by Wright [1980]:

- **Holistic nature.** A comprehensive view of human problems (i.e., recognizing the interrelatedness of all aspects of a person's life);

- **Self-determination.** The individual is at the center and controls the rehabilitation process;

- **Societal contribution.** The belief that each individual has an innate desire to be a productive member of his/her community;

- **Right to be equal.** Full civil and citizenship rights extend to people with disabilities;

- **Human spirit.** A belief in the capacity of individuals to persevere and rise above obstacles;

- **Focus on assets.** The rehabilitation focus on maximizing strengths as much as remediating deficits;

- **Motivation for good.** The belief that individuals are capable of changing and will naturally desire to improve their situation;

- **Influence of environment.** The focus of rehabilitation activities on modifying environments, as well as developing individual skills;

- **Intrinsic value.** A belief in the essential worth of a person, solely by virtue of his or her humanity, independent of social/financial/educational status, etc., and;

- **Concern for individuals.** Service provision is based on individual desires and needs, not categorical groupings or diagnosis.

Shafer [1988] spoke of rehabilitation philosophy as having an orientation towards productivity and self-sufficiency. Bitter [1979] identified three essential principles of vocational rehabilitation: equality of opportunity, a holistic and coordinated service approach, and an orientation towards individuality. The basic concept of rehabilitation counseling has evolved, as has the emphasis of the legislation and the advances in treatment strategies and technology. The core concepts of individual and group counseling and a partnership approach to the implementation of a rehabilitation plan may serve to separate out rehabilitation counseling from some of the other rehabilitation professionals, particularly those relating to physical rehabilitation.

Another way of conceptualizing rehabilitation principles as they relate to practice, is to examine the relationship between the helper and the client as it unfolds in a rehabilitation process versus what has been frequently found in a more traditional health care or medically focused model. Anderson [1975] identified four aspects of "the helping process" that can be analyzed in this light:

- Activity level of the helper/client,

- Basis of trust,

- Strategy for problem solving, and

- Helpee's capacity for future problem solving after the relationship has terminated.

In a more traditional health care model, the helper is active, while the individual being helped is passive; the rehabilitation construct reverses these roles [Anderson 1975]. In the traditional health care model, trust often is based on expertise; in the rehabilitation context, trust reflects the development of a mutual relationship. The problem-solving strategy of the traditional health care model draws on the helper's knowledge to solve problems; the rehabilitation approach works more on the identification of and access to resources and supports jointly by the rehabilitation counselor and the individual with a disability. Finally, the traditional health care model encourages a return to the helper for future problem resolution, whereas a rehabilitation practitioner presumably helps the individual develop skills that would allow him or her to solve future problems independently or with minimal assistance.

The core tenets of rehabilitation, which directly influence practice in the community, are based on underlying assumptions about human behavior and the personal change process. Four major areas have been identified by Whitehead and Marrone [1986] reflecting the individual in control, productivity as not solely related to employment but to other levels of personal achievement, support being willingly offered and accessible, and the rehabilitation process reflecting varying rates of advancement and times of plateau. Each is discussed in greater detail.

The Individual with a Disability Is in Control

The value of an active role for the individual in the decision-making and planning processes clearly runs through all the varying rehabilitation philosophies. This value is frequently seen as delineating the rehabilitation process from the more traditional health care processes. Concurrent with this belief is the implied corollary—that if individuals make choices, then they must accept the consequences attendant to those choices. With the changes in the current rehabilitation practice—that is, the increased emphasis on the provision of rehabilitative services to persons who are more severely disabled—this principle may be subject to misinterpretation. Often people with severe disabilities come into the process with limited life experience to base their choices and decisions on. Therefore, implicit for the rehabilitation counselor at this stage of the process is first to ensure that the person has some concrete experiences on which to base decisions, even if the helper initially has to create these. To offer choice when there is no understanding of what options are available or what these options may imply, is not offering informed choice but only a roll of the dice or a best guess. The rehabilitation counselor must assist the person who is disabled in acquiring the necessary knowledge and experience so that the choice process can be meaningful and informed. Exploration and experiential activities can be a central component of the rehabilitation process, especially for those who throughout their lives have had little or no opportunities to experience work, community living, or leisure recreational activities.

Roessler [1989], using some of the theories developed through the social learning literature [Bandura 1986], advances the view that motivation, a person's desires and actions towards a goal, is a function of both values and expectancy. For the individual with a disability, a lack of motivation to work may reflect a history of low expectation on the part of others. This is something the rehabilitation counselor must consider when confronting issues of motivation. Some attempt should be made to ensure that both elements in the motivational process have been attended to:

- Does the individual have a value of, or a desire to, work?

- Does the individual have a sense that efforts toward this goal will be successful?

The challenge in providing rehabilitation services to people with severe disabilities is to develop strategies and approaches that look at motivation and sense of success in light of individuals' limited experiences and accomplishments. The risk at times will be to feel that the individual who has no interests or experiences, and thus who is unable to articulate a clear or apparently realistic employment goal, is unmotivated and therefore not a good candidate for rehabilitation services. With the development of such approaches as supported employment and the use of assistive technology, people who previously were considered unemployable or unmotivated can now benefit from rehabilitation services. The caution here is to avoid equating lack of knowledge or experience with lack of motivation in the rehabilitation process, especially as it relates to persons with severe disabilities.

Productivity and Personal Achievement

The importance of productive activity to a person's physical and mental well-being has been well documented [Kiernan et al. 1989]. Work and productivity have often been perceived as similar or the same in Western society. Productivity, however, is not necessarily synonymous with gainful employment, but rather implies a degree of personal satisfaction and a sense of achievement related to employment and other activities. Hence, while employment and productivity may be closely allied in one's consciousness, the capacity for an individual to feel productive in volunteer, social, or family activities is consistent with the mission of rehabilitation. Paid work, therefore, is a significant, but not essential, goal of the rehabilitation process. Or, stated another way, vocational rehabilitation is a crucial element of rehabilitation, but it does not represent the totality of that process.

For some individuals for whom gainful employment may not be a realistic option (perhaps due to age or health-related issues) and for whom employment is not a personal goal, the concepts, values, and services provided through the rehabilitation process remain appropriate. This expanded view of the rehabilitation process differs somewhat from the origins of vocational rehabilitation as presented in the initial section of this chapter where the outcome was a return to work. As people with increasingly more severe disabilities who are not interested in entering employment or who are retired from the workforce enter the rehabilitation service delivery system, this broad view of the rehabilitation process is essential. The cornerstone of the rehabilitation process reflects the view that, even in the face of obstacles and disincentives, most people will value the opportunity to be productive.

Accessible and Willingly Offered Supports

Often the inability to seek needed support is the primary difficulty for people with disabilities. Barriers include embarrassment, fear, shyness, and lack of knowledge. Support provided over too limited a time frame may be of little value for the individual having complex needs. It may be essential to offer ongoing or at least protracted periods of support for certain people in the rehabilitation process. Beyond the issue of duration of support, it is crucial that the support offered be responsive to the needs of the individual. The final decision as to whether to seek access to the supports offered is made by the person with a disability, while it is the rehabilitation counselor's responsibility to assure that the support offered is timely and appropriate to the need expressed.

Growth in Rehabilitation Is Realized at Differing Rates

The rehabilitation process reflects varying rates of advancement and times of plateau. There are two concepts underlying this value. First, people achieve major goals by setting up a series of intermediate objectives. Second, progress will be slowed predictably from time to time as the individual "catches his or her breath" and develops stability in one area before moving ahead. It is important to differentiate this concept from that of the "continuum of services," prevalent for years in the developmental disabilities field. The plateauing principle refers not to a specific series of steps to be moved through sequentially, but rather to the need for individuals to manage changes in their lives without being continually disoriented and overwhelmed.

In addition to the four principles just described, three other core principles about the human condition and the change process are central to rehabilitation philosophy and practice. These principles, briefly outlined below, are achieving positive changes, focusing on strengths, and development of action steps.

Achieving Positive Changes Through the Rehabilitation Process

Change involves the helper effecting change in the person, the environment, or both—a simple, yet elegant rehabilitation precept. A rehabilitation practitioner does not try to teach a person with quadriplegia to walk; rather, the professional may help build a ramp or teach the person to operate a wheelchair. In the employment context with people with mental retardation, one bypasses some of the skill deficits through advocacy, job restructuring, or adding a job coach to the environment.

Focus on Strengths

For the rehabilitation process to be effective, there must be a focus on the individual's level of adaptive functioning, not disability or dysfunction. While this sounds like an unrealistic platitude, it clearly has major practical implications for rehabilitation practice. A rehabilitation counselor does not spend an inordinate amount of time identifying deficits and remediating them. Rather, the approach, while not ignoring assessment and remediation, emphasizes the following:

- The identification of assets and strengths,

- Consideration of the development of compensatory skills,

- The identification of alternative strategies, and

- The development of environmental modifications.

In implementing a rehabilitation plan, it is not uncommon to ignore or work around irreversible individual deficits.

Development of Action Steps

The development of a rehabilitation plan has a bias towards action, rather than process and discussion. Part of this approach stems from the practical and applied focus that is the foundation of the rehabilitation process. Also, since the rehabilitation process is outcome oriented, there is constant reevaluation and redirection. This emphasis often leads to what is commonly perceived by other disciplines as a "trial and error" approach. In the hands of skilled practitioners, this action-oriented approach is a way of developing client/environment specific functional data that are useful in planning effective rehabilitation interventions.

The principles of the rehabilitation process reflect a philosophy with the following emphases:

- The needs of the individual,

- The development of a working relationship between the counselor and the individual,

- The identification of strengths and abilities rather than deficits,

- The emphasis upon compensatory strategies rather than remediation in many instances, and

- The acknowledgment of the need to both develop individual skills and modify environments, thus looking for optimal fit between the individual and a specific environment.

The focus is on the individual and his or her ability to perform across work, community living, and leisure/recreational environments to maximize participation and enhance the quality of life of the individual.

Services Provided in Various Settings

As noted previously, the rehabilitation counselor's role varies and is influenced by the nature of the agency or organization employing the counselor.

The vocational rehabilitation counselor employed in a state vocational re-habilitation agency often provides the following services:

- Determination of the nature and extent of the disability and how it affects the individual's employment potential,

- Assessment of the individual's capacity to enter into or return to employment,

- Identification of the needs for specific skills training at the postsecondary level or in specialized training areas,

- Adaptations necessary to assist the individual to become more independent, and

- The identification of personal needs and personal support skills to allow the individual to function more independently in a community living or independent environment.

The services offered by the state vocational rehabilitation (VR) agency include assessment, counseling, case management, job development, job placement and postemployment supports. The rehabilitation counselor employed by the State VR Agency often will provide short-term counseling interventions that lead to vocational outcomes.

For the rehabilitation counselor employed in a community-based reha-bilitation center, counseling supports can be delivered on an ongoing basis. For persons with developmental disabilities, counseling may reflect an emphasis upon career exploration, community experiences, individual vo-cational skill mastery, case management, personal adjustment, or family supports. The rehabilitation counselor, along with other professionals in psychology and special education, often assists the individual and the fam-ily in identifying career goals, assessing individual needs, and obtaining com-munity resources that are responsive to those needs.

More recently, the rehabilitation counselor has played a role within private rehabilitation agencies, primarily in the areas of resource or case management. The rehabilitation counselor can assist individuals who have experienced traumatic injury or work-related job injuries in returning to work. The rehabilitation counselor may assist the family and the individual in adjusting to a condition as well as identifying potential career opportunities for the individual as he or she returns to employment. Additionally, the rehabilitation counselor may work with the employer, the employee assistance programs in industry, or the private practitioner in assisting the person with the disability to return to or adjust to a return to work.

The most recent role for the rehabilitation counselor is one of assisting students with disabilities to transition from school into employment. With the passage of the new education act (P.L. 101-476), as well as the Rehabilitation Amendments of 1992 (P.L. 102-569), an increased emphasis is placed on development of vocational or adult living goals while the student is in his or her high school years. The role of the rehabilitation counselor in the school system is an evolving one. The mandatory education law stipulates that the rehabilitation counselor serve as a member of the interdisciplinary educational team that assists the student and family to develop goals directed toward transitioning from school to adult life no later than the student's 16th birthday, and, preferably, at 14 years of age. The rehabilitation counselor in this role can assist the student, family, and other team members to identify realistic career goals, as well as to participate in career-oriented educational programs that will lead toward the development of more refined employment goals.

The services offered by the rehabilitation counselor vary considerably depending upon whether the counselor is an employee of the State VR Agency, a community-based comprehensive rehabilitation agency, a private rehabilitation agency, or a local school system. Although the scope and emphasis of the services offered may differ, the types of services offered, including assessment, counseling, personal adjustment training, and job placement, are consistent regardless of the place of employment. The rehabilitation counselor is playing an increasing role in developing life plans and identifying strategies to assist people with disabilities to realize their specific goals.

Relationship to Other Disciplines

The rehabilitation counselor relates to a variety of professionals, including those in health care (physicians, nurses, psychologists, social worker, physical therapists, occupational therapists, etc.); education (special educators, vocational educators, school counselors, general educators, etc.); and within the human resource departments of industry (employee assistance profes-

sionals, job accommodation specialists, equal employment opportunity officers, and employee relations professionals).

In acute hospital settings, the role of the rehabilitation counselor is less
clear and often relates to the issues of discharge planning and the identification of other resources the individual will need after leaving the hospital. In
those instances, the rehabilitation counselor may work with social workers,
psychologists, and nurses as a support and information resource in the discharge planning process.

In contrast to the acute hospital setting, the rehabilitation counselor
plays a much more active role in the tertiary care or rehabilitation hospital
setting. Here the counselor often serves as a member of a rehabilitation
team consisting of physicians, psychologists, therapists (physical therapy,
occupational therapy and speech pathology), social workers, and, in some
cases, special educators (especially for younger children). As a member of
an interdisciplinary team the counselor can assist in assessing functional
capacities, identifying (along with other team members) technology supports and devices and providing individual career and future planning supports, as well as more traditional individual and group counseling supports.

With the increased emphasis upon the need to assist students with disabilities to move from school into employment, the relationship of the rehabilitation counselor to the special educator is becoming more critical.
The rehabilitation counselor must work directly with the special educator
to identify and develop functional curricula that will assist the student to
move from the school into adult life. By working directly with special and
general educators in the development of curricula to foster increased skills
and capacities in the area of employment, community living, and integrated
leisure recreational activities, the rehabilitation counselor can begin the transition process to adult life earlier and involve others in this life-planning
process. Although not a curriculum expert, the rehabilitation counselor can
assist educators in identifying those critical skills necessary for students to
assume a productive and integrated role in society upon graduation. Thus,
in conjunction with the special educator, the rehabilitation counselor can
assist in identifying the competencies and skills that must be addressed
through the instructional (classroom and community-based experiences)
activities in the school.

In community-based rehabilitation agencies, the rehabilitation counselor often works directly with a social worker and/or psychologist to pro-

vide family supports, personal adjustment training, and case management. Some of the roles that the rehabilitation counselor assumes will at times be somewhat narrow. For example, when the counselor works for the public VR service system and the primary emphasis is on return to work, the rehabilitation counselor may work directly with the social worker as a member of an interdisciplinary support team for the family and the person with the disability. The rehabilitation counselor, working cooperatively with other allied health professionals, represents the needs and interests of the individual, while the family needs are represented by the social worker. As a team recognizing both individual and family issues, a comprehensive intervention plan can be developed to respond to the needs, strengths, and concerns of both. This type of team approach has proven effective in responding to the whole life needs of the individual and family and has served to coordinate the resources around a specific set of goals and objectives that are person specific.

Similar to relating to social work professionals, the rehabilitation counselor also relates actively with professionals in psychology. While the psychologist addresses the identification and resolution of needs and conflicts, the rehabilitation counselor focuses upon capitalizing on the strengths of the individual and creating environmental changes to assist the person with the disability to meet individual goals and objectives. The rehabilitation counselor and the psychologist together can address internal conflict while locating community resources to begin to implement a plan for return to work and participation in daily community life activities.

Although the coordination and team work with social work, special education, and psychology is more apparent than with other disciplines who may be members of an interdisciplinary team, the rehabilitation counselor can and should play an active role with other team members. However, when considering the implementation of a rehabilitation service plan, the rehabilitation counselor frequently finds himself or herself working most closely with other education and allied health professionals. This is not to say that the rehabilitation counselor does not coordinate with other disciplines, but rather, in the development of services to students with disabilities transitioning from school to work; individuals with disabilities entering or returning to work; or individuals with disabilities who are moving towards increased interdependence, productivity, and integration within the community, the coordination among special education, social work, and psychology is apparent. It should be noted that the relationship with other team members from other disciplines does not reflect the composition of the whole rehabilitation planning team. The individual who is disabled, family members, and other interested parties also must be involved actively and continuously in the development and implementation of a rehabilitation plan.

Key Issues Regarding Participation in Teams

Interdisciplinary teamwork has been of great concern to practitioners in the field over the years partly because the nature of rehabilitation theory and practice is so eclectic. Also, since the major venue of rehabilitation practice until the last 10 to 15 years has been the state VR system, concerns in the field, in general, often have been synonymous with issues in VR agency practice specifically. Due to the fact that VR systems usually work with a wide variety of community agencies for both referrals and service delivery, effective collaborative practices have been examined quite extensively.

The University of Denver Regional Rehabilitation Research Institute, the Research Utilization Laboratory of the Jewish Vocational Services, and the Knoxville (Tennessee) Area Comprehensive Rehabilitation Consortium have all examined teamwork issues as they affect interagency cooperation and linkages [RRRI 1976; Research Utilization Laboratory 1977]. Examining interdisciplinary collaboration in rehabilitation, medicine, social work, and education agencies, these studies have identified a variety of barriers and incentives to effective cooperative activities. The major barriers identified reflect clinician concerns and fears (loss of control, apprehensions about change, worries about outside criticism), lack of communication (about functions, differing service philosophies, chain of command, fears), and environmental factors (such as funding, staffing, competitive environment, and personal histories). On the other hand, a variety of factors reinforce the participation of the rehabilitation counselor and other professionals in interdisciplinary teams: complexity of presenting needs for certain clients (medical, emotional, and social); outside pressures (such as resource scarcity, consumer demand, interagency agreements); prevailing atmosphere (such as internal leadership, history of cooperation, modeling at the top, general compatibility of objectives); and self-interest (status from associating with more valued professions, tangible gain, surplus resources).

Questions that need to be addressed in collaborating on teams where rehabilitation practitioners are included involve a variety of professional practice and role issues. Since, as noted in previous sections, rehabilitation practice tends to be defined more than most professional disciplines by the environment in which it is performed, it is important to distinguish the areas that affect teamwork from a philosophical as opposed to an organizational perspective. Interdisciplinary teams composed of professions represented in other chapters of this book usually interact with rehabilitation counselors in either one of the following ways: as part of an interagency team involving the public VR system or as part of an intra-organizational, interdisciplinary team. Therefore, the issues germane to this topic will be discussed in light of both situations.

Some factors that other team members need to keep in mind in understanding the dynamics of interacting with rehabilitation counselors working for a public VR agency reflect **legislative mandates and organizational structures**. The VR system is an eligibility determination system, not an entitlement service. Eligibility involves access to the planning services of a professional rehabilitation counselor. Being eligible for VR services, based on the federal definition of vocational handicap and reasonable expectation of success, does not imply any specific commitment of agency resources beyond the development of a plan of action and the provision of vocational counseling. This distinction often causes friction within the team as the other professionals participating usually define themselves as client advocates on the team.

Over the years, VR legislation has stressed the employment aspects of the VR system. This does not mean that the only services provided are vocational, but rather that every service requested has to be judged on the basis of whether it will aid in the achievement of a specific vocational goal. The public VR counselor often plays the role of gatekeeper for the provision of specific services, a role that can place the counselor in conflict with the other team members who see needs that will have little if any relationship to a vocational or employment outcome.

There is a tendency in VR systems, as with all large bureaucracies, to make people with disabilities fit the system rather than the reverse. However, the core of the VR model is that the person who is disabled is entitled to an individual program of services, based on his/her unique needs. In fact, the Individualized Written Rehabilitation Program (IWRP) that carries the client's signature is the legislative prototype, developed in the 1973 Rehabilitation Act, for the other individualized service plans (e.g., Individual Education Plan, or IEP; Individual Service Plan, or ISP; Individual Habilitation Plan, or IHP) used currently by many professional disciplines.

The premise of most VR service delivery is the identification of individual consumer needs that are provided for through individual purchase of service funds. Once again, this means that the VR counselor's role is different from many others on the team. The role of gatekeeper to funding activities or services surfaces again. Also, many other team members either have no capacity to provide purchased services from third parties directly, or, if they have access, it is to place the client on the waiting list for services.

Vocational rehabilitation services have always been closure and outcome focused in terms of **job placement**. VR counselors have always felt pressure to meet outcome goals for clients, which, in itself, is not problematic. However, what tends to happen is that problems in achievement often get addressed by changing the client mix of people served (i.e., the search for "more appropriate referrals"), rather than improving individual skills or modifying the system. Needless to say, this tension is exacerbated when a team is trying to attend to an individual who is severely disabled, in an era of dwindling or nonexistent resources. This dilemma has given rise frequently to the accusation that the public VR system does not serve the individual who is truly severely disabled since there is not a "quick" vocational outcome, i.e., a job for such a person. In part this criticism has been valid, especially since the VR system has for more than five decades been touted as a mechanism for persons with disabilities to return to work and that the "return on investment" from vocational rehabilitation far exceeds the costs [Kiernan 1979]. As persons with more severe disabilities enter the VR system, the cost per rehabilitation is increasing and the number of persons served declining [Kiernan et al. 1991]. The emphasis upon serving individuals who are more severely disabled has placed many pressures upon the public VR counselor.

How the rehabilitation role affects interdisciplinary teamwork obviously flows from the set of **values and beliefs** about people that were presented earlier in this chapter. With the fundamental belief that the individual who is disabled should control his or her plan and accept the consequences relating to decisions made, the rehabilitation counselor can be at odds with other health care and educational disciplines. The tradition in many of the other helping professions, while clearly client centered, is usually one where the helper is presumed more knowledgeable and competent in decision making than the person being helped. Situations are further complicated when the team is assisting someone who is in late adolescence or someone who has severe cognitive problems, where the decision-making capacity is clearly circumscribed. It is in situations such as these that creative approaches to consumer decision making are needed.

The rehabilitation belief in the **intrinsic value of a person's being productive** is usually at least given lip service in environments where a rehabilitation counselor is included on a team. However, tension arises in deciding on how to set priorities on a variety of activities that may be needed (e.g., where vocational, medical, educational, residential requirements exist). In a situation where there is a consensus around vocational goals, the dilemma of determining whether certain activities (such as evaluation, more treatment, day habilitation, etc.) are critical prerequisites to eventual success can lead to disagreement among team members.

Another area where rehabilitation values affect team functioning is in the core premise that **rehabilitation outcome is affected by interventions directed at both the person and the environment**. A rehabilitation approach looks at the limitations present as caused not just by deficits in the person but also reflective of the barriers that may be present in the setting. Often the problem is identified as within the individual (i.e., an absence of skills or social competencies), and thus the intervention is directed at "fixing" the individual. In many instances, the barriers that exist in a setting or environment may inhibit the inclusion of the person with a disability. For such cases, the appropriate response may be to adapt the environment rather than the individual. In all instances, there is a need to look at both the individual and the environment and to consider environmental modifications as well as individual skill development to improve the fit of the individual to the setting.

Given this belief, a rehabilitation counselor within the team will insist on addressing not just the client's diagnosis or problems, but will see one aspect of the equation as a deficit in functioning that can be remediated, at least partly, through a skills acquisition model. Concurrently, a rehabilitation counselor will stress the need to bring other resources to bear on the situation (e.g., staff, equipment, adaptations), as a way of modifying the environment. Staff trained in disciplines that stress more of a unidimensional consumer focus may arrive at differing opinions of effective solutions to the specific problems.

The **"plateau" concept of significant personal change** referenced previously, which incorporates the need for intermediate objectives with the expectation of periods of disengagement from the change process, has major implications, particularly in a team decision about the need for active intervention as opposed to a "wait and see" approach. Especially in teams that have an orientation to aggressive treatment, the advocacy of a point of view that seems to treat "regressive" behavior as normal, or identifies an exacerbation of client symptomatology as healthy, may be viewed by other members of the team as problematic.

Conversely, the rehabilitation approach has a **bias towards action, rather than talk**, when interventions are needed. Other disciplines may have a greater tendency to process, analyze, assess, etc., prior to taking action. The rehabilitation approach often can be viewed by such professional colleagues as inordinately risky, or not well thought through. But functioning, in a rehabilitation model, is seen as environmentally specific. Therefore, a rehabilitation practitioner may view the assessment and analysis of a course of action without taking some concrete steps towards the goal as essentially flawed or at least incomplete.

The value placed on the **natural need for hope and support** as an important element of the rehabilitation approach is usually shared in its intent by all members of an interdisciplinary team. However, the mechanics of how this belief system is put into action occasionally creates some tension. In teams involving medical professionals, who work in a field where science and technology have dominated over the last 40 years and whose work is increasingly being scrutinized for cost (including professional time), the priority of this human dimension is often debated. When personnel resources are scarce, the capacity of a team to focus on the individual's hope and support demands is often stretched. When choices are confronted between effective technical interventions and labor-intensive support applications, the dilemma of these different perspectives becomes apparent. In teams including medical and nonmedical disciplines (e.g., rehabilitation counselors, social workers, psychologists), it is customary for nonmedical professionals to be seen as the primary caregivers of hope and support. Sometimes, this role differentiation, while logical in terms of the professional precepts espoused, can cause friction in light of questions arising as to the relative importance or social status of team members "relegated" to what is many times interpreted as a secondary role to that of "treater."

Finally, the rehabilitation emphasis on **functional capacity**, as opposed to disability or dysfunction, is shared usually in spirit by all team members, but is demonstrated differently within the context of the demands of the various professional roles. Particularly in teams where the individual and/or family members are not active participants, the focus of much team planning is usually problem identification and problem resolution. The capacities of individuals with disabilities to mobilize their personal resources, as well as those within their natural support network, are commonly overlooked in the desire of many teams to quickly analyze, assess, and prescribe. Once again, it is important to recognize that many helping professions do not have a tradition of honing in on strengths as part of their development. To some extent, this relatively recent tradition flows as much from the "consumerism" movement that has evolved within U.S. society in the last 30 years, as from the clinical, philosophical base of the rehabilitation profession [Schalock 1990]. Also, especially in medical or educational contexts, the individual with a disability is often seen by helpers as part of the problem to be addressed rather than a resource to be tapped. In some instances, such natural resources can in fact be problematic and of limited utility in the development and implementation of the rehabilitation plan, although this is more the exception than the rule. It is up to the members of the team as well as the family and other natural resources to create a sense of coordination and cooperation if a comprehensive rehabilitation plan is to be implemented effectively. A rehabilitation counselor should be trained to think in these terms and thus, should play an advocacy role on behalf of consumer and family involvement in the interdisciplinary team process.

Levels of Training, Licensure, and Certification

As was noted previously, the role of rehabilitation as a service was established several years prior to the emergence of rehabilitation counseling as a professional discipline. With passage of the Rehabilitation Act of 1967, programs were established at the master's level in rehabilitation counseling [Emener 1986]. The American Rehabilitation Counseling Association (ARCA) has suggested that graduate rehabilitation education include the following:

- Concern for the quality of professional rehabilitation counseling that leads to better services for those with disabilities,

- Concern for the improvement of rehabilitation counseling programs through self-study, and

- Concern for a clear outline of standards for professional education [ARCA 1968].

At about the same time the Council of Rehabilitation Education (CORE) was established to accredit master's degree programs in rehabilitation counseling [Houser et al. 1991]. The purpose of CORE "is to promote the effective delivery of rehabilitation services to individuals with disabilities by promoting and fostering continuous review and improvement of master's degree level Rehabilitation Counselor Education (RCE) programs" [CORE 1983]. Standards for RCE programs were established by CORE. These standards define the course of study for students in the program. The content areas addressed by the standards include the structure of the rehabilitation system; counseling theories and practices; planning, career development, job accommodation, and placement strategies; medical, psychological, and social aspects of disabilities; case and community resource management; and legal and ethical issues in rehabilitation.

The Commission on Rehabilitation Counselor Certification (CRCC) is the national certification body for rehabilitation counselors. The certification process ensures that rehabilitation professionals have met uniform requirements in the areas of education, training, and work experience. The primary objective is to provide assurances that rehabilitation counselor practitioners meet acceptable standards in their work performance. Similarly, this process is designed to assess whether rehabilitation counselors have developed competency and skill in the major core areas of practice. These skills are reflected in the major content areas outlined in the previous paragraph. Since 1974, CRCC has adopted a plan of certification maintenance by which all certified rehabilitation counselors must maintain and renew their certification titles. This can be accomplished through documentation of 100 clock hours of continuing education or sitting for a re-examination every five years.

Typically, certification is not a requirement for hiring in most rehabilitation counselor settings, but is valued and encouraged. There has been a strong movement within the field to advance the practice of certification and to move toward licensure as a way to enhance the profession. At the present time, rehabilitation counselors are not required to obtain a license to practice professionally; however, in addition to the certification process noted above, many states have passed licensure laws for rehabilitation counselors. Thirty-four states have some form of counselor licensure that influences the role and functions of the rehabilitation counselor [Wolfe 1992]. Often rehabilitation counselor licensure is tied to the licensure of other mental health professionals. Most states have stipulated the type of preservice, continuing education, and work experience requirements for licensure as professional rehabilitation counselors.

Professional Organizations and Leading Journals

The two major professional organizations for rehabilitation counselors are the American Rehabilitation Counseling Association (ARCA) and the National Rehabilitation Counseling Association (NRCA). The National Rehabilitation Association (NRA), of which NRCA is a division, provides the most comprehensive representation of the interests and needs of professionals involved in working with people with disabilities in the field of rehabilitation. Other divisions of NRA include National Rehabilitation Administration Association (NRAA), Job Placement Division (JPD), National Association of Rehabilitation Instructors (NARI), and Vocational Evaluation and Work Adjustment Association (VEWAA). NRA also has state chapters throughout the country. Other relevant professional organizations concerned with rehabilitation include the American Personnel and Guidance Association; American Psychological Association (with specific divisions for Counseling and Rehabilitation Psychology); National Federation for the Blind (NFB); American Speech-Language-Hearing Association (ASHA); American Orthotic and Prosthetic Association; Council for Exceptional

Children (CEC); International Association of Psychosocial Rehabilitation Services (IAPSRS); and International Association for Persons in Supported Employment (ASPE).

There are a number of publications available in the field of rehabilitation. Many of these are relevant for all of the disciplines involved in the delivery of rehabilitation services. Some specifically address the role of service, while others address the role of training in the rehabilitation process. As can be seen from the list below, several address the discipline of rehabilitation counseling specifically.

Archives of Physical Medicine and Rehabilitation
Canadian Journal of Rehabilitation
International Journal of Rehabilitation Research
Journal of Applied Rehabilitation Counseling
Journal of Counseling Psychology
Journal of Rehabilitation
Journal of Rehabilitation Administration
Journal of Rehabilitation of the Deaf
Journal of Vocational Rehabilitation
Psychosocial Rehabilitation Journal
Rehabilitation Counseling Bulletin
Rehabilitation Digest
Rehabilitation Literature
Rehabilitation Psychology
Vocational Evaluation and Work Adjustment Bulletin

As noted earlier, the role and function of the rehabilitation counselor can be varied. If the counselor is to remain knowledgeable concerning "best practices," then regular review of special education, psychology, and medical journals is critical. Since much of the focus of rehabilitation counseling is on employment, knowledge of the business and human resource journals is likewise essential. Many of the practices and approaches used by Human Resource Departments to support employees, such as staff development, employee assistance programs, and personnel management, are consistent with the approaches used by rehabilitation counselors.

Several associations in rehabilitation provide newsletters as well as journals in the field. The National Rehabilitation Association and its Rehabilitation Counseling division, as well as such disability-specific organizations as the American Association for Mental Retardation, Association for Persons with Severe Handicaps, the Paralyzed Veterans Association, the National Spinal Cord Injury Association, the National Head Injury Foundation, the Association for Retarded Citizens, the United Cerebral Palsy Association of America, the Epilepsy Foundation of America, Alcoholic Anonymous, and numerous others provide both information and an advocacy platform for rehabilitation. Allied groups such as the Council for Exceptional Children; American Psychological Association; American Medical Association; American Speech-Language-Hearing Association; and other professional associations also provide information through newsletters and journals on disciplinary and interdisciplinary practices that influence the role and function of the rehabilitation counselor.

Standards of Ethics

As an integral component of the certification process described previously, the Commission on Rehabilitation Counselor Certification has adopted "The Code of Professional Ethics" for certified rehabilitation counselors, which has also been adopted by many of the pertinent professional organizations for their membership. The emphasis within rehabilitation upon assisting individuals with disabilities to realize their maximum potential and to promote increased independence and productivity through employment is the underlying tenet of the code. The code was primarily developed to promote the well-being of people being served through the identification and enforcement of ethical behaviors expected of rehabilitation professionals. The code consists of two types of standards, canons, and rules of professional conduct. The canons express general beliefs and principles that serve as models for exemplary professional conduct, whereas the rules, which are more specific, provide guidance in specific circumstances that rehabilitation counselors may encounter [ARCA 1987]. Additional information on the canons can be found in Appendix A.

Summary

The role of the rehabilitation counselor has evolved over the past several years and reflects the continued emphasis upon movement of individuals with disabilities into or back to employment. The rehabilitation counselor must work with a wide range of disciplines including, but not limited to, special education, social work, psychology, and other medically focused disciplines, such as physical therapy, occupational therapy, speech pathology, and medicine. The actual duties of the rehabilitation counselor reflect the nature of the agency as well as the counselor's perception of his or her role. Regardless of the agency counselor's perspectives, the rehabilitation counselor must work directly with the individual, the family, other professionals, and the community in general if a comprehensive rehabilitation planning and implementation process is to be undertaken.

References

American Rehabilitation Counseling Association, Commission on Rehabilitation Counselor Certification, and National Rehabilitation Counseling Association. (1987). Code of professional ethics for rehabilitation counselors. *Journal of Applied Rehabilitation Counseling, 18* (4), 28-32.

American Rehabilitation Counseling Association. (1968). Professional preparation of rehabilitation counselors. A statement of policy. *Rehabilitation Counseling Bulletin, 12*, 20-35.

Anderson, J. P. (1975). An alternative frame of reference for rehabilitation: The helping process versus the medical model. *Archives of Physical Medicine and Rehabilitation, 56*, 101-104.

Bandura, A. (1986). *Social foundations of thought and action*. Englewood Cliffs, NJ: Prentice Hall.

Barker, J. T. (1988). *Coordination of efforts between vocational rehabilitation and mental health systems*. Switzer Monograph Series. New York: National Rehabilitation Association.

Bitter, J. A. (1979) *Introduction to rehabilitation*. St. Louis, MO: C.B. Mosby.

Brill, N. (1976). *Teamwork: Working together in the human services*. New York: Lippencott.

Cavalier, W. (1986). The history of rehabilitation. *Archives of the American Association for Recreation Therapy, 5*, 23-31.

Council on Rehabilitation Education. (1983). *Accreditation manual for rehabilitation counseling programs*. Chicago, IL: Author.

Emener, W. G. (1986). *Rehabilitation counselor preparation and development.* Springfield, IL: Charles C. Thomas.

Houser, R. A., Seligman, M., Kiernan, W. E., King, M. A., & Pajoohi, E. (1991). A survey of class time devoted to required core curriculum content areas by RCE programs. *Rehabilitation Education, 5,* 11-18.

Jaques, M. E. (1970). *Rehabilitation counseling: Scope and services.* Boston: Houghton Mifflin.

Kiernan, W. E. (1979). Rehabilitation planning. In P. Megrab & G. O. Elder (Eds.), *Planning for services to handicapped persons: Community, education, health* (pp. 137-171). Baltimore, MD: Paul H. Brookes Publishing.

Kiernan, W. E. (1991). *Natural supports in the work setting.* Boston: Training and Research Institute for People with Disabilities, Children's Hospital.

Kiernan, W. E., McGaughey, M. M., Lynch, S. A., Schalock, R. L., & McNally, L. C. (1991). *National survey of day and employment programs: Results from state VR agencies.* Boston: Children's Hospital, Training and Research Institute for People with Disabilities.

Kiernan, W. E., Schalock, R. L., & Knutson, K. (1989). Economic, demographic, and legislative influences on employment. In W. E. Kiernan & R. L. Schalock (Eds.), *Economics, industry and disability: A look ahead.* (pp. 3-16). Baltimore, MD: Brookes Publishing.

Lowe, J., & Herranen, M. (1978). Conflict in teamwork: Understanding roles and relationships. *Social Work in Health Care, 3* (3), 323-331.

National Council on Rehabilitation. (1944). *Symposium on the processes of rehabilitation.* New York: Author.

Rehabilitation Services Administration. (1979). Organizational cooperation provides effective rehabilitation services. *Rehab Brief, 11*(3), 5-7.

Research Utilization Laboratory. (1977). *Guidelines for inter-agency cooperation and the severely disabled.* Chicago: Jewish Vocational Services.

Roessler, R. T. (1989). Motivational factors influencing return to work. *Journal of Applied Rehabilitation Counseling, 20*(2), 14-17.

RRRI Center for Social Research and Development. (1976). *Interagency linkages in vocational rehabilitation.* Colorado: Denver Research Institute, University of Denver.

Schalock, R. L. (1990). *Quality of life: Perspectives and issues.* Washington, DC: American Association on Mental Retardation.

Shafer, M. S. (1988). Supported employment in perspective. In P. Wehman & M. S. Moon (Eds.), *Vocational rehabilitation and supported employment* (pp. 55-66). Baltimore, MD: Paul H. Brookes Publishing.

Whitehead, C., & Marrone, J. (1986). Time-limited evaluation and training. In W. E. Kiernan & J. A. Stark (Eds.), *Pathways to employment for adults with developmental disabilities* (pp. 163-176). Baltimore, MD: Paul H. Brookes Publishing.

Wolfe, R. (1992). *What's new in licensure.* Washington, DC: National Rehabilitation Counseling Association.

Wright, G. (1980). *Total rehabilitation.* Boston: Little, Brown, and Co.

Gerontology

By Marilyn Adlin & Gary Seltzer

A Brief History of Gerontology

Since 1960, the population over the age of 65 has grown more than twice as fast as the younger population. Currently, the elderly comprise 12% of the population [Rice & Feldman 1983]. By the year 2030, the proportion is expected to increase to 22%, almost doubling within 40 years. The number of older elderly (those over the age of 75) is increasing even more rapidly. Between 1960 and 1980, the number of persons aged 75-84 rose 65%, while the number of persons age 85 and over rose 174% [Rice & Feldman 1983]. It is anticipated that by 2030 the number of persons over age 75 will triple. Some of these demographic changes are due to declining death rates from heart disease, stroke, and influenza, as well as other causes of death. As more people live longer, however, chronic diseases have become a major cause of long-term disability.

The recognition that aging persons have unique characteristics, and therefore unique needs, has developed only recently in this country. While Great Britain identified specialty training in geriatrics more than 40 years ago, the United States did not begin to develop training programs in geriatrics until the late 1970s. The medical establishment may not have done so at all were it not for the changing demographics within the country.

Since its development in this country, geriatrics has incorporated team assessment as a model for care and service delivery for two reasons. First, diseases often appear atypically in the elderly, and information needs to be obtained from other disciplines to accurately assess the relationship between decline in health status and disease. Second, the traditional biomedical approach does not consider the functional implications of chronic illness. The

Marilyn Adlin, M.D., is Assistant Professor in the Section on Geriatric Medicine at the University of Wisconsin-Madison. Gary Seltzer, Ph.D., is Professor at the Waisman Center of the University of Wisconsin-Madison.

expertise of multiple disciplines is required to understand the complex interactions among medical conditions and psychosocial functioning and the physical ability to perform activities of daily living. Team collaboration results in interventions that target problems related to multiple illnesses and the social, psychological, and physical environment.

Most geriatric teams treat frail elderly, who have multiple coexistent medical conditions, functional limitations, and precarious social environments. These elders are likely to need help from community health and social service agencies to remain in the community and out of long-term care facilities. Although the cost of implementing the multidisciplinary service recommendations of geriatric teams is high, it is less than the cost of providing nursing home care.

Many of the community health programs developed to reduce the cost of hospital care for elders. In 1984, in a cost containment initiative, the federal government introduced a prospective reimbursement plan for Medicare. This plan, known as Diagnosis-Related Groups (DRG), imposed limits on the total reimbursement that hospitals could receive for a specific primary diagnosis. This reimbursement schedule provided the impetus for hospitals to shorten hospital stays for elderly persons on Medicare, and thus to reduce the cost of hospital care. Many hospitals developed multidisciplinary geriatric assessment teams to assist hospital staff to provide more efficient and, hopefully, more effective care for elderly patients. The DRG system thus provided a stimulus to disseminate the concept of geriatric team to a key health care establishment—the acute care hospital.

Current Philosophies of Treatment and Service

The Functional Approach and Quality of Life

In geriatric practice, an approach to care is needed that investigates the breadth of the problems posed by many geriatric patients who have one or more chronic health problems. The functional approach to health care focuses not only on the illness, but also on the functional limitations consequent to the illness; i.e., the effect that illness has on the daily routines and fulfillment of social and psychological roles [Granger et al. 1987]. The patient's ability to function or perform a number of activities of daily living is assessed, as are the psychological correlates of performance, such as motivation and cognitive limitations.

The prevalence of chronic health conditions increases as the population ages. Among persons age 85 and older, 40% are disabled to the degree that they need daily help [Williams 1990]. The demographic shift toward an aging population means that the prevalence of persons with functional limitations is increasing at an unprecedented rate. Functional limitations, unattended, have a profound effect on the quality of life of the affected individual, and an impact on affected families and on society at large.

Health care professionals are beginning to appreciate the need to focus on the consequences of disabling conditions on the daily routines and role performances of older persons whose lives are threatened by the loss of functional independence. Most recently, the Institute of Medicine [1991] issued a report that adopted a functional model as its framework for promulgating a national agenda for the prevention of disability in America. This report went beyond the World Health Organization's development of the International Classification of Impairments, Disabilities, and Handicaps [1980] and adopted the Nagi [1976] model of disability concepts, which includes an examination of pathology, impairment, functional limitations, and disability. To this analytic functional model the Institute of Medicine report added risk factors and quality of life as two important domains in the investigation and prevention of disability.

Medical practitioners, most of whom have little or no training in geriatrics, disability, or rehabilitation, are beginning to recognize the need to seek consultation in order to treat functional limitations and disabilities. Some channel their patients to appropriate resources, such as geriatric assessment teams, to develop treatment protocols that target the restoration or compensation for functional losses through the use of rehabilitation techniques and environmental manipulations. By examining functional changes associated with aging and chronic illness, they are likely to prevent excess disability and decline in this age cohort.

The geriatric team investigates the organic, psychological, and social factors that, in combination, account for limitations in function. The geriatric team recommends interventions that preserve the range of normal activities through medical and physical restoration, psychological treatment, environmental modifications, or boosting of social supports. Functional interventions include the following:

- Teaching persons to manage medical crises,

- Using adaptive technology to assist in the executive of daily routines,

- Teaching time management,

- Helping persons to adapt to the uncertainty and the possible downward trajectory of one's health,

- Assessing the impact of functional limitations on the family system,

- Supporting the strengths of natural support systems, and

- Buttressing the loss of social support by increasing contact with formal supports, such as day care and senior centers.

In sum, the geriatric team recommends interventions that restore, retain, or slow the deterioration of function, and thus enhance older persons' quality of life.

Quality of Life

Although most geriatric clinicians and researchers agree that "quality of life" is a meaningful construct, the term generally provokes debate on its definition. Differences in meaning are derived from the personal nature of life quality: the experiences that we share when preserving the life quality of intimates—friends and family members. Professionally, variability in the meaning of life quality relates to the heterogeneous array of professionals— sociologists, geriatricians, nurses, lawyers, social workers, political scientists, psychologists—who study quality of life. Some examples of disciplinary quality of life terms include "life satisfaction," "adaptive behavior," "moral well-being," and "subjective health." Andrews [1986] notes that, although the terms differ according to one's professional affiliation, they all have overlapping conceptual links.

Empirically, too, there are differences in operational definitions across disciplines in measurements of quality of life. Some researchers take an ecological approach and measure how the behavioral manifestations of life quality are affected by environmental contingencies [Mueller 1980; Seltzer et al. 1988]. This ecological approach differs from approaches that focus on a person's perception of life satisfaction [Campbell et al. 1976; Handal et al. 1983; Michalos 1979], or approaches that aggregate social indicators, such as access to community services, quality of social institutions, and other community characteristics [Allardt 1978; Andrews & Withey 1976].

For geriatric clinicians, quality of life is strictly influenced by the older person's desire to remain autonomous, make his or her own decisions, and retain as much personal independence as possible [Williams 1990]. In exemplary geriatric team practice, clinicians seek the older person's subjective evaluations of personal life experiences, which take into account the person's perceptions of life satisfaction, along with objective medical information. The geriatric team, represented by different professional orientations to quality of life, gathers a multifaceted perspective on life satisfaction. Subjective evaluation of quality of life includes a specific assessment satisfaction with health care service, social services, housing, daily activities, family and friendship patterns, leisure activities, finances, law and safety, and spiritual practices. It may also include the subjective evaluation of a person's self-esteem and other measures of self-worth, self-acceptance, and self-image. The geriatric team formulates a treatment plan that takes behavioral measures of function together with these subjective measures and develops recommendations that are targeted to maintain or improve an older person's quality of life.

Services Provided in Various Settings

Geriatric teams provide services in a variety of settings, including the acute care hospital, the outpatient setting, long-term care facilities, and the home. They may offer consultative services to generic staff, a process that includes diagnosis and problem identification, as well as treatment recommendations. Geriatric teams may also exist on separate evaluation units, an arrangement that provides ongoing geriatric care within a specialized setting.

This section reviews a variety of studies that examine the impact of an interdisciplinary geriatric team approach on the assessment and treatment of elders' health and well-being [Barker et al. 1985; Campion et al. 1983; Rubenstein et al. 1984; Zimmer et al. 1985]. Most of these studies, unfortunately, are methodologically flawed [Schmitt et al. 1988]. Few adequately define team care, and outcome measures are inconsistently selected across studies, rendering comparisons of outcomes among many studies difficult. Many studies have selection problems; a description of why persons were selected for interdisciplinary geriatric care is often omitted, or those selected for such treatment may not be those individuals most likely to benefit from team intervention [Schmitt et al. 1988]. In spite of these limitations, we review selected studies because they raise critical issues about the efficiency and efficacy of geriatric interdisciplinary team practice in a variety of health settings.

Acute Care

Persons over the age of 65 occupy 34% of acute care hospital beds [Kovar 1977]. The rate of hospitalization among the elderly is four times that of the general population [Brody 1984]. Almost 20% of persons over the age of 65 are hospitalized each year, and more than one-quarter of them are rehospitalized within the ensuing 12 months [Brody 1984]. When hospitalized, elderly patients are at greater risk for iatrogenic illnesses (medical problems induced by a physician's or other health care personnel's actions). These iatrogenic problems, more common than we would like to believe, prolong recovery time and negatively affect treatment outcome and hospital discharge plans. For example, extended bedrest without bedside exercises for hospitalized elders can lead to deconditioning and functional skill loss, an iatrogenic outcome of hospitalization that places many older persons at risk for institutional placement following hospital discharge.

Iatrogenic outcomes occur because many acute care health professionals lack the knowledge necessary to provide adequate care for older persons with multiple chronic illnesses or disabilities. Although improving, many health sciences and professional schools' curricula are deficient or absent of gerontological and geriatric education.

Interdisciplinary geriatric teams have evolved within acute care hospitals to improve the outcome of the medical care to hospitalized elders and to provide a mechanism for teaching health care professionals about the special needs of the elderly. These teams may be part of a geriatric consultation services or exist as a separate geriatric evaluation unit within an acute care hospital setting.

Geriatric Consultation Service

In 1981, Steel and Hayes were the first to describe the use of a multidisciplinary health care team to provide comprehensive geriatric consultation within the acute care hospital. The effectiveness of these consultative services has been studied by several investigators. Campion et al. [1983] studied 46 consecutive patients over the age of 75 who were admitted to the general medical unit at Massachusetts General Hospital and received a Geriatric Team Consultation. They compared these patients to another group of patients over 75 years old who were admitted to other general medical units at this hospital. Patients who were seen by the geriatric consultation team received more physical, occupational, and speech therapy without increasing their length of stay. The geriatric consultation team taught interdisciplinary teamwork and improved awareness of functional problems. However, the geriatric team consultation did not decrease the rate of hospital readmissions. These findings suggest that the nonspecialized use of a geriatric team consultation with older patients increases the use of rehabilitation services and provides opportunities for training, but does not affect the high rate of readmission to the hospital of geriatric patients over the age of 75.

In a study that examined the effects of a geriatric consultation team on iatrogenic outcomes, Becker et al. [1987] randomly assigned 185 hospitalized patients over the age of 75 to a geriatric consultation team and to a standard treatment group. The type of rate of iatrogenic complications were the same in both groups. The incidence of these complications remained quite high, 38%. Functional status on admission and admission to a psychiatric service were found to be predictive of iatrogenic illness. The results of this study suggest that a geriatric consultation team does not reduce iatrogenic complications in persons for whom at-risk selection criteria were not applied a priori.

Barker et al. [1985] conducted a study in which 4,328 newly hospitalized patients in six acute care hospitals, over age 70 were screened for conditions that placed persons at risk for lengthy hospital stays. Geriatric consultation by an interdisciplinary team was conducted on a selected group of

366 elderly persons who were determined to be at risk for prolonged hospital stays. At-risk criteria included two or more of the following characteristics at the time of admission: living alone, age over 80, low income, mental impairment, and physical disability. Patients receiving geriatric consultation were older, more likely to be female, widowed, resided in sheltered housing, and likely to have had an emergency admission. An average of three recommendations were made for each patient who received a geriatric team consultation. Recommendations included changes in care plans to restore and preserve functional independence in anticipation of discharge. Other types of recommendations included medication changes, physical therapy referrals, patient and family education, socialization, bowel and bladder training, and planning for appropriate long-term care. Patients complied with recommendations 50 to 70% of the time. During the time in which these consultation services were available to high-risk elderly patients, the census of elderly patients backed up in the hospital declined 21%. In this study, screening for high-risk elderly improved the efficacy of geriatric team consultation and justified the use of additional resources for persons experiencing increasing dependency.

Geriatric Evaluation Units

A separate unit within an acute care hospital, a geriatric evaluation unit is sometimes developed to provide access to specialized services for the older patient. This type of unit may be more effective than a consultation team for some hospitalized elderly. These units allow for more direct control over patient care. An interdisciplinary team consisting of physicians, social workers, and nurses provide ongoing care. Frequently, the unit serves an educational role for medical students, residents, and geriatric fellows. Rehabilitative services such as occupational therapy, physical therapy, and speech therapy are usually available on the unit. The intent is to improve functional status, strengthen social supports, and augment community resources in order to allow the elderly individual to return to independent living. Benefits of these units are many and include enhanced identification of treatable disorders, reduction in total number of prescribed drugs (limiting the potential for side effects and drug interactions), improved functional capabilities, and improved discharge planning, with more patients being discharged to a home setting than to a long-term care facility [Lefton et al. 1983; Rubenstein et al. 1981].

Rubenstein et al. [1984] randomly assigned frail elderly who were likely to be placed in nursing home to a geriatric evaluation unit and to a traditional acute care hospital unit. The evaluation was expected to provide better diagnostic assessment, therapy, rehabilitation, and discharge planning, all of which were delivered by an interdisciplinary team. A one-year follow-up of patients revealed that those who had been on the geriatric unit had lower mortality, were less likely to have been discharged to a nursing home, had fewer acute care hospital readmissions, and fewer nursing home days than patients in the unit. In addition, patients on the geriatric unit were significantly more likely to show improvement in functional status and morale. Over the following year, the additional costs of providing geriatric evaluation unit services were recovered by savings in the use of other services, such as nursing home care and acute hospitalization. This study supports the efficacy of an interdisciplinary team approach offered on a geriatric evaluation unit to markedly improve outcomes for elderly hospitalized patients—outcomes that appear to be long lasting.

Long-Term Care

Approximately 5% of the American population over the age of 65, and 20% of those over the age of 85, currently reside in a nursing home. Within their lifetime, 25% of those over the age of 65 will spend some time in a long-term care facility. By the year 2030, the number of nursing home beds will need to increase from 1.5 million to more than 5 million to accommodate the needs of the escalating number of frail and dependent elderly.

In preparation for the anticipated increase in long-term care, the teaching nursing home became a site for the training of health care professionals in interdisciplinary team care [Thompson et al. 1988]. Thompson et al. described a nursing home curriculum that involves faculty and students from nursing, pharmacy, and medicine providing patient care using a multidisciplinary team approach. Weekly conferences are designed to demonstrate collaborative decision making. Instruction on improved management of chronic disease outside of the hospital setting is also a primary curricular goal. Nonpharmacological therapeutic strategies are explored and medications eliminated, when there is a possibility to reduce risk of toxicity and drug interaction. Nursing and social work students are encouraged to facilitate the identification and resolution of family concerns.

Interdisciplinary teams in nursing homes are generally found within academic settings. Limited resource and time availability restrict widespread use of interdisciplinary teams in most community-operated long-term care facilities. Parallel care by individual disciplines is more commonly found within these nursing homes. However, case conferences that include nursing, social work, physical and occupational therapy (when appropriate) are increasingly becoming available at nursing home facilities. Physician involvement is variable, with the medical director participating in some settings.

Outpatient Setting

Interdisciplinary geriatric teams function in the ambulatory setting, both as outpatient geriatric evaluation units and as primary care geriatric clinics that provide ongoing care. Some controversy exists as to whether the resources of an interdisciplinary team need to be extended to all elderly outpatients or reserved for a more select group of frail elderly with multiple health problems.

The goals of geriatric teams in the ambulatory setting are listed below:

- To diagnose and manage chronic health problems,

- To provide health care maintenance through appropriate health screening and prevention, and

- To avert hospitalization and institutionalization.

The ability to provide comprehensive geriatric team evaluation outside of the hospital eliminates the iatrogenic risks associated with inpatient admissions in the elderly [Millman et al. 1986]. Ambulatory sites are increasingly becoming the focus of geriatric education, as well, since this affords a more representative view of the elderly population than hospitals or nursing homes [Millman et al. 1986].

Outpatient Geriatric Evaluation Units

Williams et al. [1987] found evidence that team-oriented outpatient geriatric consultation can provide improved quality of care at reduced overall cost, when targeted toward frail elderly persons. In a randomized experiment, overall institutional costs were reduced 25% in the group treated by an outpatient geriatric evaluation unit. Approximately 10% of the subjects generated most of the costs. The reduction in health care costs resulted almost exclusively from a reduction in number of hospital days for those patients who had received an outpatient geriatric assessment.

Primary Care Geriatric Clinics

Kerski et al. [1987] compared medically stable, community-dwelling elderly males, who were followed by an interdisciplinary geriatric team, to a matched sample assigned to a general medical clinic without an interdisciplinary team. Both groups of patients initially were evaluated at an outpatient geriatric evaluation unit by an interdisciplinary team. One group continued to receive care from an interdisciplinary geriatric team, while the other group received conventional care that did not include an interdisciplinary team. Mortality, number of hospitalizations, community placement, and use of services did not differ between the two groups. No additional advantage was found for those patients who continued to be followed by an interdisciplinary team. The provision of ongoing care by a more costly interdisciplinary geriatric team, in a medically stable population, may not offer an additional advantage over traditional care. This study did not include frail elderly patients with a more tenuous health status who may indeed benefit from the continuing involvement of an interdisciplinary health care team.

Home Care

A randomized study of an interdisciplinary team approach to home care for chronically or terminally ill elderly is described by Zimmer et al. [1985]. The team in this study consisted of a physician, nurse practitioner, and social worker delivering health care in the patient's home. The team held weekly conferences to discuss care issues and to ensure coordination of services. Patients who received these interdisciplinary team home care services had fewer hospitalizations, nursing home admissions, and outpatient visits than controls. Although functional abilities were not found to be different than controls, patients receiving home care and caretakers reported significantly higher satisfaction with the care they received. This was despite the fact that more team patients spent their days of highest care needs at home, where much of the service was provided by family caretakers. Overall cost of home care was not statistically more costly than the cost of care for controls.

Over the past few years, many home health agencies have been developed to provide services to homebound elderly. Some agencies supply health professionals from a variety of disciplines, including nursing, physical therapy, occupational therapy, and speech therapy; however, a true team approach of regular team conferences to address care needs, discuss the results of treatments, and coordinate treatment plans usually does not transpire. Another deficiency of most home health services is the lack of physician involvement. Although physicians frequently have a role in prescribing home services and may speak on occasion to the direct care providers, medical care is typically parallel care rather than team focused. Unfortunately, lack of coordinated home health team services for the elderly can lead to episodic emergency room visits and crisis hospitalizations.

Relationship to Other Disciplines

One of the major limitations in geriatric team care is the lack of continuity between interdisciplinary teams functioning in different settings. As discussed previously, the evolution of team care for the elderly has been largely dependent upon the setting in which a particular team has formed. As a result, teams within such institutions as hospitals or nursing homes may have no formal mechanism for interacting with geriatric teams in the ambulatory or home setting. Multiple doorways to services can lead to duplication of effort, as each team conducts independent assessments. In some cases, it may be appropriate for teams to perform separate evaluations. In most cases, however, better communication between teams functioning in different settings would benefit the client. The assignment of an interdisciplinary geriatric team to follow a client over time and in a variety of settings may enhance the continuity of care. Such coordination may result in better attainment of team goals for individual clients.

Another area of potential conflict is the relationship between the interdisciplinary geriatric team and the primary physician who has the responsibility for providing ongoing care. Some medical specialties do not recognize geriatrics and gerontology as a special field with a unique knowledge base. Physicians may see geriatric medicine as a compilation of knowledge from different specialties and presume that their own training and experience is sufficient to treat their patients. Since medical evaluation rarely trains skills in interdisciplinary teamwork, the type of insights that arise from team collaboration may be unfamiliar to a practicing physician. Recommended interventions may not be instituted by the primary physician for this reason. A major goal for interdisciplinary geriatric team care should be to improve the relationship with physicians in other specialties by disseminating knowledge gained from geriatric teamwork. The following sections present a description of selected team members, in order to illustrate their specific function and their relationship to other disciplines. We have chosen to describe professions that are most likely to be represented on a geriatric interdisciplinary team. Clearly, the selection is not representative of all teams and the many other professionals involved with delivery of geriatric interdisciplinary team services.

Role of the Physician on the Geriatric Team

The geriatrician on the interdisciplinary geriatric team is responsible for the diagnosis and treatment of potentially reversible conditions. This requires knowledge of the physiological changes of aging, as well as knowledge of the specific illnesses and disabilities that occur in the elderly. Some of the common conditions in the elderly include incontinence, sensory losses, immobility, falls, confusion and dementia, adverse drug reactions, osteoporosis, and cardiovascular and cerebrovascular diseases.

Many of the early studies on age-related change showed gradual declines in most organ systems beginning in early adulthood. These studies used a cross-sectional design and compared groups at different ages [Andres & Tobin 1977; Svanborg et al. 1982]. More recent longitudinal studies have found fewer age-related declines [Svanborg et al. 1982] and a stronger link to specific diseases [Lindeman et al. 1985], environmental factors, and deconditioning, due to disuse [Fiatarone et al. 1990]. The principal change that occurs with aging appears to be a declining ability of the human body to respond to stresses, such as acute illness. Some authors have coined the term "homeostenosis" to reflect a narrowing of the body's ability to maintain homeostasis [Besdine 1988]. Geriatricians identify reversible and treatable conditions, rather than attributing deterioration in health or function to "old age."

The geriatrician must also have a good understanding of the disease/disease interactions that occur when there are multiple coexisting chronic diseases present. Disease/drug associations, as well as drug/drug interactions, are also important factors in discerning the complex elements that influence the health and functioning of older individuals.

Disease in elderly persons can often present in an atypical fashion, or with vague, nonspecific complaints. Confusion, cessation of eating or drinking, dizziness, falls, lethargy, and incontinence are symptoms that frequently denote underlying illness. The geriatric physician must identify these functional changes as indicators of disease and investigate the etiology through appropriate physical assessment and diagnostic studies.

In addition to identifying treatable conditions, the physician on the team has an important role in ensuring comfort and maximizing function in elderly persons with chronic conditions. Within geriatric medicine there is a shift from the prevailing medical paradigm emphasizing "curing" disease, toward a model of "caring." This involves the recognition that many conditions experienced by the elderly, while not curable, may be amenable to palliative (i.e., alleviating but not curing) and symptom management. Chronic illness requires the same level of investigation in order to improve functional abilities, reduce pain, and limit the period of disability.

Health and illness cannot be viewed as merely the presence or absence of disease. Physicians share the task of maintaining health with other members on the team. Psychological, social, and economic considerations greatly affect illness. The geriatrician must recognize the value in perceiving the individual patient as a whole person with a complex array of needs. The physician needs to promote collegiality within a team that will enable shared decision making and problem solving to best meet the multidimensional needs of the elderly patient.

Role of the Geriatric Nurse

The nurse on the geriatric team generally has special training and experience in working with older adults. She or he has knowledge of the aging process and the interaction of health, aging, and illness [Gunter 1985]. The geriatric nurse specialist places special emphasis on preserving abilities, functions, and capabilities in the elderly. Nurses assist the physician in diagnosis by contributing valuable additional medical history, frequently obtained from family members or other care providers. Functional assessment performed by the geriatric nurse specialist can identify areas for intervention either by medical or rehabilitative services. In addition, nurses frequently can anticipate the impact of proposed diagnostic or therapeutic interventions on functional capabilities, thereby assisting the team in determining appropriate recommendations.

Geriatric nurse specialists also have an important role in medication management. They can help identify drug side effects, determine medication compliance, and recommend nonpharmacological treatments.

Health maintenance is another prominent role for the nursing specialist. Nurses promote health conducive behaviors in the elderly by educating patients and families to enable them to understand the normal aging processes and by suggesting coping strategies, such as adjusting the environment to accommodate for sensory losses.

For patients with terminal illnesses, the nurse on the team often can suggest supportive measures to enhance comfort. Counseling patients and families who are facing chronic disability or terminal illness is also an important function of the nurse specialist.

Role of the Geriatric Social Worker

The geriatric social worker is trained to help patients and their families learn to cope with the social and emotional problems associated with aging and functional losses. Geriatric social workers play a pivotal role in planning, coordinating, and delivering health care services to older persons.

The social worker typically has a background in family dynamics, social policy, community organization, and human behavior. Many social workers in general hospitals are trained at the bachelors' level, as are many of the geriatric workers in nursing homes. Increasingly, though, the Master's of Social Work (M.S.W.) degree is required. The completion of two years of postgraduate study with emphasis on normal and abnormal behavior is necessary, as well as casework and other practice methodologies, research and grant writing, policy analysis, and "hands-on" field experience. On the geriatric team, the social worker interviews the patient, family members, and other relevant persons in order to obtain an overview of the patient's current social situation and supports for maintaining psychosocial functioning, Information is obtained on living arrangements, family relationships, financial status, vocational/avocational/leisure activities, and future goals. The social worker also assesses the patient and his or her family members' attitudes toward aging as a means of evaluating the internalized stereotypes that may impede treatment planning.

Social workers' training also includes an emphasis and sensitivity to populations that traditionally have had difficulty gaining access to quality medical services. The assessment process includes a focus on cultural and ethnic values and norms. This focus is particularly important for persons of color, who, because of institutional racism, poverty, and housing problems, may experience health problems and thus an environmentally induced precocious aging process. These persons and their families are characteristic clients for social workers who assist them to bridge the health system with that of the welfare system. In these circumstances, the geriatric social worker often functions as a case manager and advocate.

When engaging in discharge planning, social workers use their knowledge of community services and the natural support systems. Often the mobilization of these resources makes the difference between placement in a long-term care facility versus a return to a community dwelling.

Social workers in outpatient geriatric teams provide information about community services, insurance coverage, transportation services, day programs, and extended care facilities. Through counseling, they can help people cope with the stress and demands of an aging and functionally limited family member. They can suggest other social supports that would forestall or delay institutionalization. The social worker can help older individuals with multiple disabilities by coordinating the various agency services provided.

Finally, it is increasingly common for social workers to be interested in the policy and research aspects of geriatric care. They are active participants and, on occasion, leaders in the design of research projects and formulation of recommendations related to findings.

Key Issues Regarding Participation on Teams

Tsukada defines geriatric teamwork as "a special form of interactional interdependence between health care providers, who merge different, but complementary skills or viewpoints, in the service of patients and in the solution of their health problems" [1990, p. 668]. Team collaboration in geriatrics encourages more creative thinking around methods to enhance functioning than would occur if individual disciplines acted independently. Convening a group of individuals with a variety of skills and differing knowledge bases enhances the process of problem solving in complex situations. NO one individual or discipline is capable of discerning the intricate interaction among physical impairments, social circumstances, psychological and emotional health, and environmental situations that are commonly seen in the elderly. Working together and allowing for the opportunity to share observations permits an increased awareness of individual client needs and fosters more inventive solutions to meet dissimilar needs simultaneously.

To achieve successful team interactions, it is important that team members share common goals and share responsibility for actions and decisions [Tsukada 1990]. The goals of geriatric teams are similar despite differences in settings. Goals usually include (a) identifying problems that affect function (i.e., physical, social, behavioral, and environmental) and potential interactions; (b) assessing available resources; (c) defining reasonable goals; and (d) planning for continuing care [Tsukada 1990]. The goals of hospital-based teams also include discharge planning.

Team care within geriatrics is shifting away from the traditional model in which medicine assumes responsibility for leadership and decision making toward a model of shared leadership and joint responsibility for decisions. It is becoming more acceptable for the team member most familiar with a particular patient or problem to assume a major role in instituting a recommendation or treatment plan after consulting with the other team members.

Levels of Training, Licensure, and Certification

Geriatrician

The first postgraduate geriatrics program for physicians in this country was started in 1974. It was not until 1985 that the American College of Medical Specialties recognized specialized training in geriatrics and set standards for competency by awarding a Certificate of Added Qualification (CAQ) in Geriatrics to physicians in Internal Medicine and Family Practice who met the following required criteria:

- Board Certification in either Internal Medicine or Family Medicine,

- Completion of a two-year fellowship in geriatrics, and

- Satisfactory performance on a written examination.

In order to enable physicians who began practicing geriatrics before these certification requirements were determined to qualify for the CAQ, it was decided that, prior to 1993, four years of geriatric practice experience or two years of practice experience and one year of fellowship could be substituted for the two-year geriatric fellowship.

Nursing

Nursing was one of the first health care disciplines to become aware of the need for a specialized approach to the elderly patient, with the first textbook in this area appearing in the 1950s. With the increased specialization of medicine in the mid-1960s and early 1970s, a shortage of primary care providers began to be identified. In response to this perceived need, nursing began to develop graduate programs to train nurse practitioners and clinical nurse specialists. As education in nursing expanded, nursing research began to identify inadequacies in the standard biomedical disease model in meeting the needs of the older patient. Nursing and social work became advocates for a team approach to help with diagnostic and management issues in geriatric care.

Certification. The American Nurses Association provides voluntary certification in advanced gerontological nursing for nurse practitioners and for generalists in gerontological nursing practice. Advanced training is available for the clinical nurse specialist (CNS) and the gerontological nurse practitioner (GNP).

Gerontological Nurse Practitioner. The GNP has an important role in providing primary care for elderly patients. A GNP is a registered nurse with a bachelor's degree who has completed an academic program and a mentored practice experience.

Clinical Nurse Specialist. The CNS usually provides gerontological consultation services in the acute care setting. The CNS is frequently responsible for program development, administration, and education. Preparation includes completion of a master's degree or doctorate.

Professional Organizations and Leading Journals

The Gerontological Society of America (GSA) was founded in 1945 to promote the scientific study of aging, to encourage exchanges among researchers and practitioners, and to foster the use of gerontological research in the formation of public policy. The Society is multidisciplinary and has 7,000 members, including leading gerontological researchers, educators, and practitioners in biological, medical, behavioral, and social sciences and the humanities, and in such professions as medicine, nursing, planning program administration, teaching, and social work. The Society has published *The Journal of Gerontology* since 1946 and *The Gerontologist* since 1961. Members of the GSA receive both of these journals with their dues.

The Journal of Gerontology is published monthly and is divided into the following sections: Medical Sciences, Psychological Sciences, Social Sciences, and Biological Sciences. Each of the sections has its own editors and editorial boards. *The Journal of Gerontology: Medical Sciences* invites manuscripts that include, but are not limited to, basic medical sciences, clinical epidemiology, clinical research, and health services research. Professionals from medicine, dentistry, allied health sciences, and nursing are encouraged to submit manuscripts. *The Journal of Gerontology: Psychological Sciences* publishes articles on applied, clinical and counseling, experimental, and social psychology of aging. It accepts manuscripts on a variety of topics, including cognition, educational psychology, industrial psychological, perception, personality, and many others. *The Journal of Gerontology: Social Sciences* publishes articles that use a variety of methodological and theoretical approaches, including quantitative, qualitative, experimental, and nonexperimental research designs. Areas in which authors are encouraged to submit articles include anthropology, social work, demography, political science, social history, sociology, and other social sciences. Finally, *The Journal of Gerontology: Biological Sciences* accepts papers on the biological aspects of aging, such as genetics, molecular biology, pathology, pharmacology, and physiology.

The Gerontologist is a bimonthly journal that accepts manuscripts in all areas of gerontology, including those with a multidisciplinary focus and those specific to practice, policy, and applied research. This journal is particularly interested in articles on practice concepts, program evaluation, humanities, and other topics that enhance the reader's understanding of human aging.

The AGS was founded in 1942 as an organization for physicians and other health professionals who were interested in the special problems of the elderly. When originally founded, a major concern was increasing life expectancy beyond the age of 65. Today, the principle concern is expanding geriatric education and increasing the number of health professionals training in geriatrics. Membership today numbers more than 6,000 worldwide and consists primarily of physicians, with representation from nursing and other health professionals. AGS is a medical society devoted to issues in geriatric medicine, with the following objectives:

- Implement geriatric education and training for physicians, nurses, health professionals, and the general public;

- Advocate for increased research on aging;

- Ensure access to geriatric medical care for the elderly; and

- Pursue a public policy effort on issues that affect the medical care of older persons.

AGS also publishes *The Journal of the American Geriatric Society*.

The American Nurse's Association (ANA) founded the Division of Geriatric Nursing Practice in 1966. In 1976, the name was changed to the Division of Gerontological Nursing, and the 1984 the division became the Council on Gerontological Nursing [Gioiella 1990].

A more recent journal is *Psychology and Aging*, published by the American Psychological Association. This journal focuses adult development and aging and primarily publishes articles based on original research, although it will accept articles on theoretical analyses of research issues and practical clinical problems. Clinical case studies that also have a theoretical orientation are appropriate.

Another practice-relevant journal is the *Journal of Applied Gerontology*. This journal, published by the Southern Gerontological Society through Sage Publications, accepts manuscripts that include applied research or review or research on the elderly and practice concepts for services for the elderly.

Standards of Ethics

Certain ethical dilemmas arise time and again in the care of older persons. Geriatric interdisciplinary teams often struggle to make a decision between two seemingly equal alternatives, although the selection of either one may not feel like a positive solution to a problem. Nevertheless, the team needs to take action and hopefully does so on the basis of some ethical principle or standard of practice. There are many ethical principles that are contradictory to one another and in geriatric care, the conflict between beneficence and respect for autonomy is a critical and common one [Howell 1989]. Simply stated, the conflict arises between respect for someone's autonomy and the intent to do good for that person. This section highlights a few of the issues that frequently cause teams to debate this and other ethical principles.

Confidentiality

Issues around maintaining team/client confidentiality for older adults can be challenging. Often it is necessary to share information with adult children and other caretakers who need to provide supervision and direct care. When competency is unclear, it can be difficult to determine how much should be shared.

Abuse/Neglect

It is difficult to gain an understanding of the extent of abuse and neglect among the elderly. Few states have mandatory reporting laws. Elderly persons often refuse investigation, due to fears of retaliation from family members. The frail elderly in particular may be unable or unwilling to report abuse and are the most at risk. Elderly persons at increased risk for abuse are those who reside with family members who have problems with chemical dependency and who are dependent on the older person financially.

While elder abuse is certainly a reality, it is important to realize that neglect can occur in well-intentioned families who are struggling to keep a family member within the home but are overburdened by the care needs. In situations such as this, team members can help the family recognize their limitations by supporting their efforts, rather than adopting a confrontational attitude. Many families struggle with financial concerns for their older relatives and can be reluctant to allow resources to be spent for institutional care. The geriatric team needs to assist family members in realizing that it is appropriate for financial resources acquired during one's lifetime to be spent in support of one's period of disability and declining health.

Competency Determination

At times, team members may have differing views on the perceived competency of a particular older patient or client. For example, a team member may have concerns about the safety of a client living alone. It is important to remember that older persons do have the right to make what others may perceive as a "wrong" decision. In the team's desire to ensure the best possible outcome for elderly clients, we need to be aware of paternalistic attitudes that can interfere with the care of older persons.

Advance Directives

One of the most important responsibilities of the geriatric team is to help the client and the family plan for the time when decision making responsibilities may need to be passed on. Most states have passed legislation for living wills or power of attorney for health care, which provide formal mechanisms for the transfer of such decision making responsibilities. Teams can encourage open discussions between elders and their families. It is important to remember that some families may have a long history of poor communication or dysfunctional interactions, and sometimes it may be necessary to bring out some of the past family conflicts to help the family reach some consensus about future plans.

Summary

This chapter has presented an overview of interdisciplinary geriatric teams as they function in a variety of health care settings. We have presented the "ideological" assumptions that underlie this practice approach. Simply stated, the whole of the team is expected to produce better clinical outcomes than the solo or parallel practice of single health care disciplines. When possible, we have presented empirical findings that do or do not support the efficacy of using this practice approach to the care and treatment of elderly patients. A consistent finding was that these geriatric teams were particularly beneficial for older persons who are at risk because of advanced age, significant functional limitations, or other health or social circumstance that required a more thorough and coordinated approach to care.

Measuring treatment outcomes in this population almost always requires a comparison group and a longitudinal design, since maintenance of function or delaying the deterioration of function are both worthwhile outcomes. Preventing losses or retarding losses associated with aging are hallmarks or geriatric practice. Medical care provided to the elderly can be improved by the support of quality team interactions that encourage shared responsibility for planning and decision making. We have described the disciplines typically represented on these teams and delineated their functions, educational backgrounds, and credentials. Practice experience, competence, and open communication are but a few of the less tangible elements that, over time, result in effective and psychologically supportive interdisciplinary teams.

References

Allardt, E. (1978). Objective and subjective social indicators of well-being. *Comparative Studies in Sociology, 1*, 142-173.

Allen, C., Becker, P. M., McVey, L. J., Saltz, C., Feussner, J., & Cohen H. (1986). A randomized, controlled clinical trial of a geriatric consultation team: Compliance with recommendations. *Journal of the American Medical Association, 255*, 2617-2621.

Andres, R., & Tobin, J. D. (1977). Endocrine systems. In C. E. Finch and L. Hayflick (Eds.), *Handbook of the biology of aging*. New York: Van Nostrand Reinhold.

Andrews, F. M. (Ed.). (1986). *Research on the quality of life*. Ann Arbor, MI: Institute for Social Research, The University of Michigan.

Andrews, F. M., & Withey, S. B. (1976). *Social indicators of well-being*. New York: Plenum.

Barker, W. H., Williams, T. F., Zimmer, J. G., VanBuren, C., Vincent S. J., & Pickrel, S. G. (1985). Geriatric consultation teams in acute hospitals: Impact on back-up of elderly patients. *Journal of the American Geriatrics Society, 33,* 422-428.

Bates-Smith, K., & Tsukada, R. A. (1984). Problems of an interdisciplinary training team. *Clinical Gerontologist, 2,* 66-68.

Becker, P. M., McVey, L., Saltz, C., Feussner, J., & Cohen, H. (1987). Hospital-acquired complications in a randomized controlled clinical trial of a geriatric consultation team. *Journal of the American Medical Association, 257,* 2313-2317.

Beloff, J. S., & Korper, M. (1971). The health team model and medical care utlization. *Journal of the American Medical Association, 219,* 359-366.

Besdine, R. W. (1988). Functional assessment in the elderly. In J. W. Rowe and R. W. Besdine (Eds.), *Geriatric medicine* (pp. 37-51). Boston, MA: Little Brown.

Blumenfield, S., Morris, J., & Sherman, F. T. (1982). The geriatric team in the acute care hospital: An educational and consultation modality. *Journal of the American Geriatric Society, 30,* 660-664.

Brink, T. L. (1984). Multi-disciplinary team success: The role of mutual respect. *Clinical Gerontology, 2* (3), 73-74.

Brody, S. J. (1984). Health services: Need and utilization. In S. J. Brody and N. A. Persily (Eds.), *Hospitals and the aged: The new old market* (pp. 25-49). Rockville, MD: Aspen Press.

Brody, S. J., & Magel, J. S. (1984). DRG-The second revolution in health care for the elderly. *Journal of the American Geriatrics Society, 32,* 676-679.

Campbell, A., Converse, P. E., & Rogers, W. L. (1976). *The quality of American life.* New York: Russell Sage.

Campion, E. W., Jette, A., & Berkman, B. (1983). An interdisciplinary geriatric consultation service: A controlled trial. *Journal of the American Geriatrics Society, 31,* 792-796.

Clarfield, A. M. (1982). A long-term geriatric teaching ward in an acute-care hospital: A three year experience. *Journal of the American Geriatrics Society, 30,* 457-465.

Clarfield, A. M. (1984). Multidisciplinary teams: Common goals and communication. *Clinical Gerontologist, 3* (2), 38-40.

Czirr, R., & Rappaport, M. (1984). Toolkit for teams: Annotated bibliography on interdisciplinary health teams. *Clinical Gerontologist, 2,* 47-54.

Fiatarone, M. A., Marks, E. C., Ryan, N. D., Meredith, C. N., Lipsitz, L. A., & Evans, W. J. (1990). High-intensity strength training in nonagenarians: Effects on skeletal muscle. *Journal of the American Medical Association, 263* (22), 3029-3034.

Gioiella, E. C. (1990). Gerontological nursing. in W. R. Hazzard, R. Andres, E. L. Bierman, & J. P. Blass (Eds.), *Principles of geriatric medicine and gerontology* (pp. 304-311). New York: McGraw-Hill.

Granger, C. V., Seltzer, G. B., & Fishbein, C. (1987). *Primary care of the functionally disabled: Assessment and management.* Philadelphia, PA: J. B. Lippincott and Co.

Gunter, L. M. (1985). The gerontic nurse. In G. H. McGuie (Ed.), *Care of the elderly: A health team approach* (pp. 113-124). Boston/Toronto, Ontario: Little Brown.

Handal, P. J., Barling, P. W., & Morrissy, E. (1983). Development of perceived and preferred measures of physical and social characteristics of the residential environment and their relationship to satisfaction. *Journal of Community Psychology, 9,* 118-124.

Howell, M. C. (1989). Ethical dilemmas. In M. C. Howell, D. G. Gavin, G. A. Cabrera, & H. A. Beyer (Eds.), *Serving the underserved: Caring for people who are both old and mentally retarded* (pp. 289-295). Boston: Exceptional Parent Press.

Institute of Medicine. (1991). *Disability in America: Toward a national agenda for prevention.* Washington, DC: National Academy Press.

Kerski, D., Drinka, T., Carnes, M., Golob, K., Craig, W. A. (1987). Post geriatric evaluations unit follow-up: Team versus nonteam. *Journal of Gerontology, 42,* 191-195.

Kovar, M. G. (1977). Health and health care of the elderly. *Public Health Rep, 92,* 9-19.

Lefton, E., Bonstelle, S., & Frengley, J. D. (1983). Success with an inpatient geriatric unit: A controlled study of outcomes and follow-up. *Journal of Geriatrics Society, 31,* 149-155.

Lindeman, R. D., Tobin, J., & Shock, N. W. (1985). Longitudinal studies on the rate of decline in renal function with age. *Journal of the American Geriatric Society, 33,* 278-285.

Maguire, G. H. (Ed.). (1985). *Care of the elderly: A health team approach.* Boston: Little Brown.

McVey, L., Becker, P., Saltz, C., Cohen, H., & Feussner, J. (1985). Impact of a geriatric consultation team on functional status: A controlled clinical trial. *The Gerontologist, 25,* 31.

Michalos, A. C. (1979). Life changes, illness and personal life satisfaction in a rural population. *Social Sciences and Medicine, 13,* 175-181.

Millman, A., Forciea, M., Fogel, D., & Johnson, J. C. (1986). A model of inter-disciplinary ambulatory geriatric care in a Veterans Administration Medical Center. *The Gerontologist, 26,* 471-474.

Mueller, D. P. (1980). Social networks: A promising direction for research on the relationship of the social environment to psychiatric disorder. *Social Sciences and Medicine, 14,* 147-161.

Nagi, S. Z. (1976). An epidemiology of disability among adults in the United States: Health and society. *Milbank Memorial Fund Quarterly, 54,* 439-467.

Qualls, S. H., & Czirr, R. (1988). Geriatric health teams: Classifying models of professional and team functioning. *The Gerontologist, 28,* 372-376.

Rao, D. B. (1977). The team approach to integrated care of the elderly. *Geriatrics, 32,* 88-96.

Rice, D., & Feldman, H. (1983). Living longer in the United States: Demographic changes and health needs of the elderly. *Milbank Memorial Fund Quarterly, 61* (3), 362-396.

Riffer, J. (1986). Geriatric units stress the team approach to care. *Hospitals, 60,* 90-91.

Rubenstein, L. Z., Abrass, I. B., & Kane, R. L. (1981). Improved care for patients on a new geriatric evaluation unit. *Journal of the American Geriatrics Society, 29,* 531-536.

Rubenstein, L. Z., Josephson, K. R., Wieland, G. D., English, P. A., Sayre, J. A., & Kane, R. L. (1984). Effectiveness of a geriatric evaluation unit: A randomized clinical trial. *New England Journal of Medicine, 311,* 1664-1670.

Rubenstein, L. Z., Wieland, G. D., English, P. A., Josephson, K., Sayre, J. A., & Abrass, I. B. (1984). The Sepulbeda VA geriatric evaluation unit: Data on four-year outcomes and predictors of improved patients outcomes. *Journal of the American Geriatrics Society, 32,* 503-512.

Saltz, C. C., McVey, L. J., Becker, P. M., Feussner, J. R., & Cohen, H. J. (1988). Impact of a geriatric consultation team on discharge placement and report hospitalization. *The Gerontologist, 28* (3), 344.

Schmitt, M. H., Farrell, M. P., & Heinemann, G. D. (1988). Conceptual and methodological problems in studying the effects of interdisciplinary geriatric teams. *The Gerontologist, 28,* 753-764.

Seltzer, G. B., Finaly, E., & Howell, M. (1988). Functional characteristics of elderly mentally retarded persons in community settings and nursing homes. *Mental Retardation, 26,* 213-217.

Steel, K., & Hays, A. (1981). A consultation service in geriatric medicine at a university hospital. *Journal of the American Medical Association, 245,* 1410.

Svanborg, A., Bergstrom, G., & Mellstrom, D. (1982). *Epidemiological studies on social and medical conditions of the elderly.* Copenhagen, Denmark: World Health Organization.

Temkin-Greener, H. (1983). Interprofessional perspectives on teamwork in health care: A case study. *Millbank Memorial Fund Quarterly, 61,* 638-641.

Thompson, R. F., Rhyne, R. L., Stratton, M. A., & Franklin, R. H. (1988). Using an interdisciplinary team for geriatric education in a nursing home. *Journal of Medical Education, 63,* 796-798.

Tichy, M. K. (1974). *Health care teams: An annotated bibliography.* New York: Praeger.

Tsukada, R. A. (1990). Interdisciplinary collaboration: Teamwork in geriatrics. In C. K. Cassel, D. E. Riesenberg, L. B. Sorenson, & J. R. Walsh (Eds.), *Geriatric medicine* (2nd ed.), (pp. 668-675). New York: Springer-Verlag.

William, M. E., Williams, T. F., Zimmer, J., et al. (1987). How does the team approach to geriatric evaluation compare with traditional care: A report of a randomized trial. *Journal of the American Geriatrics Society, 35,* 1071-1078.

Williams, T. F. (1990). Geriatrics: A perspective on quality of life and care for older people. In B. Spiker (Ed.), *Quality of life assessments in clinical trials* (pp. 217-223). New York: Raven Press.

Williams, T. F. (1986). Comprehensive assessment of frail elderly in relation to needs for long-term care. In E. Calkins, P. J. Davis, & A. B. Ford (Eds.), *The practice of geriatrics* (pp. 84-92). Philadelphia, PA: W. B. Saunders & Co.

Winograd, C. H., Gerety, M., & Brown, E. (1988). Targeting the hospitalized elderly for geriatric consultation. *Journal of the American Geriatrics Society, 36,* 1113-1119.

World Health Organization. (1980). *International classification of impairments, disabilities and handicaps: A manual of classification relating to the consequences of disease.* Geneva, Switzerland: Author.

Zimmer, J. G., Groth-Junker, A., & McCusker, J. (1985). A randomized controlled study of a home health care team. *American Journal of Public Health, 75,* 134-141.

Appendix A: Codes of Ethics

Physical Therapy
Code of Ethics

Principle 1:   Physical therapists respect the rights and dignity of all individuals.

Principle 2:   Physical therapists comply with the laws and regulations governing the practice of physical therapy.

Principle 3:   Physical therapists accept responsibility for the exercise of sound judgement.

Principle 4:   Physical therapists maintain and promote high standards for physical therapy practice, education, and research.

Principle 5:   Physical therapists seek remuneration for their services that is deserved and reasonable.

Principle 6:   Physical therapists provide accurate information to the consumer about the profession and about those services they provide.

Principle 7:   Physical therapists accept the responsibility to protect the public and the profession from unethical, incompetent, or illegal acts.

Principle 8:   Physical therapists participate in efforts to address the health needs of the public.

APTA, House of Delegates, June 1981, Amended June 1987, Amended June 1991.

Standards of Ethical Conduct for the Physical Therapist Assistant

Standard 1:   Physical therapist assistants provide services under the supervision of a physical therapist.

Standard 2:   Physical therapist assistants respect the right and dignity of all individuals.

Standard 3:   Physical therapist assistants maintain and promote high standards in the provision of services giving the welfare of the patients their highest regard.

Standard 4:   Physical therapist assistants provide services within the limits of the law.

Standard 5:   Physical therapist assistants make those judgments that are commensurate with their qualifications as physical therapist assistants.

Standard 6:   Physical therapist assistants accept the responsibility to protect the public and the profession from unethical, incompetent, or illegal acts.

APTA, House of Delegates, June 1982, Amended June 1991.

Occupational Therapy Code of Ethics

Principle 1: Occupational therapy personnel shall demonstrate a concern for the welfare and dignity of the recipient of their services.

Principle 2: Occupational therapy personnel shall actively maintain high standards of professional competence.

Principle 3: Occupational therapy personnel shall comply with laws and Association policies guiding the profession of occupational therapy.

Principle 4: Occupational therapy personnel shall provide accurate information concerning occupational therapy services.

Principle 5: Occupational therapy personnel shall function with discretion and integrity in relations with colleagues and other professionals, and shall be concerned with the quality of their services.

Principle 6: Occupational therapy personnel shall not engage in any form of conduct that constitutes a conflict of interest or that adversely reflects on the profession.

Council for Exceptional Children Code of Ethics

I.   Special education professionals are committed to developing the highest education and quality of life potential of exceptional individuals.

II.   Special education professionals promote and maintain a high level of competence and integrity in practicing their profession.

III.   Special education professionals engage in professional activities which benefit exceptional individuals, their families, other colleagues, students, or research subjects.

IV.   Special education professionals exercise objective professional judgment in the practice of their profession.

V.   Special education professionals strive to advance their knowledge and skills regarding the education of exceptional individuals.

VI.   Special education professionals work within the standards and policies of the profession.

VII. Special education professionals seek to uphold and improve where necessary the laws, regulations, and policies governing the delivery of special education and related services and the practice of their profession.

VIII. Special education professionals do not condone or participate in unethical or illegal acts, nor violate professional standards adopted by the Delegate Assembly of CEC.

Code of Ethics for Social Work

I.   The social worker's conduct and comportment as a social worker.
  A. Propriety - The social worker should maintain high standards of personal conduct in the capacity or identity as a social worker.
  B. Competence and professional development - The social worker should strive to become and remain proficient in professional practice and the performance of professional functions.
  C. Service - the social worker should regard as the primary the service obligation of the social work profession.
  D. Integrity - The social worker should act in accordance with the highest standards of professional integrity and impartiality.
  E. Scholarship and research - The social worker engaged in study and research should be guided by the conventions of scholarly inquiry.

II. The social worker's ethical responsibility to clients
  F. Primacy of clients' interests - The social worker's primary responsibility is to the clients.
  G. Rights and prerogatives of clients - The social worker should make every effort to foster maximum self-determination on the part of clients.
  H. Confidentiality and privacy - The social worker should respect the privacy of clients and hold in confidence all information obtained in the course of professional service.
  I. Fees - When setting fees, the social worker should ensure that they are fair, reasonable, considerate, and commensurate with the service performed and with due regard for the client's ability to pay.

III. The social worker's ethical responsibility to colleagues
  J. Respect, fairness, and courtesy - The social worker should treat colleagues with respect, courtesy, fairness, and good faith.
  K. Dealing with colleagues' clients - The social worker has the responsibility to relate to the clients of colleagues with full professional consideration.

IV. The social worker's ethical responsibility for employers and employing organizations
    L. Commitment to employing organization - The social worker should adhere to commitments made to the employing organization.

V. The social worker's ethical responsibility to the social work profession
    M. Maintaining the integrity of the profession. The social worker should uphold and advance the values, ethics, knowledge, and mission of the profession.
    N. Community service - The social worker should assist the profession in making social services available to the general public.
    O. Development of knowledge - The social worker should take responsibility for identifying, developing, and fully utilizing knowledge for professional practice.

VI. The social worker's ethical responsibility to society
    P. Promoting the general welfare - The social worker should promote the general welfare of society.

National Association of Social Workers. (1980). NASW code of ethics. *NASW News, 25,*(24-25).

Code of Professional Ethics
for Rehabilitation Counselors

Canon 1: Moral and Legal Standards. Rehabilitation Counselors shall behave in a legal, ethical, and moral manner in the conduct of their profession, maintaining the integrity of the Code and avoiding any behavior which would cause harm to others.

Canon 2: Counselor-Client Relationship. Rehabilitation Counselors shall respect the integrity and protect the welfare of people and groups with whom they work. The primary obligation of rehabilitation counselors is to their clients, defined as people with disabilities who are receiving services from rehabilitation counselors. Rehabilitation counselors shall endeavor at all times to place their clients' interests above their own.

Canon 3: Client Advocacy. Rehabilitation Counselors shall serve as advocates for people with disabilities.

Canon 4: Professional Relationships. Rehabilitation Counselors shall act with integrity in their relationhips with colleagues, other organizations, agencies, institutions, referral sources, and other professionals so as to facilitate the contribution of all specialists toward achieving optimum benefit for clients.

Canon 5: Public Statements/Fees. Rehabilitation Counselors shall adhere to professional standards in establishing fees and promoting their services.

Canon 6: Confidentiality. Rehabilitation Counselors shall respect the confidentiality of information obtained from clients in the course of their work.

Canon 7: Assessment. Rehabilitation Counselors shall promote the welfare of clients in the selection, utilization, and interpretation of assessment measures.

Canon 8: Research Activities. Rehabilitation Counselors shall assist in efforts to expand the knowledge needed to more effectively serve people with disabilities.

Canon 9: Competence. Rehabilitation Counselors shall establish and maintain their professional competencies at such a level that their clients receive the benefit of the highest quality of services the profession is capable of offering.

Canon 10: CRC Credential. Rehabilitation Counselors holding the Certified Rehabilitation Counselor (CRC) designation shall honor the integrity and respect the limitations placed upon its use.

T E A M W O R K
About the Editors

Fred P. Orelove (right) is Professor of Education at Virginia Commonwealth University in Richmond, Virginia, and Executive Director of the Virginia Institute for Developmental Disabilities. Dr. Orelove's teaching and research interests are focused on teamwork and learners with severe disabilities. He is the co-author (with Dr. Howard Gardner) of *Teamwork in the Human Services: Models and Applications Across the Life Span* and of several books on educating children with multiple disabilities and on inclusive education. Dr. Orelove is a founder of the Virginia Coalition on Abuse and Disabilities, an interagency, interdisciplinary group devoted to increasing knowledge and skills of professionals on maltreatment of individuals with disabilities. He is immediate Past President of the American Association of University Affiliated Programs.

Howard G. Gardner (left), Professor of Education at Virginia Commonwealth University (VCU), has been on the faculty there since 1973. In addition to his teaching responsibilities, he also serves as Director of the VCU Training and Technical Assistance Center for School Personnel Serving Students with Disabilities. His past experiences include serving as Director of the Virginia Institute for Developmental Disabilities, director of a residential program using the teamwork model for youth with emotional and behavioral problems, a principal of a special education school, and a high school teacher of U.S. government. Dr. Gardner's professional interests include achieving real teamwork in programs for children and youth, behavior management, and social skills education. He is the author of four books and numerous articles on teamwork, including *Teamwork Models and Experience in Education, Teamwork in Human Services,* and *Helping Others Through Teamwork.*

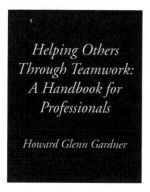

Helping Others
Through Teamwork:
A Handbook for
Professionals
Howard Glenn Gardner

Helping Others Through Teamwork was written to help practitioners who work on interdisciplinary teams understand the team approach, so that behavior resulting in real teamwork produces effective services. In a light, nonjargon style, the author addresses all helping field—child care, education, social work, physical therapy, counseling, and specialized therapies—as well as all professionals in these fields who deal with clients, patients, or students. A teamwork enthusiast, Garner explains the differences between team and departmental structure, why teamwork is the preferred system, and how to practice it.

To Order: 1998/0-87868-305-4 Stock #3054 $16.95

Write: CWLA c/o PMDS Call: 800/407-6273
P.O. Box 2019 301/617-7825
Annapolis Junction, MD 20701
e-mail: cwla@pmds.com Fax: 301/206-9789

Please specify stock #3054. Bulk discount policy (not for resale): 10-49 copies 10%, 50-99 copies 20%, 100 or more copies 40%. Canadian and foreign orders must be prepaid in U.S. funds. MasterCard/Visa accepted.